STRATEGIC SURVEY 1992-1993

Published by BRASSEY'S for

**THE INTERNATIONAL
INSTITUTE FOR
STRATEGIC STUDIES**
23 Tavistock Street
London WC2E 7NQ

STRATEGIC SURVEY 1992–1993

Published by Brassey's for
The International Institute for Strategic Studies
23 Tavistock Street, London WC2E 7NQ

Director	Editor
Dr Bo Huldt	Sidney Bearman

This publication has been prepared by the Director of the Institute and his Staff, who accept full responsibility for its contents, which describe and analyse events up to late March 1993. These do not, and indeed cannot, represent a consensus of views among the worldwide membership of the Institute as a whole.

First published May 1993

ISBN 1 85753 003 9
ISSN 0567 932X

Strategic Survey (ISSN 0567 932X) is published annually by Brassey's (UK) Ltd, 165 Great Dover Street, London SE1 4YA. All orders, accompanied by payment, should be sent directly to Turpin Distribution Services Ltd, Blackhorse Road, Letchworth, Herts., SG6 1HN, UK. The 1993 annual subscription rate is: UK and overseas £18.00, single copy £21.00; North America $29.00, single copy $32.00. Airfreight and mailing in the USA by Publications Expediting Inc., 200 Meacham Avenue, Elmont, New York 11003, USA.
USA POSTMASTER: Send address changes to Strategic Survey, Publications Expediting Inc., 200 Meacham Avenue, Elmont, New York 11003, USA. Application to mail at second-class postage is pending at Jamaica, New York 11431. All other despatches outside the UK by Printflow Air within Europe and Printflow Airsaver outside Europe.

PRINTED IN THE UK by Halstan & Co. Ltd, Amersham, Bucks.

CONTENTS

Perspectives

Almost everything that could go wrong did go wrong. It was a year in which the pendulum swung far in an undesired direction. The freedom encouraged by the collapse of communist rule transmuted into freedom for ethnic-nationalist demands to stir up wars of a particular savagery and brutality. Multilateral solutions to the world's ills, from the UN to the EC to GATT, failed to come near to the high hopes that had been invested in them. Russia was in political and economic chaos, gravely endangered by the irreconcilable split between democratic free-marketeers, trying to move the country into a brighter future, and neo-totalitarians, striving to conserve vestiges of their power or driven by nostalgic illusions of the past. Peace talks in the Middle East were in abeyance. Peace accords in Angola and Cambodia were shredded. Famine, caused as much by sectarian and ethnic disagreements as by natural causes, stalked much of Africa.

Amidst the gloom there were a few bright spots. The quadrennial presidential elections in the United States brought into office a president and administration who quickly demonstrated a refreshing will to tackle economic and social problems which had increasingly threatened to disrupt American life and act as a restraint on the necessary US international leadership role. Despite calls for sacrifice and tax increases, confidence and hope have returned to the US. Unlike the stubborn recession still gripping most of the other industrialized countries, in the US an economic recovery is gathering steam. In Central Europe encouraging signs of forward motion were seen in Poland, and while Czechoslovakia split into new Czech and Slovak republics, the division was a peaceful, bloodless one. Extraordinary arms control agreements were signed, giving rise to achievable dreams of a world with fewer weapons of mass destruction.

All of these, however, are hostages to fortune. Unless the Clinton formula for recovery proves to be sound, and quickly, the ever volatile American public can be expected to turn. There will be many who will still believe in sacrifice, but somebody else's sacrifice. A familiar gridlock between Congress and the administration will once again take hold. Poland and the Czech Republic are beginning to be able to see light, but they are still in the tunnel. If Russia regresses politically, its new leaders will probably not be willing to seal and deliver the promise of the arms control agreements its former leaders signed. In that event, Ukraine, which is already indicating considerable reluctance to give up its nuclear status, is certain to insist on maintaining it.

Most serious of all is the buffeting that multilateral solutions to international problems are taking from narrow nationalist interests. Many of the more rosy-hued hopes for multilateral approaches were indeed naive, but some of the projections were sounder and more realistic. An interdependent world must not allow the failure of the best to drive out the promise of the good. Too often during the past year the travellers on the rocky path to international cooperation in Europe, GATT and the UN have stumbled badly. They seem to have been temporarily so blinded by the brightness of the ultimate goal that they forgot to keep their eyes fixed on the uneven path. At times it is better to step sideways, or even slightly back, to assure forward progress.

Take the UN

The UN is a case in point. In the past five years, it has been called on by the major powers to deal with increasingly difficult problems. The end of the Cold War resulted in the break-up of the logjam created by the antagonisms of the old bipolar world, freeing the Security Council to act. In some cases it rushed in without full appreciation or preparation for the task. In others it chose either the wrong instrument for action, or burdened a proper instrument with mandates that hobbled its effectiveness.

That the UN has been unsuccessful in curing so many of the world's ills, in so short a time, is not surprising. But continual failure is dangerous. It undermines the credibility of the organization, particularly with regard to those who most need to feel respect for the world body; that this is acknowledged has led to some signs of movement.

Part of the difficulty is built into the UN itself and its resistance to meaningful reform. The Secretary-General recognizes that many reforms need to be undertaken, although he appears hesitant to undertake them. Part of it is due to the reluctance of the major powers to provide the UN with sufficient funds, even as they ask it to take on ever greater burdens. The Clinton administration has announced that it will clear US arrears and will thenceforth pay on time its large share of running the UN; if it does, and is followed by others, the UN will be on a sounder financial footing. Part is due to the way in which the UN has chosen to respond to the challenges. It now accepts that in a chaotic situation like Somalia or Bosnia-Herzogovina, the provision of very few peacekeepers with insufficient logistical support, restrictive rules of engagement and a mandate that prevents them from acting, merely allows local aggressors to ride roughshod over an increasingly meaningless gesture.

If carried through, these reforms may be enough to recoup some of the UN's lost ability to make a difference, if the lessons learned in the last year are properly absorbed and acted on. The evolution of the situation in Somalia provided a salutary one. The force that the UN, after much delay, initially put in place in Somalia totalled only 500 men with strict orders to take action only when it was necessary in self-defence. They were classic peacekeepers, but in a country where there was no peace to keep, no government to deal with, no police force or national army to support or on which to rely. In the midst of anarchy and freebooting this UN force was supposed to help secure and deliver relief aid and to organize some return to normality. The wonder is that it took so long to acknowledge the impossibility of achieving these aims with the means provided, in the Wild West atmosphere of Somalia.

The American-led multinational force of some 37,000 men, that was inserted in December to dampen the hell-fires and ensure delivery of aid to the people, showed what needs be done in comparable circumstances. It is necessary to arm the sheriff and his posse and allow them to use those weapons to enforce a peace that the local fighters themselves are unwilling to keep. The UN seems to have taken that on board. It is to replace the multinational force with UNOSOM II which will have about 28,000 men, plus a 'tactical quick reaction force' provided by the US, and a more reasonable and workable mandate. None of this will guarantee that the UN can do the job, but it will at least have a fighting chance.

The Limits and Alternatives to Intervention

For some of the other disorders and disasters of today's world a different question must be asked. It is not so much whether the UN or other multinational bodies should invest more troops, invigorate their mandates and insure more caring governments, but whether they should not be trying other methods that might succeed without the risk of a long-term *de facto* occupation and trusteeship. At those crossroads of ancient empires, like the former Yugoslavia, competing groups of memory-laden peoples are now asserting their right to self-determination and a personal, restrictive homeland on the same piece of land. The passions that have been stoked are fierce, there are blood-soaked historical scores to be settled and the terrain is inhospitable to foreign troops.

There is good reason for Western military leaders to be wary about deeper military involvement in places like Bosnia-Herzegovina. It is exceedingly dangerous to be the outsider trapped between two implacable foes. The number of troops needed for the operation would be large and the costs high. With most members of a possible coalition short of both money and manpower, it is doubtful if a proper force could be raised and maintained. There is not even a clear and conclusive end to be seen. Nor is there a consensus within the UN on whether an intervention should be mounted. The Serbs could perhaps count on their Slavic brothers, the Russians, to champion their cause; the Croats might hope to play on historical ties with the Germans; the Bosnian Muslims could expect to awaken sympathy in the Islamic nations and, for humanitarian reasons, much of the rest of the West. Any peace that could be imposed from the outside would be certain to penalize at least one, and perhaps two, of the three contending sides.

In the cold terms of *Realpolitik* it is difficult to see what interests of the outside powers are threatened by the fighting inside Bosnia-

Herzegovina. There is of course a surge of moral outrage at the sight of bloodshed that the media has brought into the living rooms of Western viewers. It is questionable, however, if governments can afford to base their policies on such emotions, praiseworthy though they are. There are simply not enough human or financial resources available to do what would be necessary to call to account all the inhumane regimes, whether legitimate or illegitimate, that, with great brutality, are oppressing the weak and the innocent around the world. For the same reasons as in medicine, choices must be made and resources must be rationed.

If choices must be made, they should not be made on the basis of media coverage. On humanitarian grounds and in defence of Western political values, a better argument can be made for intervening in Burma than in Bosnia-Herzegovina. In Burma a corrupt military leadership seized power and refused to allow those who had overwhelmingly won a popular election to form a government. Intervention there would have a clear aim, a finite end, and the support of the majority of the people. It would right a wrong. But it will not be undertaken, despite the illegitimate government's vicious suppression of the people, because the media has not focused the attention of the citizens of democratic Western countries on these injustices. Because those governments are not under pressure, and because they cannot see their security interests under threat, their moral outrage is muted.

European countries do have a security interest in the fighting in the former Yugoslavia. There is a threat to the long-term hopes of a 'European Security Order' which the Charter of Europe pointed towards in 1990. There is a risk that it could spread, as it has in the past, to others who would wish to support one side or the other. This threat, however, will not be affected by the methods that have been adopted over the last year by the European states, or the United Nations. Tortuous negotiations that do not address the underlying problem have merely resulted in cynical manipulation by the protagonists of the good offices proffered by well-meaning and hard-working negotiators. Leaders of the combatant groups appear not to distinguish between a signature and an autograph: cease-fires are happily signed, and then unsigned through force the next day. Efforts to deliver food and medicine to beleaguered towns are stymied because starvation is one of the tools of the aggressor, and the UN cannot use force to ensure deliverance. There can be no mistaking the bravery and goodwill of those trying to make a real difference. Their efforts, however, have merely made the institutions they represent look weak and ineffective, and the international community has suffered a setback.

The interests of Europe and the community would have been better served if, in the first instance, they had relied on different methods. To prevent the spread of the contagion they should have concentrated on isolating the area, physically if possible, but certainly diplomatically and economically. A tight sanctions policy, preventing all arms and war supplies from reaching the belligerents, would have paid greater dividends than the present policy. There is evidence that, despite the porous borders, even the unenforced sanctions against Serbia have had considerable effect. They should be tightened by invoking serious penalties against countries who engage in sanctions-busting, either purposively or by ignoring the actions of private entrepreneurs that they could control if they wished.

Alongside punitive sanctions the international community should promise diplomatic aid as and when the parties to the conflict are ready to end the fighting and negotiate seriously. Economic aid would follow. The outside powers would have to be prepared to wait until the fighters had exhausted themselves and their abilities to continue the slaughter, and that will not be easy. But even if these powers were prepared to enforce a stop to the fighting by inserting a significant body of troops, no imposed settlement from without would last beyond the time the outside force was removed. The UN, and other regional consortia, must be careful to choose to intervene bodily only in those situations where they can earn something besides opprobrium.

In the case of Yugoslavia, the UN and the international community have now agreed to guarantee a peace, if one can be reached. If and when there is an agreement on the Vance-Owen plan by the three competing sides, there will have to be a UN/NATO force prepared to uphold it. Having come this far with what was probably not the more effective option, it is necessary for the backers of the Vance-Owen plan to do everything possible to see that it is carried out.

Incipient Chaos in Russia

The world is littered with domestic political struggles that external forces are relatively powerless to bend to their satisfaction. Only some are important to the security concerns of the rest of the world. To those, attention must be paid, but to be most useful it must be early attention, when judicious input can possibly have a significant effect. In no other country are the West's interests at risk from a failure of the nation's political and economic reforms as they are at risk in Russia. Sadly, in the case of Russia, between the rhetoric of economic aid and its deliverance, fell a shadow. For most of the year US attention was fixed on the presidential election. Europeans were consumed by their own continuing economic downturn and the cautionary tale of Maastricht ratification. Japan also had its recession to worry about, and this reinforced its reluctance to advance Russia economic aid before a political settlement on the Northern Islands.

When the simmering clash between those trying to reform Russia's political and economic structures and those who feared the consequences of such reforms boiled over in March 1993, there was a scramble by the democratic nations to promise support to Boris Yeltsin. Provided earlier, the aid might have had a bigger impact in helping to reduce the pain of the social and economic dislocations

which had resulted from the slow pace of positive change and had
destroyed a good part of Yeltsin's popularity. Nevertheless, although
late, it was better than never, for thrown into the balance it might just
keep the scales from tipping in the wrong direction.

The forces that opposed Boris Yeltsin, Russia's first freely elected
president, have fed on the people's discontent. These forces, themselves, are split on everything except opposition to Yeltsin. It is, a
source of his strength that they have been unable to provide a reasonable programme to replace the reforms that, against the odds, he has
been trying to effect. It is a source of his present weakness that, more
than a year ago when his popularity was at its highest he did not move
to create a new constitution to replace the Brezhnev one, or to hold
new elections to replace those delegates from the Soviet era that now
form the majority in the Congress of People's Deputies, or to begin to
build a party which would provide him with continuous support for his
bolder measures.

Whether he moved too late, when, in pursuit of just these goals, he
struck out in late March to leapfrog over the Congress to appeal to the
people, has yet to be seen. The Congress has thrown up obstacles by
rewriting the questions in the referendum to his disfavour and have
required a majority of 50% of the entire electorate to assure a winning
result. The apathy of the people, who are more concerned with food
and the bare necessities of life than in which of the quarrelling politicians in Moscow is victorious, makes such a turn-out, and vote, unlikely.

Despite the risks, Yeltsin had little choice. A year of nibbling at his
control of events by the Congress under the clever tactical manipulation of its power-hungry Chechen Speaker, Ruslan Khasbulatov,
threatened complete emasculation. Like Gorbachev, Yeltsin has been
forced to recognize that trying to compromise with, or accede to, the
demands of the nay-sayers in Russia is a formula for disaster.

Unlike the end of the Gorbachev era, however, when there appeared
a healthier choice in the shape of the reforming faction anxious to
move Russia forward, away from the stultifying command economy
and rigid political norms of past decades, those now waiting in the
wings wish only to move back. A combination of crypto-communists,
revanchists with a nostalgia for a Greater Russia, proto-Stalinists
whose battle cry is law and order, cynical manoeuvrers for raw power,
and the odd honest, if misguided, legislator shaken by the suffering of
the elderly and the poor have brought Russia to disaster's edge.

Boris Yeltsin's shiny armour is tarnished, but he still appears the
best man in Russia for this season. If he is forced from power, or
hamstrung in his exercise of it, the consequences for Russia, its neighbours and the world are grave. The economy, now swinging uneasily
between privatization and subsidized support for inefficient state industries, can be expected to spiral out of control. Important provinces
and smaller regions, already seeking greater autonomy, will seize on

the collapse of central government to assert complete control over their own affairs. It is possible that no matter which group wins the current struggle, there may be no Russia in its present form to rule.

The new nations that rose from the rubble of the Soviet Union or emerged from the shadows of the Warsaw Pact will feel threatened by the strengthened voices calling for a recovery of a Russian Empire. Their efforts towards political and economic modernization, which are in some cases hesitant and feeble enough, will be jeopardized. And while chaotic conditions in Russia may ensure that the democratic world will not be faced with the kind of military and ideological threat the USSR posed, those nations will have lost the promise of partnership in the search for a better world polity.

It is true that under most circumstances it is a mistake in international politics to rely on specific personalities in the pursuit of foreign policy goals, but in this case it may be necessary to revise this axiom. In Russia, Yeltsin, even though he has appeared irresolute and too willing to compromise, still represents the reforming cause. Despite the many mistakes he has made, without him it is difficult to see it surviving. Thus if the West wishes to aid the cause it will need to aid Yeltsin. It is for this reason that President Clinton carefully said, 'Boris Yeltsin is the elected president of Russia . . . sticking up for democracy and civil liberties and market reforms, and I'm going to support that.' This is not the time for the statesmen of the West to flinch. A general Western policy towards the Russian reform process that goes beyond erratic crisis management has still to be confected.

How Many Nuclear Powers?

One of the telling arguments for helping to sustain a reforming Russia lies in the nuclear field. In 1992 the agenda for arms control moved from negotiation to cooperation to implementation. The nine years of tortuous negotiation required to produce the ground-breaking START I treaty were mocked by the rapidity with which the START II treaty was reached. This treaty sliced further into nuclear arsenals than anyone would have dreamed possible only a few years ago. What was now required was implementation, while the confidence built by the reductions made it possible to cooperate in further reductions.

The impending climax to the Yeltsin–Congress battle casts a long shadow over these achievements. Many of those who oppose Yeltsin have placed his 'kowtowing' to the West, in arms control as well as other areas, high in their litany of his sins. Not only would they be unwilling to agree to further reductions, they would trash agreements already reached. It is doubtful that they could find any spare change to improve on present nuclear arsenals, but they would make certain that Russia would keep everything it now has.

Equally serious is the impact this would have on the other countries that acquired nuclear weapons when the USSR sundered. Belarus and Kazakhstan agreed in early 1993 to dismantle the weapons left on their territory, but Ukraine has consistently held out. Part of its reluctance was to ensure increased Western aid in exchange for destroying the weapons, but part was a real fear of Russian intentions. This fear will be enhanced if Yeltsin is replaced. Russian Vice-President Aleksandr Rutskoi, who could inherit the presidency, has never hidden his view that at a minimum Crimea is part of Russia and should be folded back into a Russian map.

The pitch of other threats to nuclear non-proliferation either remained high or rose. Neither Pakistan nor India was willing to abandon programmes that are very close to weapons construction, if they have not already done so. Both countries continue to refuse to join the Nuclear Non-Proliferation Treaty regime, thus preventing IAEA inspection and control. Although this did not alter the existing situation, it did disappoint hopes of taking a step forward. Worse was the decision by Pyongyang in March 1993 to take a step back. To avoid an impending IAEA inspection of a suspect site, North Korea became the first country to withdraw from the NPT.

The dam that the world has been trying to build against a rapid expansion in the number of nuclear-capable countries has thus sprung a leak. It will not be easy to find an effective patch. North Korea lives up to the historical name for Korea: the Hermit Kingdom. It has long been isolated diplomatically and economically, leaving few pressure points for outside powers to push. Talk about surgical strikes by US aircraft against suspect installations worries South Korea considerably. The fanatic leadership in the North could be expected to retaliate with an attack towards Seoul, only 40 miles from the border, without hesitation.

It is possible that a compromise can be reached, although it is difficult to see what it might be. The United States has decided to use the 90 days period before the withdrawal of North Korea from the NPT takes effect to use all diplomatic means to encourage a reversal of the action. The two nations have begun talks in Beijing. Although China has declared that it will not allow discussion in the UN Security Council of sanctions against North Korea, this has more to do with Chinese reluctance to encourage interference in a country's internal affairs than with a desire to see Pyongyang with a nuclear bomb. There is some evidence that the Chinese position on this vital question is the same as the rest of the world: North Korea is too erratic a power to entrust with weapons of mass destruction. The Chinese, North Korea's only remaining 'friend', are concerned that their country could be involved in a North Korean adventure which they would not approve.

Other neighbouring countries will be much more concerned than that, for they might be the objects of such an adventure. South Korea, and in the longer term even Japan, might feel obliged to follow North Korea's unwelcome lead. Even though both countries have a nuclear patron, it seems likely that, if necessary, they would prefer to put their trust in their own ability to respond in kind than to rely on the US to do the right thing. Nor would either country have difficulty joining the club. The secret has long been out. All that is necessary now is a technical engineering base, sufficient money, and a little time.

The surprise announcement by President de Klerk of South African that his country had built six atomic bombs and had dismantled them three years ago was a sharp reminder that it can be done, and done in relative secrecy. The bombs might have been crude ones, but they were sufficiently devastating to have worried any neighbouring country which knew that Pretoria had them. There was no question why the South Africans had given them up. It was not from a sudden realization that it was wrong to be among the proliferators in today's world, nor a feeling of horror of nuclear weapons, but a cold calculation that the South African government must sooner than later be led by black ANC members. There is some question of how it planned to use them, however.

North Korea is a very different kind of regime. The danger of it using weapons of this kind if it had them for something other than demonstration purposes is considerably higher than for South Africa. The consequences for regional security, and for the non-proliferation efforts on the wider world scene, are ominous. There may be no remedy short of force in one form or another, but the seriousness of this North Korean action requires an equally serious response. The international community should prepare itself to face up to the challenge and to face down the challenger.

Old-Fashioned Nationalism

It was not wholly unexpected that the collapse of artificial political constructs like the former Soviet Union and Yugoslavia gave rise to new peaks of ethno-nationalism. Somewhat less expected was the resurgence of nationalist feelings within Europe as parliaments and people were forced by the calendar to face the momentous decisions reflected in the Maastricht Treaty. These old feelings had been submerged for decades in the need to face the common danger of communist antagonism; with that threat lifted there was a stepping back and review. This hesitancy was reinforced by the spread and depth of the economic recession. In the flush of earlier affluence, opening up borders to a single market had appeared an easy task. At the end of 1992, when ratification by all signatories of the Maastricht Treaty was supposed to have been concluded, it no longer looked like that.

The failure of the Danish referendum did not quite shred the Treaty. Compromises, along the lines of the British opting-out mechanism, have been agreed which may overcome Danish (and British) misgivings by summer 1993. Even if they do, these compromises reflect the underlying reality. The drive for political and security integration has slowed considerably, as politicians, who had allowed their enthusiasm to race ahead of the feelings of the electorate, were not accorded the degree of support they had expected. It is now in danger of petering out as nationalist concepts of economic and security protectionism return.

Complicating efforts by true believers to reverse these trends is the weakened stature of governments throughout Europe. In Germany, France, the UK and Italy parties too long in power and led by politicians the people are tired of are hard put to energize themselves, let alone realize hopes for a better future. These leaders have run into a solid wall of rising unemployment, ailing industries, increasing tension over immigration and wrenching national self-doubt. Until a mood of healthy confidence returns, more of the people and their leaders will view internationalism, and regional integration, as unaffordable luxuries.

One Bright Light

The United States is also struggling under the weight of many of the same economic and social pressures, but there a new sense of possibility has swelled. The newly elected president and administration have pulled people's heads out of the sand. In place of the constant expressions of rosy optimism by previous administrations this one has begun to tell at least some of the truth about what is wrong, and more importantly, to argue convincingly that what is needed is relatively costly individual sacrifice. To the surprise of the Jeremiahs in the press and Congress, this has been accepted with good grace and has awakened new spirit. It has reaffirmed an old truth: those who are willing to lead will find followers. In America, however, the desire for quick payoffs makes for particularly fickle followers. Whether Clinton can produce enough results to assure that they will sustain the zest needed to carry through his programme will be a challenge.

In his treatment of international issues there was a change of tone from the US as well. During his campaign Bill Clinton had emphasized that he would change the priorities of the US government from George Bush's stress on foreign affairs so that it could concentrate on solving domestic problems. But the US cannot retire from the world. Fortunately, the new president has shown no indication of wanting to. His approach to the problems he has inherited seems different from that of his predecessors, but he will need some time to extricate himself and the country from some positions that the previous administration tried to lock into place. One of the last international acts Bush took as president was to bomb positions in Iraq and to lay the blame for such retaliation, once again, on Saddam Hussein. Clinton clearly wants to de-personalize this conflict, but he must move slowly, almost stealthily, to wriggle out of the straitjacket in which the country has been bound. The problem of Haiti's political future and its refugees is another unwelcome inheritance where he intends to introduce a different policy, but again it is one where the pace is dictated by earlier decisions.

In two other areas the administration has moved more positively to reassert a US lead. With regard to Bosnia-Herzegovina the clarion call to military action stuttered because of opposition both internally, from the US defence and Congressional leadership, and externally, from reluctant allies. But even the hesitant US actions to bring pressure to bear against the aggressors and to succour the victims marked a change from non-involvement in the year past. There was no hesitation in the push to support Boris Yeltsin and the reforms in Russia. Like Yeltsin's own awakening to the dangers it comes late in the day, perhaps too late to keep from slipping into a very dark night.

Get Thee Behind Us, Nationalism

These indications that the US under Bill Clinton has no intention of withdrawing from providing a moral lead in international affairs must be greeted with at least two cheers. The third should be withheld until it is clearer that the new administration is not sinking into a nationalist-driven, protectionist economic role. If the US follows its recent harsh rhetoric demanding adjustments in trade matters to accord with US desires, the Uruguay round will truly founder, GATT may become a footnote to history, and a more sensible international economic order will not be built. It may be that the dissonant sounds coming from Washington are tactical ploys, aimed at a domestic audience. The climax has yet to be reached, and decent compromises may yet steady the threatened edifice. There is very little time left, however, for statesmen to start acting in a statesmanlike manner.

The world has fallen once again into bad habits. The international community that was slowly knitting together is in serious danger of unravelling into skeins of squabbling neighbours. The Western multilateral structures remain, but much of the life that infused them has dissipated as the unifying force of a clear outside threat dissolved. Global institutions, and especially the UN, have to be given the resources to match the hopes that people place in them or their reputation will fade and the international community will have no credible organization to act in its name.

Given the economic and even political recession in the West, it is difficult to depend for international security on benign political and military management by Western powers whose direct national interests are not always at stake. And yet regional organizations are not sufficiently strong to deal with local instabilities. The disinterested do not have the will or sometimes the power; those that are immediately implicated either do not have the capacity or sufficient credibility. Unless that security gap is breached, the fractionating tendencies in the world will overwhelm the need for integration.

Strategic Policy Issues

THE CHALLENGE OF SELF-DETERMINATION

The struggle for self-determination is one of the most powerful forces shaping the strategic landscape today. In its name waves of suddenly released feelings have in just a few years accelerated the collapse of the Soviet Union and Yugoslavia, replaced totalitarian and authoritarian regimes with democratizing or democratic regimes, and ignited and sustained civil wars all around the globe. It threatens to tear apart such newly formed or reborn states as Russia, Georgia and Moldova, and even to trigger regional wars in the Balkans, the Middle East and the Caucasus. And yet, self-determination remains a principle which is largely misunderstood.

Some Definitions

Self-determination is usually taken to mean that a 'people' determines its own future. This definition begs two questions. What is a 'people' (i.e., which community is entitled to claim the right to self-determination)? And how is a 'people' to exercise the right to self-determination (i.e., to determine its own future)? The answers to these questions have changed radically over time and there is still no consensus.

And yet there have been two constants in self-determination. First, it is seen as a dynamic and not a finite process: it should be exercised continuously without interruption. Second, self-determination has two dimensions: an internal one which regulates relations between rulers and ruled within the community; and an external one which regulates relations between the self-defined community and the outside world. The internal dimension makes 'the people' (the citizens) the source of state legitimacy and thus requires a democratic form of government. In this sense, self-determination is analogous to the existence of popular sovereignty. The external dimension makes the community a distinct political entity entitled to shape its ties with other political entities, whether states, minority groups, or international organizations. Independent statehood is only one of many forms these ties can take.

The definition of who is entitled to claim self-determination and how it can be exercised has changed since the concept first emerged out of the American and French revolutions of the eighteenth century. While the American revolution was directed primarily against British rule, the French revolution was directed against the absolutist monarchy. The first aimed at achieving internal and external self-determination, in the forms of democracy and independent statehood, while the second aimed only at internal self-determination. During this period and throughout the nineteenth century, there was no serious questioning of what constituted a 'people'.

The ideal of self-determination quickly spread to Latin America and the rest of Europe, sparking wars of national liberation which ultimately led to the emergence of new states. It was not until the First World War, however, when US President Woodrow Wilson promoted the concept as 'an imperative principle of action, which statesmen will henceforth ignore at their peril', that it became a principle of international relations. Self-determination was offered as a formula for a peaceful and harmonious world. It would give each 'people' living in the former territories of the defeated empires (German, Austro-Hungarian and Ottoman) their own state with their own democratic government. The 'people' that Wilson had in mind were pre-existing national communities, but not those living under the rule of the victorious Allied powers.

Although the 1920 League of Nations Covenant did not once mention self-determination, it set up two separate mechanisms to promote it: internationally supervised plebiscites in contested border areas; and the international protection of national minorities. The League was not concerned with producing democratic forms of government; it only promoted the external dimension of self-determination. Because of the inherent difficulties in establishing objective criteria for nationality (what constitutes a 'people') and because of great-power interests, the post-war settlement was a selective and *ad hoc* application of the principle.

In contrast to the League, self-determination became one of the purposes of the United Nations. It was mandated to promote self-government in non-self-governing territories, both colonies and trust territories. The principle of self-determination was redefined by UN resolutions (like General Assembly Resolution 1514 in 1960) as a right to self-determination. Rapporteurs of UN Commissions spoke of it as a 'peremptory' right.

This right, however, did not supersede that of governments to preserve the sovereignty and territorial integrity of the states they governed, once these states became independent. Internationally recognized states were allowed, and even helped, to quell any attempt at secession, as in Congo–Katanga in 1960, and Nigeria–Biafra in 1967. East Pakistan's secession from Pakistan in 1970–71 to form Bangladesh was for some time the exception which confirmed the rule. That secession was recognized only because the UN Security Council considered this the only way to ensure international peace and security which was threatened by war between India and Pakistan. It was not until Croatia and Slovenia seceded from Yugoslavia in 1991 that the international community again recognized the sovereignty of states created without the agreement of the existing central government.

The UN has been involved in a number of referenda on self-determination, including most recently Namibia (carried out successfully in 1989), Eritrea (scheduled for April 1993) and the Western Sahara (date not yet determined). The UN's experience in Eritrea and the Western

Sahara will affect the way the international community deals with future claims to self-determination. The UN-sponsored exercise of deciding who has the right to vote in the Western Sahara's proposed referendum may set a precedent for how to define what constitutes a people. In both the Western Sahara and Eritrea voters will determine the international status of the two territorial entities: whether to opt for independence or union with a neighbouring state.

During the Cold War, the Conference on Security and Cooperation in Europe (CSCE) helped to resurrect the original concept of self-determination. It restored the link between the internal and external dimensions of self-determination in the Helsinki Final Act (1975) which recognized that, on the basis of the right to self-determination, all peoples can determine their own internal and external affairs. The CSCE, however, also restated the principles of the inviolability of frontiers, the territorial integrity of states and the peaceful settlement of disputes. By lumping all these principles together, it took the first step on the road to redefining the right to self-determination as one which has to be reconciled with the requirements of international peace and security.

With the end of the Cold War, the CSCE took the next step along the same road. It generated detailed agreements to protect 'the rights of persons belonging to national minorities' which, it recognized, 'do not constitute exclusively an internal affair of the respective state.' The Charter of Paris for a New Europe (1990) and the Concluding Document of the CSCE Copenhagen Conference on the Human Dimension (1990), along with the recently created post of High Commissioner for Minority Issues, are the main threads of an international safety net meant to reassure ethnic groups that their concerns can and should be met without resorting to violence and within the borders of existing states. The CSCE is attempting to help ethnic groups exercise external self-determination short of independent statehood by regulating their relations within the state in which they live. In doing so it is establishing direct relations between itself and ethnic groups, thus bypassing sovereign governments.

The Power of Self-determination

It was primarily the explosion of ethnic, nationalist and religious feeling unloosed by the collapse of the Soviet empire and the disintegration of Yugoslavia which turned the CSCE's collective mind to the problem of self-determination. Its attraction had always been very powerful, but has now grown stronger. For the democratic nations of the West, the challenge presented by the power of self-determination had to be met if any semblance of a 'new world' were to be created.

One reason for the many recent claims to self-determination is that it brings with it international recognition and stature. Based on the rich legal tradition behind the modern understanding of self-determination, movements and communities can claim the right to be recognized as legitimate participants in international relations, and self-proclaimed territorial entities can seek recognition of their statehood. Such recognition opens up membership in international organizations, and gives direct access to foreign governments through the diplomatic recognition which usually follows. It can also have a domestic side-effect of helping the leadership by shoring up its prestige internationally. Above all, it represents a certain degree of political support by foreign powers. This support may even go as far as military aid, although the case of Bosnia-Herzegovina shows that international legitimacy and access to military support do not always go together. Recognition of a state or an organization involved in a civil war can also help bring about intervention in favour of the beleaguered community.

Nevertheless, most of the advantages of claiming the right to self-determination are harvested in the ripe field of internal politics. Leaders and movements claim the right primarily because it is an effective mechanism to mobilize the population they seek to lead. Self-determination is offered as a programme, or a substitute for a programme, which will take care of the problems plaguing the population. In the Casamance region of Senegal and in New Caledonia, it is a rallying cry for those who oppose the exploitation of the natural resources of their region by outsiders. In the Transylvania region of Romania and in Quebec, it is offered as a way to defend the people's culture. In the Kosovo region of Serbia and Indonesian-occupied East Timor, it is put forward as the only answer to endemic and large-scale abuses of human and collective rights by the state. The movements spearheading claims to self-determination do not attract recruits ready to sacrifice their lives solely on the basis of the ideological appeal of the concept, even though this is an important part of it, but because it promises to free them from their many every-day problems: poverty, abuse, discrimination and repression.

Movements also claim self-determination because it allows them to bring together a number of disparate factions. Partly because of the sheer ambiguity of the term, it is the one unifying aim in a coalition of otherwise competing political forces. The Sudan People's Liberation Movement, the militia forces of 'Somaliland' and the Palestine Liberation Organization are examples of such movements united by their common claim to self-determination, but by little else.

Political leaders use their call to self-determination to protect themselves from attacks by more extremist politicians and to allow themselves to mobilize popular support by riding a nationalist wave which they have helped to create. The Palestinian leader Yasser Arafat is one politician who has made good use of this tool. The transformation of the Serb leader Slobodan Milosevic from Yugoslav communist patriot to Serb nationalist is another example.

The Scope of Conflict

At the root of many ethnic conflicts are irreconcilable, or seemingly irreconcilable, claims to self-determination. When, and if, foreign powers and international organizations decide on the appropriate re-

their repression of Kurdish separatist movements. Armenia, a co-signer of treaties with the Russian Federation and the beneficiary of much Russian sympathy, and Azerbaijan, a state with increasingly close ties to Turkey which along with Russia is the guarantor of the Nakhichevan enclave of Azerbaijan, are busy consolidating support from international coalitions in their war over the self-determination of Nagorno-Karabakh.

Western Interests

The strategic, moral, political and economic consequences of self-determination often justify and require Western and international intervention. At the very least, these conflicts raise the issue of the recognition of a new state or of a political organization as a representative of a people entitled to self-determination. At the other end of the spectrum, they force governments to decide whether or not to intervene militarily in the conflict and if so, how and to what extent. Between these two extremes lies a series of policy options, including economic sanctions, arms embargoes and peacekeeping operations.

The primary strategic Western interest at the moment is to ensure that self-determination conflicts do not lead to the reversal of the positive developments of the last two years in Russia. There is a justified concern that demands for self-determination in the Russian Federation will help bring about either a nationalist, anti-democratic backlash or the collapse of state institutions and the outbreak of many civil wars. The importance of this strategic interest should be balanced by a realistic assessment of what the West can do to avert any of those outcomes.

There are two other more general strategic interests which need to be evaluated on a case-by-case basis. The first is the danger of internal conflicts over self-determination escalating into regional wars by drawing in a neighbouring state or states. A conflict between Serbs and Albanians in the Serbian province of Kosovo, for example, may draw Albania into a war with Serbia; or the Armenian–Azeri conflict over the Nagorno-Karabakh enclave's right to choose may draw Iran, Turkey and Russia into the conflict. The fear of these conflicts escalating into regional wars is often overstated, especially by those parties hoping to garner international support. Regional powers, although sometimes eager to intervene in civil wars for reasons of domestic politics, limit their ambitions and often manage to cooperate tacitly to avoid a regional conflict (India–Sri Lanka, Israel–Syria, Morocco–Algeria).

The last strategic consideration is the diffusion of self-determination wars within and across borders. Claims can spread through the 'demonstration effect'. If one group succeeds in establishing its claim to the right of self-determination by force against a central government, others will be encouraged (Abkhaz and South Ossetian separatism in Georgia; Russian and Gagauz separatism in Moldova; and North Caucasus separatism in the Russian Federation). Self-determination wars can also spread by 'contagion', by introducing weapons and militias into a neighbouring country which hitherto had been at peace (the state of Tamil Nadu in India, in Bangladesh near the border with Burma).

In addition to these strategic interests, there are moral, political and economic considerations which may call for a Western and international response to self-determination. The ideal is correctly associated with democracy and the collective rights of ethnic minorities. It is usually invoked in the face of abuses of human rights. Yet self-determination conflicts also often produce human tragedies: massacres, violent expulsion of populations from their homes, and massive refugee flows. Western governments have a political interest in intervention because public opinion in their countries sympathizes with most claims to self-determination. And the West has an economic interest in limiting self-determination conflicts because instability is the enemy of commerce and civil wars destroy potential markets.

What Can Be Done?

Self-determination conflicts should not be ignored and self-determination claims should not be dismissed wholesale as many observers are quick to do. Even if the international community produced a consensus to oppose all future claims, it would not stop them from being made, often violently. They are not the result of an alleged 'permissive' international environment; they have more to do with the existing state of relations between ruling governments and ethnically distinct populations.

Once Western governments and the international community make the decision to avoid or limit the pernicious aspects of a particular case of self-determination, they have to address its root causes. Where it is fuelled primarily by national myths and ideologies of nationalist expansion (the 'Greater X' variety) the options are limited to offering varying degrees of support to the opposing side. Where the claims are facilitated by economic exploitation, human rights abuses or collective rights abuses (or fear thereof), the first step must be to neutralize them. Then an appropriate mechanism must be found to mediate, adjudicate and enforce settlements. Furthermore, the outside powers have to offer creative solutions and engage in 'constitutional engineering' while at the same time developing the ability to guarantee the viability of the agreements brokered. The costs of regulating self-determination are certain to be enormous, but the costs of inaction may be even greater.

The problem with many cases of self-determination is that satisfying concerns within existing borders demands very intrusive activity by the international community. Until regional security organizations and international law permit greater intrusiveness, it is unlikely that the root causes of such claims will be dealt with before they take a violent form. It is here that the nexus between changes in international law and international security is most evident.

INTERNATIONAL LAW AND SECURITY

The sovereignty of the state is the basis of two of the most important principles of the post-1945 international legal order: that the territorial integrity of each state is inviolable; and that each state is entitled to be free from outside intervention in its internal affairs. The continuing significance of these principles has been borne out by many of the events of the last few years. One of the reasons why Iraq's invasion of Kuwait posed such a challenge to the international community was that it entailed a fundamental repudiation of the principle of the territorial integrity of states. In evicting Iraq from Kuwait the international community was not so much seeking to create a new world order as to defend one of the central pillars of the existing order. As for the principle of non-intervention, this was reaffirmed by the International Court of Justice in the 1986 case of *Nicaragua v. United States*, in which the Court described the duty to respect the political integrity of each state as a natural corollary of the protection of territorial integrity.

Nevertheless, while the core of these principles remains intact and retains its importance, recent events are forcing a re-examination of some of the rules which were thought to flow from them. The dissolution of the USSR, Yugoslavia and Czechoslovakia into more than 20 states, many of which contain regions or ethnic groups which want to secede and create new states in their turn, has raised fundamental questions about statehood and the inviolability of frontiers, while the extent of the principle of non-intervention has come in for renewed scrutiny as a result of recent events in Somalia, Iraq and Liberia, as well as in the former Yugoslavia.

Self-Determination

The idea of self-determination is not particularly new but few concepts have undergone such a radical transformation in so short a time. The references to self-determination in the United Nations Charter (Article 1(2) and Article 55) are essentially an assertion not of the right of a people to create a state, but the right of existing states to determine their internal affairs free from intervention. It was only as a result of a process which took many years (and which reached its apotheosis in the 1960s and 1970s) that self-determination developed into the principle that the people of a colony had the right to determine the future of that colony, a right which was normally exercised by the creation of an independent state. Self-determination in this form was perceived as a right of the whole population of a colonial unit, irrespective of ethnic or cultural diversity and the whimsical nature of colonial boundaries, not as a basis for redrawing maps on racial or other grounds. Moreover, it was at this stage seen as a right which a people exercised only once, when they achieved independence from colonial rule, not a continuing right to determine, for example through a democratic process, the future of the new state which was thus created.

Most important of all, self-determination was treated as a right pertaining only to a people living under colonial or quasi-colonial rule. Most states, especially those which had come into existence as a result of the exercise of this right, were firmly of the view that it could not affect the territorial integrity of existing states and thus gave no right of secession to groups within those states. So far as secession was concerned, international law was, at most, neutral. An entity which attempted to secede from an existing state – as Biafra did from Nigeria in the late 1960s or Bangladesh from Pakistan a few years later – was treated as having no right to do so but nor was it prohibited by international law and if, as in the case of Bangladesh, the secessionists were successful, international law accepted that fact and the international community recognized the creation of a new state.

If the right to self-determination had remained within these confines, it would swiftly have become of only historical interest as the decolonization of the 1960s and 1970s came to an end. In practice, however, the attempts to restrict the scope of self-determination in this way proved untenable and the concept gradually began a second mutation, developing into a more extensive right, the shape of which is still far from clear.

Ironically, the seeds of this change were sown in the 1960s when the 'decolonization' view of self-determination was at its height. Article 1 (1) of the International Covenant on Civil and Political Rights, which was adopted in 1966 and now has over 110 states as parties, provided that:

All peoples have the right of self-determination. By virtue of that right they freely determine their political status and freely pursue their economic, social and cultural development.

This provision has subsequently been interpreted by the United Nations Human Rights Committee (which, within an admittedly confined jurisdiction and with very restricted powers, is charged with supervising the implementation of the Covenant) as the recognition of a continuing right to self-determination in the form of a right on the part of the people of a state to determine the political, social and economic destiny of that state.

It would, of course, be idle to pretend that the reality of the political process in many (perhaps most) states comes anywhere near this ideal, or that the Human Rights Committee will be able to compel compliance with this modern notion of self-determination. Nevertheless, to dismiss this development as being of purely academic importance would also be wide of the mark. An increasing number of states are making aid dependent (at least in part) on movement towards some kind of democratic process. This step can be defended in the UN and elsewhere as compatible with the principle of non-intervention precisely because of the evolution in the right of self-determination, for it is not a breach of that principle to insist that a state comply with its international obligations.

A different and, in the short term at least, more important development is that the right to create a state in the exercise of self-determination has appeared in the last few years to be breaking free from its roots in decolonization. As the USSR and Yugoslavia began to dissolve, more and more states spoke of the federal units within those states as having a right to self-determination. This was particularly the case with Western reaction to the attempts by the Baltic states to reassert their independence after 1989 (although the right of these countries to re-establish themselves as independent states rested on the illegality of their incorporation into the USSR in 1940, rather than the right to self-determination). It reached its peak with the insistence of the European Community states on recognizing Bosnia-Herzegovina as an independent state and securing its admission to the UN in May 1992, even though its government never controlled more than a fraction of its territory and Bosnia-Herzegovina did not meet the traditional criteria for recognition. The stark contrast between the international community's acceptance of Bosnian independence and its treatment of Biafra 25 years earlier reflects the evolution of the concept of self-determination as well as the different political circumstances of the two cases.

Yet the application of the principle of self-determination in the USSR and Yugoslavia still has much in common with the practice in the decolonization era. Self-determination is still seen as the right of the people of a defined territory and not as a right belonging to ethnic groups or minorities. Thus, the people of Bosnia and Croatia were treated as possessing this right, but the Arbitration Commission established by the Peace Conference on Yugoslavia ('the Badinter Commission') rejected a submission that the Serbian minorities in these republics also possessed a right to self-determination, although it sought to soften the effects of this ruling by stating that the Serbs in the two republics possessed significant minority rights which the majorities in the two new states were obliged to respect. Similarly, the Vance-Owen plans for a cantonal constitution for Bosnia (like the UN Secretary-General's proposals for Cyprus) are built around the notion that minorities can be granted internal autonomy but denied a right to secede. Laudable as such aims may be, the likelihood of their success must be open to question. If, as some have suggested, the right of self-determination now means that units within a federal state have a right under international law to secede from the federation but that no such right extends to communities within such federal units (or, presumably, to communities within a unitary state), that limitation is likely to appear as artificial as the traditional limitation of self-determination to colonial peoples and will probably be as difficult to sustain.

A further problem is that the practice of the international community, and particularly of European institutions such as the EC and the Conference on Security and Cooperation in Europe (CSCE), in applying the principle of self-determination in the Balkans and the USSR is based upon the principle that frontiers are inviolable. Applied to existing international boundaries between states, this principle is, of course, of fundamental importance. To apply it to internal frontiers within a federal state, however, is more problematic. In the USSR, in particular, these boundaries were often highly artificial and relatively unimportant. The result is that there are scores of boundary disputes between the states which emerged when the USSR dissolved, and numerous cases of ethnic groups which find themselves a minority within one of the new states and attempting, often by force, either to carve out a state of their own or to ensure the transfer of the territory in which they live to one of the adjacent states.

Nevertheless, it is easier to criticize the approach taken to the right to self-determination than to suggest an answer to the problems thus identified. In this era of what one writer has called 'post-modern tribalism', the best hope probably lies in seeking to make secession seem less attractive by stressing the other side of self-determination, namely the right of all the people of a state to participate in the governance of that state and the right of minorities to respect for their separate identities.

State Succession

The disintegration of the USSR and Yugoslavia has also raised important questions about the law relating to state succession. These questions were of particular significance in the case of the USSR, since the obligations of that state (particularly in relation to disarmament) were many and substantial, and the UN Charter allocated one of the five permanent seats on the Security Council to the USSR by name. The speed of the Soviet collapse was such that the choice of who should occupy that seat at the Council was one which had to be made quickly. In the circumstances, the other permanent members (particularly the UK and France who have an obvious interest in not opening any discussion on permanent membership of the Council) were happy to accept the Russian Republic's contention that it was the continuation of the former USSR and thus automatically inherited its seat in international organizations. The other states which emerged from the USSR, however, were to be treated as successor states which would assume a share of the rights and duties of the USSR but (with the exception of Ukraine and Belarus which, for historical reasons, were already members) would have to apply for membership of the UN and other international organizations.

Only a few months later, in April 1992, a different approach was taken in the case of the former Yugoslavia. The republics of Serbia and Montenegro combined to form the Federal Republic of Yugoslavia (FRY), which they claimed was the continuation of the old Socialist Federal Republic of Yugoslavia (SFRY) from which the Republics of Bosnia, Croatia, Macedonia and Slovenia had broken away. This claim was rejected by the United Nations and the Peace Conference on Yugoslavia, which insisted that the FRY was a new state and that none of the states which had emerged from the collapse of the SFRY could claim to be the continuation of that state. The result was that the Yugoslav seat at the UN was still empty at the beginning of 1993. The Yugoslav case was, of course, different from that of the USSR – the Russian Republic was a larger and more important part of the USSR than Serbia and Montenegro were of the SFRY, and the history of the two states was different – but it is clear that for many states the rejection of the FRY's claims was a way of punishing Serbia for the atrocities and the continued fighting in Bosnia and of bringing pressure to bear to put a stop to these.

On a less dramatic plane, international lawyers are likely to be busy for some time to come in attempting to determine how the assets and obligations of the USSR and Yugoslavia should be shared out between the successor states, and it is not entirely clear what legal standards will be applied. Although two international conventions on questions of state succession were produced by the International Law Commission during the 1970s and 1980s and adopted at international conferences, they have attracted only a handful of ratifications and are, in any event, very much the product of decolonization.

Humanitarian Intervention

Perhaps the greatest change in the law relating to state sovereignty, however, has been in the area of humanitarian intervention. Developments here have been prompted by two different concerns. First, there have been a number of cases, of which Somalia is the best known, in which the population of a state has faced starvation and it has proved impossible to deliver relief supplies without some kind of military involvement. Second, there has been increasing pressure for military intervention to prevent the widespread abuse of human rights in some states. The traditional approach to these questions, based upon the twin principles of territorial integrity and non-intervention, was that humanitarian aid could be delivered to the people of a state only with the consent of the government of that state and, *a fortiori*, any kind of military intervention by one state in the territory of another was absolutely prohibited. Intervention by the United Nations was, in principle, a different matter. Notwithstanding the ban (in Article 2(7) of the UN Charter) on UN intervention in the internal affairs of a state, the UN Security Council has always had the power, under Chapter VII of the Charter, to take enforcement action if the situation in a state posed a threat to international peace and security. Until recently, however, no real use was made of that power apart from the imposition of an arms embargo against South Africa in the 1970s.

In April 1991, however, the United States and a group of Western countries intervened in northern Iraq to ensure the delivery of relief supplies to the Kurdish refugees there and subsequently to compel Iraq to withdraw its forces from that part of the country in order to create a 'safe haven' to which refugees could return. This action took place against the background of Security Council Resolution 688, which identified the situation in Iraq as a threat to international peace and demanded that Iraq cease attacks upon its civilian population. Resolution 688 was not, however, a Chapter VII resolution and, unlike the resolutions adopted in respect of Kuwait, contained no mandate for the coalition states to enforce its terms. Although the states taking part in the operation were initially vague about its legal basis, it gradually became clear that they were asserting a right of humanitarian intervention in a case of what UK Foreign Secretary Douglas Hurd termed 'extreme humanitarian need'. This justification was made explicit by the UK in the summer of 1992 when the same states imposed the 'no-fly zone' in southern Iraq, and in January 1993 when their aircraft attacked Iraqi missile sites in both southern and northern Iraq. It may be noted that the US, while also advancing the argument put forward by the UK, went further and claimed a mandate from the UN to take action against Iraq because of Iraq's violations of the cease-fire resolution (Resolution 687) adopted by the Council in the aftermath of the Kuwait conflict. This argument was supported by the UN Secretary-General. One US attack, on a nuclear production facility outside Baghdad, could only be justified on this basis, since it had no relevance to the protection of the Kurds or the Shi'ites.

The Economic Community of West African States (ECOWAS) also relied on humanitarian arguments to justify its 1990 intervention in Liberia, where it deployed a peacekeeping force and installed an interim government following the death of President Samuel Doe. Neither the Iraq nor the Liberian interventions aroused the storm of protest or legal challenge which they would once have done. The Security Council has now given a measure of support to the ECOWAS operation by imposing an arms embargo on Liberia at the request of ECOWAS.

The Security Council measures in Liberia can easily be accommodated within the terms of Chapter VII: there was a clear threat to international peace as the fighting in Liberia was spilling over into neighbouring Sierra Leone. The measures taken by the Security Council in Somalia are less easily justified. Initial UN action was undertaken with the consent of the Somalian government (although that government had for all practical purposes ceased to exist), but by late 1992 the humanitarian effort had become bogged down in the faction-fighting in the country. In December 1992, therefore, the Council adopted a Chapter VII resolution authorizing the United States to use 'all necessary means to establish . . . a secure environment for humanitarian relief operations in Somalia' (Resolution 794). This time, there was no obvious threat to other states and the preamble to the resolution made clear that it was the 'magnitude of the human tragedy' in Somalia which itself constituted the threat to international peace. Resolution

units'), the immediate establishment of a $50m peacekeeping reserve fund, and the establishment of a pre-positioned stock of basic peace-keeping equipment. Particular emphasis was placed on the concept of 'preventive deployment' as a means of pre-empting potential inter- or intra-state conflicts. Lastly, the report stressed the need for the UN to initiate practical cooperation with regional organizations, thus giving life to Chapter VIII of the Charter.

Even as the Secretary-General and his closest advisors were preparing the report there were more visible indications of the organization's new-found activism. By the time it was finished the Security Council had authorized three new major operations: in Croatia, Cambodia and Somalia. In February 1992, the first in a series of promised reforms designed to streamline the Secretariat was enacted, cutting the number of top departments from 20 to 8, and reducing the number of first- and second-level jobs from 48 to 32.

By the end of 1992, however, the mood had changed. The continuing war in Bosnia, the complete failure of the United Nation's Operation in Somalia (UNOSOM), the relapse of Angola into civil war and the growing difficulties encountered by the UN Transitional Authority in Cambodia (UNTAC) had seriously deflated the sense of optimism with which the year had begun. In addition, the slow pace of UN reform reduced the effectiveness of operations everywhere. Within the Secretariat the half-hearted response of the international community, especially the Permanent Five, to the proposals contained in the 'Agenda for Peace' and continuing financial instability, added to a growing sense of frustration and uncertainty.

Eroding Traditional Assumptions

In the abstract, 'peacekeeping', 'peacemaking' and 'peace-enforcement' are easily distinguished and logically connected. Peacekeeping is a holding action; a temporary measure aimed at defusing tensions and reducing the incentives for parties to resume violent conflict. Peacemaking covers all conflict resolution and mediation techniques set forth in Chapter VI of the UN Charter and is designed to bring hostile parties to agreement. Peace-enforcement involves measures to compel a recalcitrant party to abide by the resolutions of an international body.

Over the past year the largely academic quality of these distinctions has become increasingly apparent. The term 'peacekeeping' is now used to describe large-scale civilian and military operations conducted in an environment in which the techniques and management structure supporting peacekeeping in its strictest sense are proving to be wholly inadequate. In Cambodia the UN has been charged with the task of rebuilding a nation ravaged by more than 30 years of war, while in Bosnia-Herzegovina UN forces are seeking to ensure that essential relief supplies reach a beleaguered population in the midst of a brutal communal war. Indeed, the UN operation in Bosnia has not been concerned with peacekeeping at all; there has been no peace to keep. In Angola the UN was supposed to have disarmed UNITA and MPLA soldiers, created a new joint army and monitored multiparty elections in a country two-thirds the size of Western Europe.

In spite of the exceptionally ambitious nature of operations undertaken in 1992, there has been no corresponding re-evaluation of UN military requirements, concepts of operations, and arrangements for a continuous and reliable system of financing. The upshot has been a depressing pattern of UN involvement with little or no consideration given to the long-term political and administrative arrangements.

When the Security Council approved 'peacekeeping missions' in the former Yugoslavia, Cambodia and Somalia, it did so on the understanding that UN forces would be neither equipped nor empowered to enforce solutions. As with 'classic' peacekeeping operations, adherence to the principles of local consent and minimum force were seen as the *sine qua non* for accomplishing the tasks entrusted to the peacekeeping force. However, in its peacekeeping efforts the UN was soon faced with a critical dilemma: while Security Council authorization of an operation assumed that traditional preconditions had been met, the consent of the parties quickly disappeared during the implementation stage.

A major part of the problem – as demonstrated above all in the former Yugoslavia – has been that although the leader of a warring faction may agree to a UN-sponsored plan, this does not necessarily translate into the consent of his local commanders and troops in the field. Under the original peacekeeping plan for Croatia, the UN Protected Areas (UNPAs) were to be demilitarized and refugees repatriated, while a joint commission would oversee the restoration of Croatian authority in the Croatian areas under Yugoslav National Army (JNA) control, largely populated by Serbs but outside the boundaries of the UNPAs. The United Nations Protection Force (UNPROFOR) has not been able to implement any of these provisions; in fact, it has failed in all its stated objectives. By late 1992, the Secretary-General could only deplore the 'conditions of brutal lawlessness' existing in all four of the UN protected areas, and the resumption of heavy fighting between Croat and Serbian forces in Krajina in January 1993. Croatian forces had stormed through the UN-monitored cease-fire line, as expected by Western diplomats and UN authorities, and Serbian forces had forced their way into UN-protected arms depots and re-equipped themselves with heavy weapons.

Similarly, the crucial premise underlying UN involvement in Cambodia has been that all four parties to the original agreement had an interest in its implementation. UNTAC deployment in Cambodia, however, ran into difficulties even before it had been partially completed. Developments since February 1992 – including battalion-size engagements between government forces and the *Khmer Rouge*, assassination campaigns by the *Khmer Rouge* against ethnic Vietnamese, and direct attacks against UN forces – demonstrated the extent to which the entire operation was based on flawed assumptions, especially since no provision was made (let alone any capabilities provided) for enforcing any aspect of the original agreement. Refusing to implement the decisions reached in 1991, the *Khmer Rouge* has continued its military struggle, exploited the corruption and social tensions created by the large UN presence in the country and succeeded in consolidating its position along the border with Laos and Thailand.

It was, however, the collapse of the UN operation in Somalia which most dramatically epitomized the bankruptcy of the 'classical' approach. Conceived as a traditional peacekeeping force with highly restrictive rules of engagement, the UNOSOM mandate was to monitor a non-existent cease-fire in the capital, Mogadishu, and to provide troops to escort food supplies to distribution centres in and around the city. The initial force was made up of 50 military observers, a 500-member security force and 79 civilians.

As the situation in Somalia continued to deteriorate throughout summer 1992, it was becoming obvious that UN efforts were failing in every respect: attempts to convene a conference for 'national reconciliation' produced no results; warring factions extorted, blackmailed, robbed and murdered relief workers with total impunity while food supplies did not reach the needy. The UNOSOM force, shackled by its rules of engagement, suffered attacks on personnel and equipment and was reduced to a reporting agency describing the devastating impact of famine throughout the country.

In a letter to the Security Council in late November, the Secretary-General finally concluded that the situation in Somalia 'has deteriorated beyond the point at which it is susceptible to the peace-keeping treatment'. Informing the Security Council that the UN could not command and control an enforcement operation to create a secure environment for the uninterrupted delivery of humanitarian assistance, Boutros-Ghali urged the Council to take action under Chapter VII of the Charter and to accept an American offer to send troops into Somalia.

This, then, was a belated acknowledgement of the limits of 'classical' peacekeeping techniques in an environment where political violence, common criminality and collapse of central authority had led to a breakdown of civil society. When the UN resumes control of the Somali operation in 1993, its mandate will have been extended to include the disarming of Somali factions under Chapter VII. Similarly, on 19 February 1993 the Security Council extended the mandate of UNPROFOR and placed that operation under Chapter VII of the Charter. These are both potentially significant departures from UN practice, away from the consensual and non-forceful pattern of previous operations.

If the Somali operation and the extension of the UNPROFOR mandate in February 1993 indicate that the UN is gradually adjusting itself to demands imposed by the changing character of the international political system, other factors continue to impair the effectiveness of UN operations. In particular, three areas of acute weakness stand out: logistic planning and support; the management of peacekeeping operations; and the UN's precarious financial situation.

Logistic Planning and Support

While the operations in Cambodia and the former Yugoslavia have both been plagued by poor logistic support, especially in the start-up phase of the operation, the collapse of the UN operation in Angola in autumn 1992 provides a more depressing illustration of existing deficiencies in the area of logistic planning and field support.

One can argue that Jonas Savimbi would never have accepted the outcome of the Angolan election even if the process had been properly monitored, and that the resurgence of civil war was the inevitable result of the failure of both sides to honour their obligations under the Bicesse accord relating to the cantonment and demobilization of troops, the formation of a new Angolan army and a neutral police force, the effective control and custody of weapons, and the extension of central administration to the whole territory. Yet there can be little doubt that the role of the UNAVEM II and the coordinating agencies at the UN headquarters in New York did little to facilitate the peace process at its most critical stage.

During the electoral stage, UNAVEM II had only 350 military and 90 civilian observers in the field. For the election itself the UN deployed 400 electoral observers in two-person teams for the observation and verification of voting. The small number of observers and the acute lack of transport made it impossible for the UNAVEM teams to visit all of the nearly 6,000 polling stations; instead they relied on sample observation, covering all 18 provinces and most of the 164 municipalities, but spending an average of only 20 minutes at each station. Observation of the counting was an even more incomplete process. At the root of the difficulties was a factor which has impaired, and continues to impair, the effectiveness of all peacekeeping operations: inadequate logistic planning and support. Even though the two major challenges in Angola – transport, especially air support, and communications – were largely overcome by borrowing helicopters and fixed-wing aircraft, no proper logistic estimate had been made beforehand. Using 45 helicopters and 15 fixed-wing aircraft (the largest airlift in its history), the UN deployed electoral teams, supplies and equipment to the more inaccessible areas of the country. Yet many of the polling booths arrived only the day of the election, while other difficulties included the late arrival of voting material and a general lack of lighting, blankets and ballot boxes.

The Secretary-General's Special Representative, Margaret Joan Anstee, declared after the election that 'organizational and logistical difficulties . . . had been overcome with good will and ingenuity'. A lesson of the Angolan operation must surely be that too much reliance should not be placed on 'good will and ingenuity'. The fact that the observers were so thinly spread made it more difficult for the international community to reject outright UNITA's allegations of fraud. This in turn complicated the attempt to isolate UNITA internationally and to grant recognition to the government in Luanda.

An implicit admission by the UN of its poor performance in Angola is evident in the mandate for the new mission to Mozambique (ONUMOZ), approved by the Security Council in December 1992. The ONUMOZ force will assist in the implementation of the peace agreement signed in Rome on 4 October 1992 by the government of President Joaquim Chissano and Renamo (*Resistência Nacional Moçambicana*) under Afonso Dhlakama. It will consist of 7,500 troops, policemen and civilian administrators who, in an attempt to end 16 years of civil war, will monitor a fragile cease-fire, protect infrastructure from looting and banditry, disarm rival armies and organize nationwide elections.

The Angolan debacle also demonstrated the weaknesses in the present UN machinery for managing peacekeeping operations, including the lack of an operations centre in New York, an ambiguous chain of command to the field mission, and inadequate training and preparation for all members of the UN force.

Mismanaging Peacekeeping Operations

The UN system for planning, organizing and supporting peacekeeping operations in the field remains largely unchanged since the end of the Cold War. As a system of management it evolved out of the specific experience of peacekeeping in the Middle East. For its effective functioning it has always relied to an unusual degree on improvisation and close working relationships among members of the Secretariat in New York, and between officers and civilian personnel in the field. Although a series of changes to the Secretariat structure were introduced in February 1992, these did not address important management problems.

Most critically, no single focal point for an operation embraces operational, logistic and financial matters. The division of responsibility between the Department of Peacekeeping Operations and the Field Operations Division located within the Department of Administration and Management and responsible for the financial, administrative and logistic aspects of peacekeeping operations, remains a serious impediment to efficient cooperation between the military and civilian components of a mission. Although the Force Commander is nominally in charge of the management in the field, he is still faced with a separate chain of command from the mission's Chief Administrative Officer to the Field Operations Division in New York. The result is that the Commander's decision on a strictly operational issue may be over-turned by his Chief Administrative Officer who controls administrative and financial resources.

Even if one allows for these unsatisfactory command-and-control arrangements (which in part represent a bureaucratic compromise), the Department of Peacekeeping Operations, as presently organized, is massively understaffed and not in a position to cope with the range of demands placed on it. The Office of the Military Advisor, which forms part of the Department, has less than 20 officers attached to it and is staffed by officers who are far too junior, while lacking a necessary component of non-commissioned officers. The conduct of operations on a day-to-day basis also suffers from a lack of computerization and information-management systems. An important consequence of these deficiencies in manpower and equipment is that the Department has been unable to develop any forward-planning capability. This has also directly affected the conduct of operations in Cambodia, Angola and the former Yugoslavia.

In order to overcome these management problems, the Department of Peacekeeping Operations must be allowed to absorb most of the current functions of the Field Operations Division, especially those relating to logistic planning and support. The Department also needs to develop a forward-planning unit and a responsive operations centre in New York which can serve as a focal point for operations.

Reform along these lines, which is currently being discussed at the UN, is required even if 'peacekeeping' continues to be based on the consent of all parties and does not move into enforcement. Only when the management issue has been addressed and the necessary reforms enacted can other more ambitious proposals be considered; such as the establishment of a permanent UN force, the designation of national contingents to be 'on call' for rapid deployments, the creation of multinational maritime forces, and the pre-stocking of heavier equipment in locations around the world.

Starved For Funds

The failure to implement reform at the UN is closely linked to the continued absence of an adequate and reliable system of financing to support the burgeoning demand for peacekeeping, which now costs over $3bn a year. The principal reason for the current financial crisis is that member states – most importantly the United States and the Russian Federation – have been reluctant to pay their dues. The US, which under existing arrangements should provide 30% of the UN peacekeeping budget, owes the UN more than $700m. As of September 1992, unpaid assessed contributions towards peacekeeping stood at $844m. President Clinton has recognized the seriousness of the situation, and the US has now promised to make up its arrears and to pay its future dues promptly.

Cash-flow problems resulting from an unusually high number of unpaid contributions (only 52 countries had paid their bills by September 1992) have directly affected UN operations. In Cambodia the planned second phase of the UNTAC mission was delayed by arguments over finance. Plans to despatch a UN policing force as a 'preventive deployment' to Bosnia were shelved in part due to lack of money. Limited funds constituted one reason why UNAVEM II was not reinforced before the Angolan elections in September 1992.

To remedy the situation, the Secretary-General, with strong backing from traditional troop-contributing countries, has suggested that three specific measures be taken. First, member states should begin to finance peacekeeping operations through their defence budgets rather than through their foreign ministries, as is currently the case. Second, a temporary peacekeeping reserve fund of $50m should be established in order to meet initial costs pending the receipt of assessed contributions. Third, he has called for the establishment of a 'UN peace endowment fund' with an initial target of $1bn to be created from a combination of assessed and voluntary contributions from governments, the private sector and individuals.

If the financial predicament in which the organization now finds itself is not alleviated, the UN's ability to initiate and sustain multicomponent operations on the current scale will diminish rapidly. Wealthy nations cannot continue to call on the UN to maintain, let alone expand, its operations without demonstrating a greater willingness to foot the bill.

The UN's Choices

The UN's difficulties in the past year are partly attributable to the intrinsic conservatism of its bureaucracy, the sheer pace of events and limited resources. They also reflect a larger failure of the organization – or more correctly, its member states – to examine how it may intervene meaningfully in intra-state as opposed to inter-state conflicts.

In *Agenda for Peace* there is a distinct tension between emphasis on 'the importance and indispensability of the sovereign state as the fundamental entity of the international community', and recognition that 'the time of absolute and exclusive sovereignty ... has passed'. While the report emphasizes that respect for the 'fundamental sovereignty and integrity' of the State remains crucial to 'any common international progress', no attempt is made to explore the meaning of 'sovereignty and integrity' in the post-Cold War environment. In each of the major operations in 1992 this issue has been at the heart of the conflict. Addressing how the UN can intervene effectively in civil wars may involve re-examining arrangements surrounding such ideologically sensitive concepts as 'non-self-governing territories' and 'trusteeships'. Under certain circumstances the UN may have to assume a long-term administrative and political role in an area riven by decades of civil war and conflict. Equally important, the UN must also accept that certain conflicts will not be solved by UN intervention, especially if political and financial support cannot be guaranteed.

SANCTIONS: EFFECTIVE TOOL OR CHIMERA?

According to Woodrow Wilson, they were to be an 'economic, peaceful, silent, deadly enemy' whose application would eliminate any need for the use of force. To many others, however, sanctions were themselves a threat to peace, another technique of coercion as likely to precipitate warfare as to prevent it. Although regularly disparaged by scholars as ineffective and even counterproductive, sanctions have been increasingly invoked by policy-makers in the nuclear age as they searched desperately for a middle ground not accounted for in Clausewitz's celebrated maxim.

Sanctions, of course, are as old as warfare, and normally accompanied it. Collective sanctions were to be a part of Sully's Grand Design in the sixteenth century for keeping order in the world, and of Napoleon's Continental System Blockade against England. By the twentieth century sanctions had emerged as the League of Nation's first line of defence for preserving world peace. Unfortunately, the effectiveness of this technique under the League was mixed and the lessons to be drawn from it unclear. While the threat of sanctions was effective against Yugoslavia in 1921, against major states a sanctions strategy was complicated, perhaps compromised, by the uncertain trumpet of great power diplomacy.

Thus the League failed to take action against Japan after the latter's invasion of Manchuria in 1931, and when it did call sanctions into play after Italy's aggression against Abyssinia four years later, the result was only to erode the credibility both of sanctions and the League itself. Important centres of opinion in the chancelleries of Europe, as well as within the League, were as much concerned to conciliate Mussolini as to coerce him. When Chamberlain assured the world that sanctions had failed, however, neither he nor his audience had any way of knowing that Mussolini was on the point of giving in to them, and the historical wisdom was born that sanctions were futile against a determined adversary.

The Cold War and After

The Cold War, in its turn, proved to be not merely an oxymoron but a strategic paradox; new means were needed to assert national interests without running unacceptable risks of military commitment. Sanctions offered one such option. Moscow, for its part, managed to conspire from the beginning in its own isolation by the creation of the Council for Mutual Economic Assistance (COMECON), a useful system for subordinating the economies of Eastern Europe, but also a self-imposed embargo from which it was to spend much effort decades later to escape.

The idea of containment, on the other hand, implied a strategic rationale for a system of sanctions and was criticized by some as unrealistic for that reason. In time, the utility of trying to isolate the Soviet bloc economically came to be questioned, particularly by America's allies. Detente militated against a strategy of sanctions – *Osthandel* and *Ostpolitik* were mutually supportive and through judicious linkage it was hoped that Soviet policy could be moderated by offering the rewards of participating in the prosperity of the Free World's economy.

If sanctions had little role to play in confrontation between the major powers, however, they offered them a useful means of dealing with third parties where outright military force was deemed unsuitable. The results were not always as anticipated. The Soviet cut-off of economic support to China resulted in a greater alienation of Beijing, not a retreat from its offending policies, while pressure on Yugoslavia drove Belgrade to mend its fences with the West. Egypt got its High Dam without American assistance and gave the Third World a lesson on how to exploit great-power rivalry. The long-standing boycott of Cuba did not topple Castro but did fix him irretrievably within the Soviet orbit. A bipolar world, in short, was not a favourable theatre for deploying the sanctions weapon. The pressure exerted by one side might always be neutralized (or at least relieved) by its rival's readiness to rush to help the sanctions target – as exemplified by the cases of Cuba, on the one hand, and Romania on the other. The certain prospect of veto, moreover, put paid to hopes of mounting collective sanctions action through the UN.

Almost all instances of sanctions between the world wars were meant to deal with examples of military aggression. Since 1945, however, sanctions have been invoked for a wide range of other purposes, acknowledged or implicit, beyond that of keeping the peace. They have been used to punish a state for its support of terrorism, to penalize it for violations of human rights, to bring down its government, to secure its support against a third party, even to alter its domestic political arrangements in the interests of democracy or justice. While often thought of as an instrument used by the strong against the weak, sanctions have also been used by the weak against the strong (as in the OPEC oil embargo) and by minor powers against each other (as in the Arab states' boycott of Israeli trade). Nor have governments a monopoly over use of the sanctions weapon, as shown by the very effective non-official agitation carried on for decades against trade or cultural contacts with South Africa.

Forms Sanctions Take

Sanctions are of different kinds and serve different ends. Most familiar and most frequently invoked are economic sanctions, designed to disrupt trade and undermine the economy in the target country. They can take the form of an embargo on exports to the target country, or boycott of its goods, or both. Normally such sanctions operate through legal prohibitions within the sanctioning state; in extreme cases, they are implemented by a blockade – a physical interdiction of exchange with the sanctions victim. Clearly, economic pressure is likely to have little effect on a society whose leadership can ignore its citizens or where the latter, used to a rudimentary level of economic life in the first place, can ignore small increments in their privation. It can be highly disruptive, as the OPEC oil embargo demonstrated, against advanced consumer societies with well-developed outlets for public opinion.

Financial sanctions aim to cut off a state's access to international investment or credit facilities, such as the World Bank and the International Monetary Fund (IMF), or to special bilateral arrangements such as Most Favoured Nation trading clauses and government loan guarantees. A more controversial form of such measures is the denial of access to the normal resources of international banking. American unilateral seizure of $12bn of Iranian assets in American-owned banks, both in the US and abroad, at the time of the hostage crisis in 1979, for example, generated considerable criticism by its claim of extraterritorial authority and precipitated an avalanche of litigation which long outlasted the crisis itself. The Democracy in Cuba Act, late in 1992, may well rekindle this controversy by its attempt to tighten restrictions on trade between Cuba and American-owned firms operating abroad.

Some have argued that interference with international banking for political purposes is dangerous to the stability of the system and should be avoided: even the Reagan administration thought better of a proposal to force Poland into bankruptcy in order to undermine the Soviet Union's status as superpower guarantor. Still, it has recently been reported that personal and official assets of the Iraqi leadership are being tracked through the labyrinth of international banking by Western intelligence services capable of monitoring bank transfers and communication. Concerted use of this laser-guided accountancy would, certainly, raise questions of national and international law and bank security which many policy-makers would rather not confront.

Economic sanctions come in many shapes and degrees of severity, from a minor, near symbolic limitation of trade to a decision to isolate a country totally by cutting its communication and air traffic, as well as its commerce, with the rest of the world. Such flexibility of response will always be attractive to policy-makers as they feel their way through events whose significance is obscure and who very often find themselves, in Alexander Pope's phrase, 'willing to wound, but afraid to strike'.

A more elusive but, in the long run, perhaps no less corrosive form of sanction is that which cuts a country's cultural links – in sport, the arts, foreign study and so forth – with the world community. The impact of such quarantine is, of course, very hard to assess. For some states, it is likely to be inconsequential: the fundamentalist regime in Iran, in fact, prefers insulation from the temptations of an infidel world, while foreign contacts have normally been rationed for security reasons by most totalitarian states.

Many other societies, however, harbour that same 'decent respect for the opinion of mankind' which led Jefferson to explain the reasons why America opted for independence. In countries whose elite have travelled, even perhaps studied, abroad, foreign opinion can count for a great deal. The late Christian Barnard, expecting to be interviewed on his pioneering work in heart transplantation, was chagrined to find that the then David Frost wanted only to talk about racism: sports-loving South Africans, meanwhile, discovered that the domestic policies of their government deprived them of the chance to see foreign teams in action or their own compete peacefully abroad. Minor irritations these may have been in one sense, but to many they were also disturbing symbols of moral obloquy that found an echo throughout the world. In the last analysis, a state must consider the judgement of the world, as well as that of its own people, if it is to be secure in its most basic requirement – the stature of legitimacy.

Do Sanctions Work?

Before the Second World War, reservations about sanctions tended to stress the risk that they might provoke rather than forestall conflict. Such fears were exploited successfully by Mussolini in 1935–36 and dramatically realized when Japan chose war in 1941 in response to an American embargo on oil. Since the end of the Second World War, however, reservations about sanctions tend to emphasize the belief that they are usually ineffective as a means of coercion: the consensus has grown that sanctions do not work.

Clearly, sceptics can call on a number of cases to prove their point. Castro has managed to survive more than 30 years – a good showing anywhere in Latin America. Iran was not forced to surrender its American hostages by the toughest measures which the latter could impose. Sanctions did not destroy Israel or topple Gaddafi or bring Ian Smith's regime briskly to its knees. Sometimes a sanction has even boomeranged. President Carter's grain embargo against the USSR, for example, not only failed to influence Soviet policy, it failed even to penalize Moscow. Instead, it operated in the Soviets' own interests, forcing them to open up new sources of supply which improved their future trading position, while leaving American farmers and tax payers to shoulder the loss of a profitable customer.

Some have argued that sanctions even benefit target governments by helping them to mobilize patriotic support – that sanctions have worked in Saddam's as well as Mussolini's favour, for example, and helped Milosevic defeat Milan Panic in the elections in December 1992. It is probably unwise, however, to divine the true state of opinion where freedom of expression is in short supply. And it is well to remember that much respectable opinion was for long categoric in assuring that sanctions against apartheid would only strengthen South African determination to resist change – an interpretation now difficult to support.

It would be hard to deny that when conditions were right, sanctions have played a significant part in the exercise of international power. The fact that US and IMF help in support of the pound was made conditional on British withdrawal from Suez certainly influenced British policy in that crisis. Many failed regimes have been undermined to one degree or another by economic pressure from abroad. If some totalitarian regimes (those of Castro, Saddam, Khomeini) have seemed proof against sanctions, others (Trujillo, Somoza, Amin) have not. The failure of Carter's grain embargo to have any impact on Soviet policy towards Afghanistan must be set against the estimate of the US Defense Intelligence Agency that fear of a major Western sanctions offensive helped to deter Moscow from an invasion of Poland in 1980–81.

It is the work of social science to analyse such things as sanctions out of the context of events, compare abstract results with announced objectives, and where possible assign a numerical value to the relation between the two. Little of this approach, however, is transferable to the real world of human affairs where the future is hard to predict, the present difficult to assess, and even the past a matter of endless controversy. Sanctions, like any other aspect of human affairs, cannot be factored out, nor should we always judge their utility to policy-makers by what the latter, in the press of the moment and in response to other considerations, may feel obliged to say. The real purpose of sanctions, for example, may be simply to proclaim where a state stands on some issue, or to distance itself from something it condemns but has no compelling interest to counter. This is by no means a meaningless gesture in a world where even great states must establish priorities for action and where even the most sophisticated leadership seldom exercises political power with that deliberateness and economy of will which the hindsight of history is likely to invest in it.

Do sanctions work? In a sense the question is too simple to answer with any realism: in almost every case one's conclusion requires some qualification. While it is true, for example, that Castro survived the American embargo, he did so at a substantial cost to the Soviet Union and at the sacrifice of his own ambitions to galvanize revolution in Latin America – ambitions which prompted Washington's hostility in the first place. Thanks to the arts of despotism, Saddam has weathered the dislocation which sanctions have imposed on his people – but he has also survived a crushing military defeat in the field – and few would argue that *Desert Storm* did not work. Without access to Gaddafi's processes of decision-making, similarly, it is difficult to assess the part, if any, which sanctions have played in his gestures of cooperation with the authorities seeking indictments for the Lockerbie bombing. It appears that sanctions have brought the Serbian economy to the brink of ruin. This must carry with it serious implications for Belgrade's security and status after a settlement, even if its present leaderships have failed to grasp them.

Using Sanctions Effectively

Wielding the sanctions weapon is not always simple or straightforward. Smuggling is as old as legal trade, and the designation of anything as contraband inevitably creates a market for it. Sanctions-busting can often mitigate the impact of sanctions, particularly in key goods, as it did for South Africa. Policing sanctions, also, is not always easy: inspection in many states can be haphazard or corruptible while skilful manipulation of multinational commercial operations can challenge even sophisticated monitoring, as shown by the last-minute interception of materiel intended for the construction of Iraq's supergun. Still, sanctions-busting is risky to the supplier and expensive to the recipient, and even in the best of circumstances unlikely to constitute a dependable replacement for interdicted trade. In the wake of the Cold War, moreover, an imposing array of advanced intelligence surveillance techniques have become a kind of war surplus, which could present a formidable threat to the sanctions-buster if turned to peacetime use. In addition to smuggling, sanctions can be blunted, also, by product substitution in the target economy or the development of indigenous sources of supply, such as practised by Rhodesia following the imposition of UN sanctions. There is, however, a limit to what such domestic enterprise can do to make up the loss of traditional trading sources, particularly in a well-developed economy.

Probably the most difficult problem for those imposing sanctions, however, is the cost they involve for innocent third-party states or even for the sanctioner itself. The penalty can occur during the boycott of a critical product: the loss of oil from Iraq and Kuwait had to be made up to prevent Western shortfalls, and the loss of imported Rhodesian chrome led Washington to fear that it was becoming dangerously dependent on the USSR for its supply of this vital metal. More commonly, sanctions will also strike at third parties whose economies are tied to that of the sanctions but whose cooperation may be vital to an effective target regime. Jordan, for example, required substantial compensation for the loss of earnings from its trade with Iraq and may well have felt the effects of the sanctions as much as its affluent neighbour.

The ingredients for a successful sanctions policy are probably the same as those called for in any other aspect of a state's foreign policy, yet the theory to support them is one of the most neglected fields of study. More than one scholar has complained that sanctions have not received the kind of academic attention they deserve; the sanctions weapon has been increasingly resorted to but little studied, while nuclear weapons have been the subject of concerted analysis and doctrinal debate, but never employed since their use against Japan.

Even without such a study there are some generalizations which can be made with little dispute. To begin with, sanctions will benefit from being integrated into some overall strategy, thus limiting the danger that they become too easy an option – a means to avoid having to develop a policy in the first place. Then, the sanctions policy must have the consistent support of the government which imposes it. While this may appear a truism, the circumstances of both the Iran/Contra and Matrix Churchill affairs suggest it is something to bear in mind.

Sanctions will be easiest to apply where the target government is responsive to its own public opinion and if that public opinion is shaped by moderately high levels of expectation. Sanctions will, obviously, also have more impact on unstable or insecure regimes which are less able to manage popular or elite dissatisfaction. Above all, an effective sanctions initiative usually requires cooperation from other states, either joining in the sanctions themselves or at least refusing to cooperate in sanctions-busting.

The Future Of Sanctions

In recent years, sanctions of one type or another have operated against a long list of states: Argentina, Burma, Cambodia, Cuba, Haiti, Iran, Iraq, Israel, Liberia, Nicaragua, North Korea, Somalia, South Africa, Syria, Vietnam, all the parties to the present disorder in former Yugoslavia, and more. In addition to those imposed unilaterally, sanctions are laid down by international or multinational authorities such as the EC, the OAS, the Arab League and, of course, the UN. In short, sanctions have been integrated into the very fabric of international relations.

There are several reasons to suppose that they will continue to be relied on in the years to come. The likely further progress of democracy throughout the world will increasingly render governments more responsive to their domestic opinion and thus more vulnerable to the effects of sanctions on their people. Perhaps ironically, economic development itself, with its higher standards of living and greater integration of economies into a world economy, will mean that more and more societies will have something substantial to lose by falling foul of international opinion.

To be sure, the end of the Cold War has not made it possible to think in terms of a world community: true interdependence, rather than an anarchy of independent sovereignties. Like most communities have always been, the world community will seldom be entirely harmonious, and certainly never unanimous. Yet recent events suggest that there may be sufficient prospect for collective action in the future to give the sanctions weapon increasing employment as the years pass. At the same time, the very experience of invoking and operating sanctions may well itself become a school for increasing levels of cooperation in managing world affairs.

The electronic news media, moreover, has added a new factor to the conduct of international affairs – the direct pressure of public indignation. Attitudes have changed since the *Washington Post*, criticized the US in 1977, for its boycott against Amin's Uganda, as setting 'a dangerous precedent. . . . arbitrarily using its massive economic power . . . to force a smaller and weaker state to alter its internal treatment of subjects'. There seems every reason to assume that governments will have to face continued public demands for action on humanitarian and human rights issues, and that, in many cases, sanctions will prove to be the only practical means of satisfying it.

Clearly many Third World countries will wonder whether such new structures of international stability, buttressed by sanctions, are merely a new imperialism to accompany the new millennium. Certainly the combined economic and cultural power of the industrialized world – or even just the United States and the EC acting together – puts it in a commanding position. But this, for good or ill, is a given in world affairs, something over which neither rich nor poor have any real control. Weaker countries, however, may take some comfort from the thought that only collective sanctions are likely to be effective and that the UN may become an increasingly powerful forum where consensus must be solicited, and bargained for, even by the major powers. Such an arrangement will no doubt lack the formal supranationalism of Sully's Grand Design, and may not, even in the next century, be transformed into the collective system of peacekeeping which he envisaged. It may, however, help in the development of an international system based on negotiation, consensus and collective action; a more limited goal, but one worth striving for.

The Americas

CHANGE AND CONTINUITY IN THE US

'We have met the enemy and he is us'. If ever this quip by the American humorist Walt Kelly applied, it applied to President George Bush in his quest for a second term of office. Rarely in American political history has a president fallen so far and so fast in the public's estimation, and had so few to blame for his fate.

Although Bush claimed to be an expert foreign policy practitioner – a claim many would dispute – foreign policy credentials were of little value in a campaign that swung on domestic issues. Long before election day on 3 November 1992 it was clear that Bush had failed to convince the electorate that he appreciated the magnitude of the economic and social problems facing the country. Instead he appeared virtually oblivious to the hardships that were the daily lot of many Americans. Bush consequently failed to convince voters that he would shift his priorities in a second term and focus his energies on domestic matters; his inability during the campaign to develop and articulate a credible programme for economic recovery demonstrated that little would change on the home front if Bush won. More generally, Bush failed to convince voters that he had either a foreign or domestic policy agenda that he wanted to pursue in a second term. To many, it seemed that Bush wanted to be president, but that there was little he wanted to do as president.

Democratic challenger Bill Clinton, on the other hand, promised to focus 'like a laser beam' on the country's economic problems. Clinton's many ideas for galvanizing an economic recovery and embarking on social reform, although not uncontroversial, convinced the electorate that this young (46 year old), dynamic leader was not content with the status quo. This proved to be a decisive consideration when most Americans believed the country was moving in the wrong direction.

On The Campaign Trail

President Bush was challenged for the Republican nomination by Pat Buchanan, whose isolationist manifesto maintained that the US should withdraw from most international military and economic commitments. The support Buchanan received during the primary season, however, was more a reflection of dissatisfaction with Bush than the appeal of the alternative. The fight for the Democratic nomination was a characteristic free-for-all, with over a half-dozen contenders in the running. Clinton – coming from Arkansas, a small state rarely in the national limelight – started from near the back of the pack. He persevered, however, through a gruelling campaign whose ups and downs resembled the fever chart of a malarial patient, and eventually pulled away from his opponents. The wild card in the pack was Texas billionaire H. Ross Perot, who launched an independent drive for the presidency in early 1992, only to pull out in the summer when critical press coverage offended his sensibilities.

The Democratic Party's convention in New York in July was a triumph in at least two respects. First, Clinton's advisors did a masterful job in showing how Clinton had come from a poor background and worked his way to the top winning scholarships to Georgetown and Oxford universities before going on to Yale Law School. The contrast with George Bush's patrician background did not have to be made explicit. Second, Clinton demonstrated boldness in selecting Senator Al Gore from Tennessee to be his vice-presidential running mate. Gore was also from a comparatively small, mid-South state, which may have lent no geographical balance or ballast to the ticket, but by featuring another bright, energetic, baby boomer the Democrats were able to position themselves as the party of the future.

The Republican convention in Houston in August was, by comparison, an unmitigated disaster. The right-wing of the party was allowed to dominate proceedings, and what should have been a showcase for the Bush presidency deteriorated into a harangue about 'family values' and repeated, harsh attacks on Clinton's wife, Hillary. Instead of giving Bush's campaign a boost, the convention undermined it.

There may have been a way to recover from this, but Bush never found it. Throughout he was an uninspired campaigner. Clinton won or held his own in all of the presidential debates, and Perot, who re-entered the campaign just before the first debate, outperformed Bush on at least one occasion. In the final weeks, Bush took to the low road that had worked so well for him in 1988. He tried to attack Clinton on 'character' issues, arguing that Clinton was unsuitable for the presidency because of his efforts to avoid the draft in the late 1960s, and because he had visited Moscow and protested against the Vietnam war while a student in England.

The voters, however, were looking for a positive agenda for the future, not a negative blast from the past. In the end, a stunning 62% voted against the incumbent: although Clinton captured only 43% of the popular vote he won 32 of 50 states; Bush won 38% of the vote but only 18 states; Perot received a surprising 19% of the vote but did not carry a single state. Bush was defeated decisively, but the vote for Clinton was less than overwhelming. Many Americans retained reservations about Clinton's ability to chart America's course.

What Can the World Expect?

Although Bill Clinton is the first US President to be born after the end of the Second World War and the first Democrat to occupy the White House in 12 years, there will more continuity than change in US foreign and defence policy under the new administration. There are two main reasons for this.

First, there is a strong consensus in the US about national interests and the role the country must play in world affairs. It is widely recognized that to prevent the development of long-term threats to US national security and to promote US economic prosperity, the United States must keep any great power from establishing hegemony in Europe or Asia, that it must keep the great powers in Western Europe and East Asia from going to war with each other, that it must maintain an open international economic system, and that it must maintain Western access to Middle Eastern oil supplies. This, in turn, means that the United States must remain actively engaged – politically and militarily – in Europe and Asia.

This consensus has persisted in the United States for some 50 years. It was born in, and grew during, the Cold War. It weathered the end of the Cold War, and it has survived the end of the Bush administration. President Clinton and his advisors, including Secretary of State Warren Christopher, Secretary of Defense Les Aspin, and National Security Advisor Anthony Lake, subscribe to the mainstream view that US national interests require it to play an active, but not necessarily hyperactive, role in world affairs. Indeed, in his first press conference after the election, Clinton went out of his way to stress that 'America's fundamental interests' would not be redefined by the new administration.

Second, while it is certainly true that US foreign and defence policy is changing in important ways, these changes can be traced to the collapse of Soviet power in Eastern Europe, the dismantling of the Warsaw Pact, the disintegration of the Soviet Union, and the end of the Cold War. The changes in US foreign and defence policy – most notably, the reduction in the number of US troops stationed abroad and the number of US military bases maintained overseas, along with ever-deeper cuts in US defence spending – can be traced to developments that took place in 1989–91. These changes preceded Bill Clinton's arrival in the White House. Because Clinton shares the mainstream view that the threats to US national security interests have changed in important ways, the new administration will not redirect the basic course of US foreign and defence policy, although it will undoubtedly fine-tune it.

In short, the foundation of US foreign and defence policy – beliefs about national interests, threats to those interests, and basic policy directions – will not be shaken by the Clinton administration. By all accounts, Clinton and his advisors are centrists. Their views are representative of the American foreign policy establishment.

The Clinton Agenda

This is not to say that all will remain the same under the new administration. First and foremost, Clinton has pledged to devote most of his

time and energy to the many domestic problems the country faces: a
slowly recovering economy, poverty, inadequate health care, a falter-
ing educational system, poor race relations, crime, drug abuse, AIDS,
and environmental pollution. If Clinton follows through on this pledge,
which he seems likely to do, foreign and defence policy will be
affected in a number of ways. The development of new policy initiatives could be hampered, for example, particularly if the president's
advisors fight among themselves for control of the policy agenda.
Policy implementation could be stultified if insufficient high-level
attention is devoted to important details or if insufficient funds are
available for foreign economic and military assistance programmes.
Money will undoubtedly be tight, given Clinton's interest in spending
more on domestic programmes while reducing the $350-billion federal
deficit.

Although foreign and defence policy issues were not the top priority
during the campaign, Clinton and his advisors have nonetheless made
enough pronouncements on these issues to identify the main items on
the new administration's international agenda.

Improving Competitiveness

One of President Clinton's top foreign policy objectives is to
strengthen the country's international economic position. During the
campaign, he argued that America's declining economic competitiveness constituted the most serious threat to its long-term international
position. He consequently believes it is vital for the US to raise export
levels and lower the balance of trade deficit.

Clinton and his economic advisors recognize that the sources of
America's economic malaise are primarily domestic. Clinton spent
most of his first month in office developing an economic recovery
plan, which he presented in his first State of the Union speech on 17
February. His proposal, which calls for higher taxes for most Americans, cuts in government spending, and an investment package designed to stimulate the economy, will be bitter medicine, but it is
medicine most Americans are willing to swallow if it helps cure the
sickness. Whether Clinton has the right prescription remains to be
seen.

At the same time, Clinton and his advisors believe that some of
America's economic problems can be traced to unfair trading practices
in Japan and Western Europe. They argue that excessively subsidized
Japanese and European exports, in conjunction with pernicious barriers to American imports, have played an important role in creating the
massive US balance of trade deficit.

How hard will the new administration push Japan and Western
Europe to change these policies? In just the first few weeks of the new
administration, it was announced that punitive tariffs would be imposed on 19 Western European and East Asian countries if they failed

to stop dumping subsidized steel on the US market. The administration also announced that sanctions would be imposed on the EC unless it repealed a new policy that would give companies based in the EC the inside track in bidding for government contracts for telecommunications and power-generation equipment. And Clinton himself denounced British, French, German and Spanish subsidies of the *Airbus* project as excessive.

Although leaders in Western Europe and East Asia were alarmed by these developments, the new administration is not protectionist. It recognizes that the maintenance of an open trading system is essential if the US is to prosper economically. It knows that a trade war would be catastrophic for all. That said, it appears ready to employ very firm tactics in dealing with what it perceives as unfair trading practices. Clinton made these points explicit in a major speech on 26 February, just prior to the administration's first meeting with the G-7, in which he attacked protectionism and called for free, unfettered competition in world markets.

President Clinton seems willing to take a fair amount of heat from Western European and East Asian allies in the short run to establish a more equitable foundation for US trade in the long run. This looks to be one of the pillars of his foreign policy strategy. It is a seemingly rational policy, with two dangers. One is that, having set this as the basis of his approach, domestic developments might force the new president to take actions which he himself would not wish to take. The other danger, of course, is that punitive sanctions could lead to retaliation and a protectionist spirit, however unintended.

Democracy and Human Rights

The promotion of democracy and human rights abroad is another area in which Clinton has started to articulate a post-Cold War vision for US foreign policy. During the election campaign, he repeatedly criticized Bush for compromising America's political ideals, coddling authoritarian regimes, and tolerating human rights outrages. Clinton's vision of what he would do, however, is still vague. Most importantly, it is not clear how his universalist principles – the promotion of democracy and human rights everywhere – would be applied in practice, given that US interests often oblige it to work with unsavoury regimes, and given that there are limits to US resources and influence in international affairs. The US has neither the will nor the capability to champion democracy and human rights in each and every corner of the world. The most immediate effects of this policy will probably involve China, Somalia and Bosnia.

During the campaign, Clinton launched blistering attacks on Bush's policies towards China. More specifically, he lambasted Bush for his refusal to link Most Favoured Nation (MFN) trading status to improvements in China's human rights policies. Most observers consequently expect Clinton to be receptive to the idea of linking MFN renewal to movement on the human rights front when the matter next comes before the US Congress. This issue is complicated, however, by the fact that the Clinton administration would also like China to cut back its exports of nuclear technology, high-performance missiles, and other weapon systems. Penalizing China over its human rights policies might undermine US non-proliferation efforts, another of Clinton's major concerns. Clinton will have to address this policy dilemma sooner than later. It may lead him to back down from, or at least downplay, his human rights agenda.

Clinton was also critical of Bush during the election campaign over his handling of the humanitarian crisis in Somalia. More could be done to help the relief effort there, Clinton felt. A couple of weeks after the election, Bush finally sent a large contingent of US Marines to Somalia to provide escorts for UN and other relief convoys. He insisted, however, that the Marines were not there to re-establish political order, which he felt was the job of the UN, and he expressed the hope that all US troops would be able to return home by 20 January 1993. Although Clinton is interested in reducing the US military presence in Somalia as soon as possible, he appears more inclined to keep some American troops as part of a multinational force to help restore political order in that troubled country.

The situation in Bosnia shows how Clinton's activist inclinations will be constrained by military and political realities. During the campaign, Clinton argued that the US should take more forceful action to ensure the delivery of humanitarian aid to civilians in Bosnia and to bring the conflict to an end on terms that would not reward Serbian aggression. Among the options he raised were: using military force to get aid where it was needed; lifting the arms embargo currently in place against Bosnia; and using US airpower to intimidate Serbia.

In February 1993, the new administration unveiled a policy towards the Bosnian crisis that was considerably more cautious than the one hinted at during the campaign. The administration decided that a military solution to the conflict could not be imposed on the participants and that the US should therefore play a more active role in the multilateral peace talks sponsored by the UN and the EC; a special envoy to the negotiations, Reginald Bartholomew, was named. To move the negotiations along, the administration suggested that the embargo on Serbia should be tightened and that the no-fly zone over Bosnia should be enforced, but specific proposals were not made. The administration said that the US would be willing to help enforce a settlement in Bosnia and that steps should be taken to keep the war from spreading to Kosovo and Macedonia, but again, specific proposals were not outlined. It did, however, mount an air drop of food and medicine for those areas in Bosnia where land-delivered supplies were blocked.

In its first major foreign policy announcement, the Clinton administration departed in only limited ways from the policies it inherited from Bush, demonstrating great wariness about using military force in such highly unsettled situations. Reflecting the views of the American people in general, the administration does not see the US playing the role of global policeman. It will be hard for Clinton to pursue his universalist principles in places where US strategic interests are few and potential costs are many. If supporting democracy and human rights is to become the centrepiece of Clinton's foreign policy, he and his advisors will have to be able to explain why the US should become involved in some crises, but not others.

Helping the Former Enemy

Judging from their campaign rhetoric, Clinton appeared to be more sensitive than Bush to the strategic implications of political and economic reform in the former Soviet Union. Clinton argued that it was in the US national interest to help the new states of the collapsed empire to strengthen and extend their reform efforts. This was absolutely essential, he felt, if the US was to reduce defence spending and devote more of the national treasure to economic development. With this in mind, Clinton and his advisors developed an economic and technical assistance programme for the republics of the former Soviet Union which forced Bush in April 1992 to throw together a belated plan of his own.

In the first few months after he was elected president, Clinton appeared prepared to bow to the budgetary constraints that made it difficult for him to provide the material assistance to the republics that he would otherwise be inclined to offer. In March 1993, however, in response to the danger that the embattled Russian President Boris Yeltsin and his reforms might be derailed, Clinton launched an effort to explain to the American people why supporting the reforms in Russia was in the US interest. This, and comments his spokesmen made, suggested strongly that he was planning to give considerable new aid to Yeltsin when they met at the Vancouver summit on 3 to 4 April 1993. In the event, Clinton promised that the US would supply $1.6bn in 1993.

Step Up Arms Control Efforts

Although the Bush administration deserves much credit for inducing Russia and the other republics of the former Soviet Union to agree to reduce their nuclear arsenals, these agreements have yet to be implemented. The Clinton administration is expected to make a concerted effort, not just to carry these measures through, but to accelerate them.

Ashton Carter, one of the leading architects of the new administration's policy in this area, has written that the US and the four republics with strategic nuclear weapons stationed on their territory (Russia,

Ukraine, Kazakhstan, Belarus) should disarm all missiles scheduled for deactivation under START I in six months, not seven years as the treaty outlines. Similarly, all strategic nuclear weapons currently deployed in Ukraine, Kazakhstan and Belarus (over 3,000 weapons) should be moved to central storage in Russia in six months, not seven years. All non-deployed strategic and tactical nuclear weapons in the former Soviet Union (a total of some 20,000–25,000 weapons) should be dismantled in three years, as opposed to the 10–12 years under the current timetable. The fissile material taken from these weapons should be placed under international control, it is said, and retired ballistic missiles should be dismantled or demilitarized. To achieve these objectives, the Clinton administration will have to put considerable pressure on Ukraine to live up to the arms control and denuclearization pledges it has already made. The administration will also have to cover much of the cost of the denuclearization effort and to take comparable steps with respect to the US arsenal, in order to weaken the hand of hardliners in Russia who feel that Moscow should not reduce its military forces.

The Clinton administration also seems inclined to devote more energy than its predecessor to controlling the proliferation of nuclear, chemical and conventional weapons. During the campaign Clinton indicated that he would like to strengthen the purview of the International Atomic Energy Agency, aggressively implement the recently-signed Chemical Weapons Convention, and press more countries to sign the Missile Technology Control Regime. He argued that multilateral agreement on tighter export control laws should be sought, and that countries and companies that violate supply-side agreements should be punished more harshly. Better intelligence will be needed if enforcement is to be improved and, with that in mind, Clinton will direct the CIA to devote more of its resources to the identification of proliferation violations.

In a departure from the US government's previously held position, Clinton has supported imposing more restrictions on nuclear testing. He proposed a two-stage process. In the first stage, the US, Russia and other parties to the agreement would lower the threshold below which nuclear tests could be conducted and impose a quota on the number of tests each party could conduct each year. If all goes well during this first phase, Clinton said he would support negotiations aimed at concluding a Comprehensive Test Ban Treaty.

Cutting and Restructuring

Clinton and Secretary of Defense Aspin believe that the Bush administration's plan to scale back US military forces in light of the collapse of the Soviet Union does not go far enough. Bush called for a reduction in the US military from 2.1 million to 1.6 million troops by 1997. Those stationed in Western Europe would go down from 325,000 to 150,000, again by 1997.

The Clinton administration maintains that a smaller force structure will be adequate, given recent developments on the international scene. The number of troops in uniform can be cut to 1.4 million. The number of US troops deployed in Western Europe can be reduced at least to 100,000. The number of ships in the US Navy can be reduced from 450 to 340, aircraft carriers in the force structure from 12 to 10, active Army divisions from 12 to 9, and active Air Force fighter wings from 15 to 10.

Since most modernization programmes for strategic systems have already been scuttled, the new administration will make few changes in US policy in this regard, except to reorient the Strategic Defense Initiative away from space-based *Brilliant Pebbles* interceptors, which are intended to throw thousands of small obstacles in the path of an incoming missile, and towards ground-based alternatives. The estimate is that these and other cuts, in conjunction with a review of military roles and missions designed to reduce duplication, will enable it to trim a total of $127bn from Bush's defence spending plan by Fiscal Year 1998.

To preserve an effective military capability, Clinton and Aspin plan to emphasize mobility and flexibility. With better airlift and rapid sealift forces, they say, the US can retain formidable power projection capabilities even though a larger proportion of US forces would be based at home. In the long run, they believe that the key to military effectiveness will be the continued development of technologically sophisticated weapons and associated systems. Thus, they support the development of advanced precision-guided weapons, advanced tactical aircraft, and improved command, control, communications and intelligence systems.

Whether Clinton can succeed in reducing defence spending and reshaping the force structure will depend in part on his relationship with military leaders in the Pentagon. This relationship got off to a very rocky start when Clinton announced that he would fulfil a campaign promise to allow homosexuals to serve openly in the military. This is a step most US military leaders bitterly oppose. In the long run, though, the tenor of the relationship will depend on Clinton's and Aspin's effectiveness in conducting a serious review of military roles and missions, and implementing the recommendations that come out of this review. To date, the military establishment has been able to stymie fundamental reforms.

How Blows the Wind?

It is far too early, of course, to make any firm predictions about the Clinton administration's prospects in foreign and domestic affairs. The administration has many strengths on which to draw. Clinton himself is bright, learns quickly, and is not uninformed on foreign and defence policy issues. And, despite his ham-fisted handling of Attorney General nominations, he is an able politician who has a track record of effectively implementing the policies he enunciates. His advisors, by and large, are knowledgeable and energetic. Most of them have had 12 years out of office to reflect on the country's policy needs.

At the same time, neither Clinton nor his top advisors have articulated an overarching vision for US foreign policy, although some of the main elements of what could become a grand strategy – promotion of economic competitiveness, democracy and human rights – are beginning to emerge. The danger is that, if Clinton focuses mainly on developing a strategy for domestic economic recovery and if his advisors fail to work together and develop a clear list of foreign policy priorities, the administration could end up reacting to international events as they unfold. The urgent could come to dominate the important. Americans are full of hope that the Clinton administration will capitalize on its potential. Many fear, however, that it might well succumb to drift and paralysis.

LATIN AMERICA: STRUGGLE FOR POLITICAL AND ECONOMIC EQUILIBRIUM

Forging economic adjustments under democratic rule has long been the major challenge in Latin America. In 1992, governments were forced to confront the usual hurdles of consolidating structural adjustment schemes, combatting drug traffickers and guerrillas, trying to ensure stable democratic rule, and generating trade and foreign investment in an increasingly competitive international economic environment.

Some countries fared better than others. Once again Mexico and Chile proved capable of taming inflation, controlling scattered incidents of popular and labour unrest, and advancing regional trade arrangements. Colombia, Brazil, Peru and Venezuela faced greater obstacles. Guerrillas, corruption scandals, economic crises and narcotics traffickers wrought havoc on those countries' plans for economic stabilization. Uncertainty continued to plague Central America as the UN-supervised El Salvadoran peace process faltered, insurgency and counterinsurgency prevailed in Guatemala, and Nicaragua's democratically elected government struggled to control both its economy and its unruly legislative branch.

Shaky Democracies

Latin America universally embraced constitutional democracy as an ideal in 1992. The practice proved more difficult. In April, Peru's democratically elected President Alberto Fujimori dissolved the legislative branch, moved to reorganize the judiciary, and suspended the constitution, claiming that corrupt congressmen not only hindered his

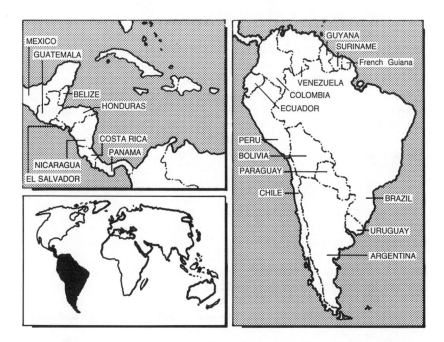

economic reforms but his battle against the guerrilla insurgency and drug traffickers. Although many of Peru's political leaders were forced into hiding, and there was some talk of imposing sanctions, neither the Organization of American States (OAS) nor much of the international community could agree to do so.

Fujimori did not keep his promise to hold a plebiscite to determine the nation's future within six months. Instead, he organized elections for a constituent assembly, rather than a full legislature, for late November 1992. In these elections, Fujimori's own *Cambio 90-Nueva Mayoria* won a majority of the seats, and the results and the establishment of the 80-member *Congreso Constituyente Democratica* were endorsed by the OAS and the Rio Group in December. Fujimori's surprising domestic popularity rests on his success in bringing inflation down to sustainable levels, from 139% in 1991 to 57% in 1992, the lowest in 15 years, and on his capture of the leader of the *Sendero Luminoso* guerrilla movement. Peru's military, however, is still restive. In November, a week before elections, Fujimori faced down an unsuccessful coup attempt which was probably backed by the military.

Venezuela's President Andrés Pérez also headed a shaky democracy. Following an attempted coup on 4 February 1992, Pérez installed a new cabinet and promised reform of the Supreme Court, political parties and the provision of social services. His new round of economic reforms, however, was soundly criticized by the Congress and the public. In June, the opposition party, COPEI, withdrew support for the administration as political and economic reforms stalled. Over 1,000 demonstrations were held against the Pérez administration, with an estimated 48% involving students. August was a busy month. A package of constitutional amendments, including a proposal to create a constituent assembly to debate the reform proposals, was introduced. There were also more rumours of planned coups, Pérez's announcement of a sweeping austerity drive, and the approval of an amendment prevented presidential re-elections.

On 27 November, a more serious coup attempt was mounted. More military and civilian participants were involved, and it brought a five-hour battle to the steps of the presidential palace. The coup leaders were identified as two admirals, an air force general, an army colonel, and a National Guard lieutenant colonel.

The government's unpopularity was widely held to have stemmed from a lack of credibility following corruption charges, and popular disenchantment with the free-market economic programme. Reductions in social services, due to declining oil revenues, and water rationing in Caracas increased the discontent. In early December, an attempt by the legislature to impeach Pérez failed. The alienation felt by the people was graphically demonstrated when approximately half of the electorate refused to vote in December's municipal and state elections.

In Brazil, corruption shook the country's democratic foundations. President Fernando Collor de Mello and his campaign manager, Paulo Cesar Farias, were implicated in the extortion of millions of dollars in payment for access to information and government contracts. Collor resigned in the midst of impeachment proceedings in December. Ironically, he had won the 1989 elections running as an anti-corruption fighter.

In Mexico, state elections in the left-leaning state of Michoacan in July were hotly contested; both the reigning Institutional Revolutionary Party (PRI) and Cuautemoc Cardenas' Democratic Revolutionary Party (PRD) claimed victory for their candidates. The PRI contender finally admitted defeat 6 October, the day before President Carlos Salinas de Gortari's scheduled meeting with President Bush and Prime Minister Mulroney in San Antonio to discuss the North American Free Trade Agreement (NAFTA).

While Mexico's electoral system was in need of reform, opposition parties were unable to take advantage of this issue. The adept economic management exhibited by Salinas left little room for radical opposition from either the right or left. In an autumn State of the Nation address, he took the initiative by promising to make electoral reform a part of the last third of his six-year term.

El Salvador made significant but incomplete progress towards a stable and lasting peace, despite a comprehensive framework overseen by the United Nations. The demobilization of the approximately 8,000 Farabundo Marti National Liberation Front (FMLN) guerrillas in the

15 UN-supervised assembly points proceeded slowly. The target date for demobilization was moved from May to October and finally to late November 1992. The FMLN guerrillas refused to lay down their weapons, pointing to President Alfredo Cristiani's failure to purge senior military officers, to disband the police forces, and to initiate land redistribution. The military remained suspicious of the arms inventory supplied by the FMLN, hinting that the former guerrillas were withholding weapons. By the November deadline, approximately 65 to 70% of the rebels were demobilized. In November, the UN assisted in producing a land redistribution scheme which called for over 400,000 acres to be given in allotments of between 3.5 and 1.2 acres to the rebels.

On 15 December the FMLN agreed to end officially the 12-year-old civil war that had claimed 75,000 lives. In return, the FMLN was rewarded with legitimate status as a political party, allowing it to participate in the 1994 presidential elections. Most observers were sceptical, however, of the ability of the peace accords to maintain stability in the country.

In Nicaragua, the coalition party elected in January 1990, held on tenuously for another year. Rumours abounded that President Violeta Chamorro, in a time of deep economic troubles, would attempt a Fujimori-type coup in order to keep political and economic challenges under control. Nicaragua faced continued US Congressional pressure over the presence of former *Sandinista* party members within the government's power structure. In June, the United States halted aid disbursements to Nicaragua, placing the nation in dire need of hard currency and economic assistance. A September earthquake brought tidal waves and destruction to the coast but the US offered only a small aid package of $5m. This economic pressure forced President Chamorro to acknowledge the US demands, and in September she dismissed Rene Vivas and 11 other top military officers.

In response to another US concern, the government announced plans in October to pay $250m in compensation to property owners whose land was confiscated during the 1979–89 *Sandinista* rule. In December, the US released $54m, or approximately one-half of the original 1992 aid package. The release of the second half of the aid was made conditional on further reform of the security forces and on completion of the compensation programme for confiscated property.

The plight of Haiti, the most impoverished nation in the Western hemisphere, continued to worsen. Neither the ousted former president Jean-Bertrand Aristide nor the US and OAS representatives could manage to change the political climate of the tiny Caribbean island.

By early 1993, the US had returned 30,000 of the over 40,000 Haitians estimated to have fled in the 16 months since Aristide's ouster. With US President Bill Clinton adhering to his predecessor's policy of forced return (despite Haitian hopes to the contrary), the crisis was not resolved. In June 1992 an OAS initiative to bring together former president Aristide, coup leader Raoul Cedras and other national leaders under the auspices of President Joaquín Balaquer of the Dominican Republican was refused. Only the Vatican recognized the current government.

Structural Adjustment

An emerging consensus among economic policy-makers over the basic tenets of free markets developed in 1992. Despite the praises of international financial officials and private investors, however, robust economic development remained an elusive goal. An estimated 180 million people, or two out of every five Latin Americans, continued to live in poverty, and the inequality of income in the region remained the worst in the world. Real investment as a percentage of GDP remained low throughout the region in 1992, although Chile and Mexico were both granted significant increases in foreign direct investment.

Latin American nations continued to grapple with the financial debt burdens of the last decade. In many, legislative discord, popular unrest and union strikes followed efforts at privatization and reducing public sector expenditures. A majority of the nations continued negotiations with commercial banks and the IMF, rescheduling debt payments and bargaining for fresh loans. Global recession, declining commodity prices, debt servicing and continued domestic fiscal crises made it clear that austere structural adjustment programmes would continue to reign throughout the near future.

Chile was again the darling of the international financial community in 1992, as the country registered an 8% increase in real economic growth, 4.5% unemployment and a inflation rate of only 14%, recording the strongest economic figures in three decades. A further opening of capital markets was decided in February 1993.

Mexico, despite sluggish growth (2.5%) and persistent inflation (15.5%), continued to have the approval of investors, in large part because of the finalization on 12 August of the NAFTA. While most observers expect that NAFTA will be revised along lines recommended by President Clinton and Congress with regard to environmental and labour issues, the agreement took a significant step towards an eventual economic partnership.

Numerous strikes forced Mexico's President Salinas to rethink measures for wage repression that are part of the structural adjustment programme. Salinas, hoping to mitigate labour unrest, negotiated a renewed version of the 1987 pact with trade union and business leaders to ensure productivity and competitiveness.

Although Argentina registered 7% growth in GDP during 1992, this achievement was dulled by inflation that hovered at 20%, and a bankrupt national retirement system which threatened to shake the economy. Consultations with Paris Club members to renegotiate debt continued throughout the year. President Carlos Saúl Menem privatized the state oil company *Yacimientos Petroliferos Fiscales* (YPF), the national airline *Aerolineas Argentinas*, the electrical power company serving Buenos Aires, and the troubled pension system.

The April 1991 economic stabilization plan remained intact, but the Central Bank was forced to support the Argentine peso in November as it fell below parity with the dollar. (The 1991 arrangement made the currency fully convertible and mandated that Central Bank reserves equal the money supply.) An extraordinary rise of 50% in the stock market between June and August forced Economy Minister Domingo Cavallo to establish a fund to stabilize the market's prices.

Brazil's economic woes deepened in 1992 as the presidential corruption scandal escalated. GDP growth slowed to 2.5%, and inflation remained high, with monthly rates averaging 20%. Despite the IMF structural adjustment constraints, the Collor government granted a pay increase of almost 80% to the armed forces in April in order to prevent a barracks uprising. The government also increased minimum wages to $100 a month, despite poor macroeconomic indicators. As a result, Brazil was unable to meet IMF targets. New economic goals were eventually negotiated, however, to enable Brazil to qualify for an IMF standby loan.

The presidential hand-over to Collor's vice-president, Itamar Franco, in November during impeachment proceedings further undermined investor confidence in Brazil. The new president, a traditional politician with populist tendencies, voiced his reservations about Brazil's privatization and structural adjustment programmes. In February 1993, Brazil's finance minister, the third in five months, resigned over disagreements with anti-inflationary strategies and was replaced by a former minister who last held a post under military rule.

Unaffected by international criticism and confident of his domestic power base, Peru's President Fujimori launched a $400-m 'economic revitalization programme' in August. Financed by increased tax revenues, the programme boosted public sector salaries, cut bank interest rates, decreased sales taxes and restored social security benefits in jungle and frontier areas. Since Fujimori launched his earlier adjustment plan in 1990, open unemployment has stood at 7.7%, although the estimated underemployment rate has been over 77%. The worst drought in 70 years deepened the economic crisis, and Peru's GDP fell by 3% in 1992.

Economic troubles were particularly acute in Cuba. The nation reported that the 30-year US embargo had cost $6.5 billion. Severe energy shortages left Havana financially constrained, despite a surprising growth in tourism. In 1989, a ton of sugar brought in 4.5 tons of Soviet oil; in 1992 that same ton brought only 1.4 tons of oil. The country's only hope for new energy is the Juragua nuclear power plant whose completion is not expected until 1994.

The policy of selling state-owned enterprises continued to provide once-only windfalls for indebted Latin American nations in 1992. The region's top four privatizers – Argentina, Brazil, Mexico and Venezuela – brought in more than $15bn in 1991 alone. While proponents touted the benefits of these programmes, such as cutting fiscal deficits and external and domestic debts, popular discontent, fuelled by workers fearing job losses and by nationalists fearing the loss of sovereignty, slowed the pace of privatization in most countries. Efforts to privatize Brazil's ports provoked a dockers' strike, while unions in Bolivia launched numerous strikes, demanding guarantees of compensation in case privatization created unemployment.

Privatization sales in Bolivia of the state airline, *Lloyd Aereo Boliviano*, and in Peru of Peru's *Cochan* Refinery attracted only one bidder each. Peru's state-run copper mine *Condestable* brought a low price. In a December referendum, Uruguay's electorate overwhelmingly rejected President Luis Alberto Lacalle's privatization plan. As an estimated one out of ten Uruguayan adults is employed in the public sector, the plans generated massive opposition.

In September, Ecuador became the first member of the 13-nation OPEC cartel to quit the organization. Ecuador claimed that it wanted to privatize much of its oil production and to increase production without cartel approval. This decision sparked demonstrations in Quito by thousands of workers, students, housewives and Indians.

Drug Traffickers and Guerrillas

In 1992, an unprecedented campaign to arrest drug traffickers and to stem the flow of drugs was waged in Latin America. The US and Latin American governments expanded their efforts to eradicate the planting of coca and to restrict the trade of the commodity. The drug problem had grown beyond mere trafficking. Drug-related violence and money laundering became important political issues in Colombia, Bolivia and Peru. In March 1992, Colombian central bankers testified before Congress that approximately $1bn of an estimated $1.9bn increase in their nation's hard currency reserves were of dubious origin. Within guerrilla organizations, extortion and money-making ventures increasingly took over from their political goals.

Pablo Escobar, Colombia's Medellín drug cartel leader who had surrendered to authorities in June 1991, escaped from jail in July. This set off a new round of violence. There was a spate of bombings, kidnappings and threats to officials of Colombia's Justice Department. Colombia's Gaviria administration not only faced drug traffickers, but also guerrilla insurgencies. An estimated 8,000 combatants made up two guerrilla armies, the Revolutionary Armed Forces of Colombia (FARC) and the National Liberation Army (ELN), which exacted money from business enterprises operating in areas under their control, kidnapped prominent figures and terrorized many local governmental offices. No serious negotiations between the government and guerrilla groups took place. The emergence of a new organization, PEPEs, or People Persecuted by Pablo Escobar – dedicated to killing Escobar and his allies – added a new twist to the macabre events.

Political violence in Colombia took the lives of an estimated 27,000 people in 1992. In November, Gaviria declared a 90-day national state of emergency and announced stringent measures intended to halt the growing insurgency: improved intelligence and communication networks, press restrictions and measures enabling the government to cancel foreign and domestic contracts with companies believed to be delivering protection money to the guerrillas. Seizures of ELN documents revealed that the organization obtained close to $30m from kidnapping and extortion in 1991 alone.

Peru shared Colombia's plague of both drug traffickers and guerrillas. For the past 12 years, the *Sendero Luminoso*, or Shining Path, which observers believe is organized and financed by the drug trade, has stalked both rural and urban Peru in a vicious campaign. Of the more than 1,600 terrorist acts recorded in Peru throughout 1992, over 1,300 were attributed to the *Sendero Luminoso*, and over 3,000 people died as a result of Peru's political violence during the year. In March, Fujimori moved to 'privatize' the war against insurgents by handing out arms to urban self-defence groups. In September, Abimael Guzman Reynoso, *Sendero Luminoso's* notorious leader and ideologue, was arrested and sentenced to life imprisonment. The government followed this with additional victories, dealing blows to two of the Shining Path's surface organizations, *Asociacion de Abogados Democraticos*, the legal services arm and *Socorro Popular*, the group's social welfare arm.

The disclosure in October 1992 of the 'Green Ice Operation', which involved the coordinated attempt of nine governments to dismantle the link between Latin American drug suppliers and European distributors, revealed the limited success of the international campaign against Latin American drug trafficking during the year. Bolivia's cocaine production is second only to Colombia's, producing one-third of the world's supply. In July the US announced it would withhold aid to Bolivia, because the coca eradication programme was reported to be far behind schedule. However, while revenues from Bolivia's cocaine trade brought in $300–$500m in 1992, US aid brought in only $200m.

The large presence of the US military, CIA and DEA agents also created domestic opposition in the region. In Peru, a US aircraft was attacked in April by the Peruvian state air forces, prompting questions about links between the military and drug trafficking. Containment also became a greater problem for the drug war in 1992. New drug corridors were set up in Chile and Venezuela whose open borders provided convenient access points for drug traffickers to get into and out of neighbouring Colombia and Bolivia.

Trade and Integration
Intra-regional trade and integration remained a popular, if elusive, goal for most Latin American countries. As European and Asian nations

strengthened their economic ties to regional trading blocs, Latin American nations had little choice but to turn to their regional neighbours. In August, the European Community announced the restriction of banana imports from Latin America to two million tons a year. This translates into a 30% reduction in Latin America's exports. The US also dropped Latin America's sugar quota by 11%, compared to 1991.

The economic gains from free-trade agreements remained largely unrealized. President Bush's 1990 Enterprise for the Americas Initiative did not develop into a viable strategy for achieving hemispheric-wide trade integration. Latin American nations recognized that they would have to broker their own trade deals to guarantee their place in the global economy.

At the close of 1992, five different trading groups within Latin America had emerged. In 1991, the Southern Cone nations of Argentina, Brazil, Paraguay and Uruguay formed a regional common market MERCOSUR, or *Mercado Comun del Sur*, aimed at reaching a zero tariff for intra-regional trade and a common external tariff by the end of 1994. The Andean Group of Bolivia, Colombia, Ecuador, Peru and Venezuela, originally created in 1971, was revived and planned to establish a customs union by 1995. Central American countries reinstated the Central American Common Market, originally formed in 1964. Thirteen Caribbean nations established CARICOM, a regional organization with an ambitious agenda, including adoption of a single currency, a common external tariff and elimination of all intra-group barriers to trade by 1993. In early 1987, Colombia, Mexico and Venezuela set up a separate subregional organization, called the Group of Three, to help the countries of the Caribbean Basin to finance oil purchases. They expect to sign a free-trade pact in 1993.

These Latin American free-trade agreements, however, did not move beyond the negotiation of initial frameworks. Members of the Andean Group had to put back their initial timetable for integration, CARICOM met resistance from various states to the common external tariff, and MERCOSUR was stalled by Brazil's domestic political troubles. MERCOSUR members did manage to cut their tariffs in half and increased the gross volume of their combined trade by 45%. Chile, still hoping to negotiate its own free-trade agreement with the US, stayed out of any of the regional trade pacts.

Finalization of the text of the North American Free Trade Agreement in August and the signing of the treaty in October by the presidents of Canada, Mexico and the US has moved the Western hemispheric trading bloc closer to realization. There are a number of obstacles, however. Opinion polls conducted during the US election campaign pointed up the likely opposition the agreement would encounter in ratification proceedings on Capitol Hill. Of the three major architects of the agreement only one is still active in pushing for ratification. Mexico's President Salinas, who expects it will result in increased investment in his nation, remains anxious to see early NAFTA implementation, but Canadian Prime Minister Brian Mulroney has announced his resignation and US President Bill Clinton promised during his election campaign to request revisions to the treaty on employment and environmental issues. That the US 'fast track' procedure is coming to an end is likely to further politicize the issue. NAFTA is another grand idea that may take more time than initially expected to come into being.

A More Hopeful Balance Sheet

Years of incompetent military governments, debilitating internal wars and static economic policies have left deep scars on the Latin American landscape. Recovery will not be easy, but the efforts are encouraging. Most of the wars have ended with negotiated solutions which are slowly being implemented. Although the tenets of democracy are still being breached in a few countries, for the first time all of Latin America, has embraced the concept. And there has been a surprising, and healthy, turn on the part of almost all governments in Latin America towards seeking more harmonious relations with the US.

Massive problems remain. Individual countries are still deep in debt, and inflationary pressures have not fully subsided. Although exports are high as a result of improved economic development, that same improvement is bringing an increased demand for imports. Drug traffickers combine with guerrilla movements in some countries, stretching the capabilities of their security forces to the limit. There are all to many ifs to take into account to feel confident about predictions, but the trend is certainly in the right direction and cautious optimism seems the best bet.

Europe

Throughout Europe, from Land's End to Vladivostok, the time was out of joint. The artificial order that had been imposed by the Cold War had dissolved after 1989; despite high hopes, the once-normal disorder had returned in 1992. Brutal ethnic and nationalist-driven wars raged in the Balkans and the Caucasus, and threatened to break out in parts of western Russia. Economic dislocation affected all of Europe, and weak, dispirited governments seemed to have run out of ideas on how to cope. It was not just a winter, but a year, of discontent.

Among the newer nations in Europe there was little but trouble. In Russia, the reformist group under Boris Yeltsin was struggling to keep control of a disintegrating situation, and there was grave doubt that it would be able to keep those who look more to the past than to the future from coming to power. In that event it will be difficult to stop the fighting from spreading from the Caucasus to western regions of Russia where strong feelings for independence have been asserted. Nor was there much reason to believe that the fighting in the former Yugoslavia will soon end. Even if present diplomatic efforts to negotiate a settlement succeed, the plans that have been advanced cannot satisfy the contradictory ambitions of the parties to the war. The settlement will have to be ensured by a large military presence from outside; when it is withdrawn the battle may well flare again.

Among the older nations of Europe, expectations that the Maastricht Treaty, leading to European unification, would be ratified in 1992 have been shattered. What had once appeared a popular idea has not only lost the support of the citizens of many of the countries of Europe, but even governments, which had championed the cause, have had second thoughts. The one positive note in an otherwise dismal year was struck in the Central European nations, where efforts to replace dictatorships with democracy, and command economies with market-driven ones, have made encouraging progress. But hopes that they would be able to join a new and dynamic Europe when those tasks are done have been set back because of the doubts which now exist as to whether there will be a new, or very dynamic, Europe in the near future.

RUSSIA IN EXTREMIS

By the end of March 1993 the ferocious, but yet unresolved, fight for leadership of Russia had cast the country into turmoil. The struggle for primacy of view and the power to effect it was joined in Moscow by the Yeltsin administration and the Congress of People's Deputies, led by its turncoat Speaker, the Chechen, Ruslan Khasbulatov. It was mirrored in the *oblasts* and *krais* by similar clashes between those who were hoping to push the country forward and those who pined for the past. Yeltsin and his colleagues, who had begun the year with much popular support, were still in charge, but they were weak and their opponents were closing in fast. In a desperate effort to recoup, Yeltsin reached out to the people for a vote of confidence. If they care to speak, they may give him just enough support to allow him to climb back, but apathy born of the economic burdens they have been carrying may rob him of another chance. As doctors often say, the prognosis must be guarded.

The Antagonists

Since the collapse of the old regime at the end of 1991, Russia has been racked by a search for an identity. Did a Russian state exist, and if so, what were its boundaries? Was there a Russian nation and if so, how was it to be defined? The confusion led to a lack of direction, focus and coherence in Russian policy.

Two main schools of thought were discernible. One group, who can be labelled the Atlanticists, wanted Russia to join the 'civilized world'. By this they meant the West. Russia should strive to become just like a West European or North American state. This implied parliamentary democracy, the rule of law, a market economy and a civil society. An added attraction was that most of the world's rich states belonged to this grouping.

The others, who may be dubbed Eurasians, rejected the view that Russia was merely a European state. Since most of Russia is in Asia, they saw it as a bridge between East and West and this required the development of its own unique type of society. Merely being a copycat was seen as demeaning to Russian national pride. Russia should rely on its own resources, its own people. Unlike the Atlanticists who placed great store on permitting the market economy to flourish, competition to expand and the successful to gravitate to the top, the Eurasians were unwilling to accept the necessity for a great gulf to develop between the haves and the have nots. They preferred a corporatist approach with a strong central government, intervention in the economy (what they called a regulated market economy), and protection for the less able and successful.

In international affairs the choices were just as stark. The Eurasians argued that ever since the beginning of the Gorbachev era Russia was being sold into bondage to Western capitalists. They wanted it to develop self-reliance. They are belligerently nationalist and feel the loss of great-power status keenly. They would use the presence of the Russian military in the successor states of the USSR to defend Russia's national interests and the over 25 million Russians living there. They would not have signed START II and would prefer not to implement START I. They hold that Russia has a special responsibility for security in the former Soviet Union, and would like to develop what might be called a Russian 'Monroe Doctrine'; they are in effect 'neo-imperialists'.

The Atlanticists approach foreign and security policy from a different angle. They believe that Russia should not lay claim to any foreign territory, or threaten aggression. They have taken Gorbachev at his word when he claimed that national security cannot be achieved if it makes another state feel insecure. The world in their view is interdependent. Although they too dream that one day Russia will again be a superpower, they accept that now it is weak. As this can only be achieved through a market economy, they are eager to accept the help, collaboration and cooperation of the West. They are 'post-imperialists'.

The Impact of Economic Hardship

By instinct a gambler, Yeltsin miscalculated the odds several times during the year and lost. He always avoided making the final, fatal mistake, however, and survived by backing off and making concessions to his more powerful opponents. In January he gambled that Egor Gaidar's economic shock therapy, liberalization and stabilization would break the power of the ministries and the strong industrial lobby by forcing bankruptcies and looser control from the centre.

The major aim of Gaidar's shock therapy had been to bring the budget deficit under control, weaken the industrial lobby and make the march to a market economy irreversible. Privatization was seen as crucially important, because if enterprises were transformed into joint stock companies, the influence of the central ministries would be emasculated. One major difficulty was that no one knew at what point reforms rendered a return to a more centrally administered economy impossible.

By the end of the year privatization had made some progress in services, housing and agriculture, but had hardly touched medium- and large-scale industry. In October, only 4% of all industrial enterprises and 5% of small trade and services enterprises were in private hands. Vouchers with a face value of 1,000 roubles, which could be used to buy shares in newly privatized companies, were distributed to the population by the end of January 1993. About 10% of Moscow's housing had been privatized; there were over 170,000 private farms cultivating about 3% of the arable land and most small shops had passed into private hands. With the help of the International Finance Corporation, the private sector arm of the World Bank, a bold initiative was launched at the end of the year to privatize 500 medium and large enterprises in the 14 of the 49 *oblasts* and *krais* in the country that were considered most receptive. The experience of Nizhny Novgorod, where auctioning of small-scale shops and enterprises had been successful, served as a guide.

The opponents of a rapid transition to a market economy staged a comeback from August onwards. By December Yeltsin was forced to ditch Gaidar as his prime minister and to accept Viktor Chernomyrdin, a former minister of the gas industry under Gorbachev. Despite this, the Gaidar reform team remained in place. It was indicative of the balance that existed between the two sides that Boris Fedorov, Russian director of the European Bank for Reconstruction and Development (EBRD) in London, returned to Moscow to take up his old post of minister of finance and to take responsibility for macroeconomic policy.

Fedorov correctly pointed out that lowering inflation was a key priority and that it had not been effectively tackled by Gaidar and his government. Gaidar was riding high in August when the monthly inflation rate fell to 9%. He had failed, however, to exert influence over the Central Bank. With many enterprises running up huge losses and facing collapse the industrial lobby swung into action and the Central Bank issued almost unlimited credit to these otherwise almost bankrupt enterprises. The EBRD estimates that the real gross domestic product in Russia declined by about 20% in 1992, while inflation averaged 1,450%. Money had become quite useless; the rouble, which was rated at 162 to the dollar in August 1992, had fallen to 649 to the dollar by March 1993.

During the year industrial production fell by 24% and output by 22%, with unemployment officially below 1%. The same labour force was producing almost one quarter less than in previous years. Little wonder then that there were acute shortages of most consumer goods. The harvest was barely adequate. Shortages of feed grains and fodder reduced livestock herds so far there were fears that by the end of 1993 herds would be down to the levels of the 1960s.

The Political Ramifications

As a consequence of the hardships now being borne by the people, Yeltsin's popularity declined, his influence over parliament waned and a danger of violent strife loomed. The heady optimism of the immediate post-coup period gave way to bitterness and recrimination. While it was true that the many problems facing the leaders were not amenable to short-term solutions, much of the blame for the deadlock that developed must rest with Yeltsin and his team.

Russia is the only ex-Soviet state which has not had elections since the attempted coup in August 1991. One major blunder was Yeltsin's failure to establish a party of reform. He regarded himself as above political parties and relied on loose associations such as Democratic Russia to propagate change. It was soon made clear, however, that the only thing that united Democratic Russia was anti-communism. Faced with fundamental questions, such as privatization, it began to fray.

Modern political parties emerge to fight elections, and the absence of elections in Russia has held back the development of these parties. Political parties and movements there remain dominated by individuals, and since there is little or no party discipline they fragment easily.

The Eurasians managed to put together a coalition, the Civic Union, which became influential both as a faction in parliament and outside. It was composed of four main groups: the Democratic Party of Russia, led by Nikolai Travkin; the People's Party of Free Russia, headed by Vice-President Aleksandr Rutskoi; the Renewal group, led by Arkady Volsky, who was also head of the Union of Industrialists and Entrepreneurs (consisting predominantly of military industrial enterprises); and *Smena* (Change). The overall grouping came into being during the summer and quickly had an impact on government monetary policy by winning large credits for beleaguered enterprises. But it soon also wavered. By December, Travkin announced that the time had come for his party to leave the opposition and to support the new prime minister Viktor Chernomyrdin. This split the party; its St Petersburg faction went off in search of liberal democratic allies who would support market reform.

To the right of Civic Union was Russian Unity, a broad coalition of conservatives and ex-communists who opposed market reforms and dedicated their efforts to bringing down the government and President Yeltsin. The communists received a boost in November when the Constitutional Court ruled that the ban on the CPSU that Yeltsin had decreed was legal at the national level, but not at the local level. If the party could prove that its buildings and property had been financed from party and not state funds it could claim them back. The moderate and far right came together during the autumn to form a National Salvation Front, which was also supported by Vice-President Rutskoi. It was banned in October by presidential decree. Also banned was the Russian Supreme Soviet private armed guard, estimated to be 5,000 strong and rumoured to be under the direct command of Khasbulatov.

The Congress of People's Deputies, the controlling parliament, with 1,033 deputies, and the Supreme Soviet, the standing parliament, with 252 deputies, gradually became more assertive during the year. These bodies were elected in March 1990 and Yeltsin's supporters made up no more than a third of the deputies. At the sixth congress in April Yeltsin was forced to step down as Prime Minister. His nominee for replacement, Egor Gaidar, was not confirmed in office by the Congress. At the same time, three conservative deputy prime ministers were added to the government.

By the time of the seventh congress in December, the reformers had lost further support. Four main blocs were discernible. About 30% of the deputies supported Russian Unity; 20% were predominantly pro-communist; 35% adhered to the bloc of the democratic centre (leading members of this bloc were the People's Party of Free Russia, headed by Rutskoi, and Civic Union dominated by the industrialists); and 15% made up the coalition for reform. Only the coalition for reform fully supported Yeltsin and Gaidar. At the congress Yeltsin was forced to drop Gaidar entirely and to accept a prime minister who was the nominee of the democratic centre.

This underlined a fundamental conflict, that between the president and the Congress. The Speaker of the parliament, Ruslan Khasbulatov, who had stood shoulder-to-shoulder with Yeltsin during the coup of August 1991, became one of his fiercest critics. Khasbulatov's goal was to subordinate the president and the government to parliament. If elections had been held in late 1991 they would have almost certainly produced a parliament that was more amenable to reform. Failure to elect a new parliament meant that a new constitution did not appear, and the power and responsibilities of the three centres of power, the president, the parliament and the government, remained unclear.

Yeltsin countered by establishing a parallel administration, accountable to him. There were presidential advisers, presidential prefects (governors) in various parts of the country, a presidential administration (*upravlenie*) and a presidential organization (*administratsiya*). Since parliament rejected so much of his proposed legislation he resorted to issuing laws and decrees under his own signature. Here he faced the same problem that Gorbachev had. While he could issue decrees, it was difficult to have these policy documents implemented, for the institutions necessary to carry out the orders did not yet exist.

Political Deadlock

The struggle that consumed much of 1992 became full-scale war at the end of the year. Yeltsin and his supporters had revealed a lack of finesse at the seventh congress in December. They miscalculated their level of support, tried unsuccessfully to deprive the Congress of a quorum and then had to accept various constitutional amendments which further restricted presidential power. While Yeltsin's opponents were successful in this regard, they could not muster the two-thirds majority (689) votes needed to carry through their motion to impeach him. Yeltsin decided to go to the people for support for a referendum that would decide key issues such as a new constitution, new parliamentary elections and whether private ownership of land and property should be carried forward.

This led to an impasse which was only broken when the Constitutional Court intervened. It mediated a compromise in which a date was set for the referendum (11 April 1993) and the constitutional amendments the Congress had passed were placed in abeyance until after the referendum. The compromise did not last long. In the period between the seventh congress in December and the eighth in March 1993, Khasbulatov lobbied hard against his own agreement, Civic Union joined in opposing it, and even Valerii Zvorkin, the head of the Constitutional Court, who had been the midwife to the agreement now disowned it.

When the eighth congress convened on 10 March, it was clear how the wind was blowing. The agenda had two items: the referendum and the need to obey the constitution. The second was obviously a direct attack on Yeltsin, who was being criticized for having said that he did not feel obligated to follow the constitution because it had been so amended since he was elected president that it was no longer the document he had sworn to uphold. After three days of raucous debate, the Congress cancelled the referendum, refused to accept the compromises Yeltsin suggested, cut further into his executive powers, and went home. Before they left, the deputies tried again to impeach Yeltsin, but again fell short of the necessary two-thirds vote.

Yeltsin may have survived as president, but his room for manoeuvre was badly constrained. He then tried an appeal to the people over the heads of the Congress. On the night of 20 March he called on the people to give him a vote of confidence in a 'plebiscite' to be held on 25 April. He planned also to ask for a vote on a new constitution, on the basis of which new elections to parliament would be held. Until then he hinted that he would rule by presidential decree. Yeltsin's dramatic action came under immediate attack by Khasbulatov, Vice-President Rutskoi and Zvorkin, who spoke out against the president even though, as head of the constitutional court, he must have known that he would be called upon to judge the constitutionality of Yeltsin's actions. The now badly politicized court was called upon by the Congress to make a judgement; in the event it ruled that Yeltsin had acted unconstitutionally, but went on to say that this was not grounds for impeachment.

Despite this, Khasbulatov called an emergency session of the Congress, which met from 26 to 29 March. Yeltsin had pulled back slightly by not issuing the decree for presidential rule, but he was standing firm on the need for a vote of confidence. The Congress failed once again to impeach Yeltsin, but this time by a narrower vote than before. It then turned on Khasbulatov, furious that he and Yeltsin had met behind closed doors on the night of 27 March in an attempt to hammer out a compromise.

On the last day, the Congress passed a resolution calling for a referendum on 25 April, but not on the questions that Yeltsin had put. There will no longer be any question of asking the people about a new constitution, which would have been certain to cause the disbandment of the whole system of congresses from which the delegates derive their power. Instead, there are four questions: do you have confidence in President Yeltsin; do you approve of his policies; do you want early elections for president; and the same for deputies of the Russian Federation. The country was back in the stalemate that Yeltsin had tried to break, and there was no sign that it would be capable of much movement until after the referendum.

The Russian Military

In the midst of the crisis generated by Yeltsin's struggle with the deputies of the Congress, General Pavel Grachev, Russian Minister of

Defence, and the heads of the other security services insisted that their forces would remain neutral. They declared that they supported the constitution; however, since the constitution can be read in support of either side, this merely meant that they wished to try to stay on the sidelines. The reasons are not hard to see. The generals cannot be sure if their officers and men would carry out their orders. The armed forces are as badly split as the rest of the country, and a request for action in favour of one or another of the factions might well result in civil war. Wait and see must have been a more appealing option.

At the December congress General Grachev made an optimistic speech in which he claimed that the decline in the combat readiness of the armed forces 'had been arrested' and that 'reliable command and control' had been restored. Both statements must be doubted. In February 1993 an All-Army Officers' Union held an illegal meeting attended by perhaps 250 men. The Union had been set up in January 1992 and banned in October, and there is no way to know if, as some claim, it speaks for a majority of officers in the army or only a few.

Grachev has started to implement the plan to reduce the military to 1.5 million men by the year 2000; he has claimed that it will be carried out as early as 1995. A reduction of some 220,000 personnel was planned by the end of December 1992. But one reason for the accelerated fall in numbers was the inability of the military to enforce the draft. According to Grachev only one in ten in Moscow, and one in five elsewhere in Russia, actually ended up doing their national service. The transition to a mixed professional force would take place over the next eight years with a goal of 50% personnel on fixed-term contracts by the end of the decade. During 1992 about 100,000 men were withdrawn to Russia and this is supposed to rise to 250,000 by the end of 1995.

The effort to bring the boys home places enormous strains on the Ministry of Defence's ability to house incoming personnel. This inability was given in March and October 1992 as the main reason for suspending withdrawals from the Baltic. Other Russian units outside Russia are now classified as 'peacekeeping forces', but in many areas they are busy enforcing a Russian-desired peace rather than keeping a locally-desired one. Russian personnel are active in Transdniestra, the Caucasus and Tajikistan.

The standing of the military within Russia has suffered. Money is short, and because the military budget will depend heavily on the economic development of the country there is little hope of a quick improvement. As a result morale has plummeted. Many units are in disarray and desertions are commonplace. There is considerable doubt that the army would be able to fight effectively. Surveying the forces under his command, General Grachev must have decided that, while issuing constitution-supporting noises, non-action was the wisest course of action.

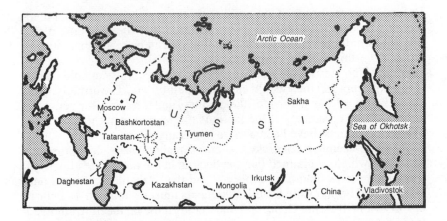

A Threat of Disintegration

The Russian Federation came into existence on 31 March 1992 when the federal treaty was signed by 19 of the 21 sovereign republics within the Federation, the Russian *krais* and *oblasts*, and the cities of Moscow and St Petersburg. The federal government was responsible for foreign policy, defence, protecting human rights and ethnic minorities. Russian was declared the official language of the Federation, but republics could also have their own official languages. Chechnia and Tatarstan refused to sign, holding out for extra concessions.

During the year since the federal treaty was signed, the pull of regionalism has grown stronger. The oil-rich Tyumen oblast in West Siberia and Sakhalin island in the Far East are determined to gain greater freedom to run their own affairs. Chechnia has in effect seceded; Tatarstan has been negotiating with Moscow for much greater autonomy; Bashkortostan, an oil-rich region next to Tatarstan, has also been agitating for less Moscow control. What was once Yakutsia, a vast republic in Siberia producing 99% of Russia's diamonds, is now called Sakha. It has been discussing some kind of possible link-up with Tatarstan and Bashkortostan in order to gain heft in their struggle against the centre.

Throughout the year, in his efforts to acquire their support, Yeltsin offered greater control over economic and many personnel decisions to the local leaders. The Congress has begun to match his promises. The only thing that can hold a federation together is the ability of the central government to provide a basic minimum of needed services: economic stability which will keep inflation down below the level that will destroy the currency; basic policing to ensure domestic tranquillity; and protection from outside threats. Moscow is having acute difficulty providing any of these now, and will be totally unable to do so in the near future, unless the political impasse is broken. In those circumstances, the richer regions that Moscow depends on for revenue can be expected to withhold the taxes they are now collecting to provide some of these services for themselves. What led to the break-up of the Soviet Union was just such a march of events. Local centres of power which wanted more control over their own affairs, a break-down of central control, and a slow accumulation by local leaders of the means to achieve their dreams.

Racing Towards the Crash

In his TV broadcast throwing down the gauntlet, Yeltsin said that the country could not afford another October Revolution. The example was picked with care for the two situations have close parallels. In 1917 a weak reforming government under Aleksandr Kerensky, loath to take drastic actions that would transgress its democratic ideals, faced the growing strength of those who would willingly take drastic action while hiding behind democratic slogans. 'All power to the Soviets!' was the battlecry. In 1993 a would-be reforming government is being slowly throttled by men who claim they are on the side of the people, upholding the constitution, and proclaiming 'all power to the Congress!'.

Conditions as a result of the economic breakdown in Russia are not as bad as they were during the war 75 years ago, and there is no determined party in sight like the Bolsheviks to push the situation to armed revolution. Yet the auguries are not good. The present impasse is certain to last at least until the referendum. Even if there are then elections for president and parliament, without a change of constitution the two centres of power will remain. Not even a strong country can be effectively run under such a system. In Russia, it is a formula for disaster.

CONFLICT IN THE CAUCASUS

For hundreds of years the Caucasus has been the uncomfortable meeting place for a bewildering variety of different peoples, cultures, religions and nations. Historically located on the mountainous edges of large neighbouring multi-ethnic empires, the Caucasus has been the haven for a number of national groups who have sought to preserve their cultural and religious freedom and independence. Over the centuries the ancient Christian nations of Armenia and Georgia have fiercely defended their distinctive religious inheritance. With just as strong a sense of national pride, the Muslim peoples of Azerbaijan and the Northern Caucasus have maintained their allegiance to the *Dar ul-Islam*, the world of Islam. Like the Balkans, the Caucasus marks the historical frontier between Islam and Christendom and has the same shattered mosaic of multi-religious and multi-ethnic societies.

The rugged independence of the Caucasian peoples was to be a considerable obstacle to Russian imperial expansion into the region in the eighteenth and nineteenth centuries. Under a succession of charismatic leaders, such as Imam Mansur and Sheikh Shamil, resistance to Russian rule was sustained for over 70 years through numerous guerrilla campaigns. It was only in 1855 that Russia completed its conquest of the Caucasus and could enjoy full control over its new territory. However, the tradition of opposition to Russian and Soviet rule never died, and renewed campaigns for independence broke out whenever control from Moscow weakened, as in the revolutionary chaos of the 1917–21 period and during the Second World War.

When Mikhail Gorbachev set out to reform and democratize the Soviet empire in the late 1980s, it was not surprising that the Caucasus proved to be one of the greatest obstacles to his ambitions. In 1988, the eruption of the Nagorno-Karabakh conflict between Azerbaijan and Armenia provided the first significant indication that inter-ethnic confrontation would prove to be a more powerful force than internationalist integration and that the Soviet Union was more likely to collapse than be reformed. Similarly, the forceful Georgian campaign for independence, which grew in strength after the bloody repression of a nationalist demonstration in Tbilisi in April 1989, confirmed that the Caucasian struggle for independence was becoming more uncompromising in its objectives and was seeking complete severance from the multi-ethnic Soviet empire.

The collapse of the Soviet Union in December 1991 was a critical turning-point in the liberation struggle for an independent Caucasus. Georgia, Armenia and Azerbaijan became fully independent and internationally recognized states during 1992. Such independence was not, however, granted to the peoples of the North Caucasus, which were left within the borders of the Russian Federation. Chechnia directly challenged this disposition in the last quarter of 1991 by proclaiming its independence from Russia. That neither Russia nor the international community has recognized Chechnia has not deterred the self-proclaimed state; it has not retreated from its declaration of independence and continues to defy the Russian authorities.

As 1992 progressed the initial euphoria of the dramatic unravelling of centralized Soviet rule in the Caucasus gradually evaporated. The speed with which power was transferred from Moscow meant that the new states of the Caucasus had inadequate political, economic and social institutions, lacked indigenous national armies and security forces, and faced severe economic deterioration. Inter-ethnic conflicts also grew in intensity. Armenia and Azerbaijan became locked ever more bitterly in the Nagorno-Karabakh dispute; Georgia became embroiled in a number of violent confrontations with some of the non-Georgian minority groups; and instability flowed over to the Russian Federation resulting in fierce fighting between the Ingush and the Ossetes in October 1992. Tragically, it was these various conflicts which essentially defined the political developments in the Caucasus during 1992.

Armenia, Azerbaijan and Nagorno-Karabakh

In the early part of 1992, the new Russian government under Boris Yeltsin ordered the full withdrawal of the Soviet troops which had been attempting to maintain peace in Nagorno-Karabakh. This decision was popular not only in Russia but also with the combatants, since Armenia and Azerbaijan had regularly complained that the troops had never been truly neutral and that they had been manipulated by conservative forces in Moscow to perpetuate and exacerbate the conflict. The withdrawal meant that the two sides could also test their respective military strength.

At the outset, the Armenian forces were clearly ascendant and won a number of critical military victories, including the opening of a corridor at Lachin through Azeri territory to the disputed enclave. The reason for these Armenian successes was the relative discipline of their forces against the chaotic and anarchic Azeri armed formations. Political instability in Baku also did not help the Azeri cause, as from February to May the Azerbaijani Popular Front (APF) battled with, and finally ousted, the ex-communist President Mutalibov. It was symptomatic of this power struggle that during the first five months of 1992 six different defence ministers marched through that office.

In the summer of 1992 the balance shifted. Azeri forces managed to return to the offensive after they had seized large amounts of equipment from the former Soviet army garrisons inside Azerbaijan. They recaptured a large part of the territory that had been lost earlier in the year. The Lachin Corridor, however, remained under Armenian control, and in the autumn the Azeri advance was halted as the Armenian defence forces in Nagorno-Karabakh consolidated and strengthened their defences. By the end of 1992, a stalemate had been reached.

Throughout this period Russia, Iran, Turkey and the CSCE took turns at mediation, but all failed to make any decisive breakthrough. Cease-fires were arranged after weeks of arduous diplomacy and then casually broken within hours of their supposedly coming into effect. There were also bitter divisions between the two sides about obligations to the disputed territory and on the right of representatives from the Nagorno-Karabakh parliament to be involved in the negotiations. The unstable political situations inside Armenia and Azerbaijan made it even more difficult for the two sides to reach any sort of compromise. President Lev Petrossian of Armenia had to contend with strong nationalist opposition to any concessions, particularly by the Dashnak Party which is the dominant force in the Armenian community in Nagorno-Karabakh. The political flux in Azerbaijan was even more destabilizing. The APF forcibly seized power in May, and its leader, Abulfaz Elchibey, was subsequently elected president in June 1992. His legitimacy and the strength of his political power-base remained far from secure, however, and he has had constantly to look over his shoulder at the growing popularity of such figures as the radical nationalist Etibar Mahmedov or the strongman of Nakhichevan, Gaidar Aliev.

The overall situation at the beginning of 1993 appears bleak. Peace seems as far away as ever, and the economic and political costs of the five-year-old war are becoming ever more apparent. Armenia is certainly suffering the greater economic hardship. The combined effects of the economic blockade imposed by Azerbaijan and the disruption of supplies from Georgia have meant that Armenia is receiving no oil and hardly any gas. The economy is, as a result, close to collapse. Azerbaijan is clearly hoping that Armenia's economic plight will be translated into increased military weakness. However, as the more acute observers in Baku realize, this expectation of an Azeri military victory is improbable, given the deeply entrenched Armenian defences inside Nagorno-Karabakh.

The only limited grounds for optimism are that the military stalemate and the undoubted war-weariness of the Armenian and Azeri populations might lead to a more profitable and sustained peace initiative. Such an initiative would depend, however, on the internal consolidation and increased moderation of the governments in power, greater centralized control over the armed formations engaged in the fighting, and energetic mediation and intervention by the major external powers and international organizations like the UN and the CSCE. It would also require greater involvement and cooperation between the three major regional powers: Russia, Turkey and Iran. Without such a concerted and coordinated drive for a peaceful settlement, there is a considerable danger that the parties in dispute will attempt to escalate the conflict by spreading the war beyond Nagorno-Karabakh into each other's territories and by seeking to drag their respective regional allies into the fighting.

Georgia – The Divided State

The inter-ethnic conflicts inside Georgia since the proclamation of Georgian sovereignty in March 1990 have been caused by one fundamental contradiction: the deeply-ingrained Georgian nationalist desire for a unitary state and the fact that over 30% of the population are non-Georgian minorities who deeply fear Georgian nationalist self-assertion. Zviad Gamsakhurdia, popularly elected president in May 1991, proved incapable of resolving this contradiction and only made inter-ethnic tensions worse by attempting to impose a unified Georgian state and to abolish the autonomous status of South Ossetia, Abkhazia and Adzharia. His increasing unpredictability and authoritarianism also led to deep fissures within Georgian society and alienated many of his former allies. In January 1992, Tengiz Kitovani and Dzhaba Iosseliani, backed by their respective armed formations, forcibly deposed Gamsakhurdia in a coup.

By spring 1992 Georgia was in a state of deep crisis with restive minorities and a polity divided between pro-Gamsakhurdia supporters based mainly in western Georgia and his opposition in the rest of the country. In order to legitimize their military takeover and consolidate their power, the new rulers invited Eduard Shevardnadze, the former Foreign Minister of the Soviet Union, to return to his native land and resume the political leadership of the country. Shevardnadze was fully aware that he had been offered a poisoned chalice. He knew that Kitovani and Iosseliani would not willingly give up their independent power-bases and would seek to circumscribe and undermine his own authority. The weakness of the government, the parlous state of the economy and the plethora of ill-disciplined armed formations would also present considerable obstacles to the consolidation of a centralized state and the development of democratic reforms and a market economy. Furthermore, Shevardnadze knew that he would have to deal with a continuing armed conflict in South Ossetia and a potentially dangerous confrontation in Abkhazia.

In the first few months after his return, Shevardnadze had a number of successes. Georgia received the recognition which the international community had denied it during Gamsakhurdia's reign. There was a constant flow of Western statesmen eager to support and resume their contact with the man who had helped to dismantle the Soviet empire. In June, Shevardnadze defused the South Ossete conflict after negotiations with Yeltsin had led to a military cease-fire and a tripartite Russian–South Ossetian–Georgian agreement on peacekeeping forces. On 11 October 1992, Shevardnadze's position was boosted by his election to the head of the Georgian state by a massive majority. Although the democratic credentials of the election were tainted by the fact that no one stood against him, the vote did represent strong popular support for Shevardnadze's leadership and strengthened his position against his other political rivals.

But 1992 was not an unblemished year for Shevardnadze. In August, he suffered his first major setback, as an attack led by Kitovani against the Abkhaz republican government in Sukhumi escalated into a major military confrontation between the Georgian and Abkhaz armed forces. The Abkhaz also managed to gain the upper hand, as their forces were strengthened by volunteers from their ethnic kinsmen in the Northern Caucasus and by the support of conservative-inclined elements in the Russian military. The Georgian armed formations, beset by ill-discipline and incompetence, also proved to be almost completely ineffective militarily. Although it is unclear how deeply Shevardnadze was implicated in the decision to attack Sukhumi, he immediately assumed responsibility for the subsequent defeats and vowed to regain the lost territory.

The Abkhaz crisis has placed considerable constraints on Shevardnadze's room for political and diplomatic manoeuvre. It has made it more difficult for him to make concessions to the Abkhaz or to other minority groups without the opposition accusing him of compromising Georgia's territorial integrity. The triangular power struggle between Shevardnadze, Kitovani and Iosseliani has been intensified in the face of the Abkhaz crisis, and none of the three can afford to appear to be betraying the Georgian nationalist cause. The acute political crisis also makes it even more difficult for Shevardnadze to develop the political and economic institutions of the country and thus build a dam against growing political anarchy and economic disintegration.

The Abkhaz conflict has furthermore undermined Shevardnadze's attempts to place Georgian–Russian relations on a more conciliatory basis after the fiercely anti-Russian policies of Gamsakhurdia. Unlike his predecessor, Shevardnadze was willing to accept, and not immediately condemn as imperialist intrigue, Russia's expressed interest in the Ossete and Abkhaz disputes. Since the Abkhaz and Ossetes have strong ethnic, national and cultural links beyond Georgia's borders with the Caucasian nations in the Russian Federation, the Russian authorities were naturally concerned about the destabilizing consequences of any escalation in hostilities. Russia not only feared the consequences of increased instability on its very borders but was aware that if it appeared to condone Georgian military action it would lose the support of the nations of the North Caucasus. This could only lead to more forceful demands for secession. Russia, therefore, has been keen to see a political settlement of the Abkhaz and Ossete conflicts, and has had a correspondingly urgent concern that Georgia should not be tempted to seek a military solution.

Shevardnadze was aware of Russia's concern and understood that only Russian–Georgian cooperation could secure a durable settlement of the North Caucasus problem. The cease-fire agreement that had dampened the South Ossete conflict had been a good example of successful coordinated action between Shevardnadze and Yeltsin, enhancing bilateral Georgian–Russian relations. Much of that good work was undermined by the Abkhaz crisis. Shevardnadze has had to take into account the widespread belief among the Georgian people that Russia deliberately provoked and inflamed the crisis to undermine the territorial integrity of their state. This sense of a Russian conspiracy is only accentuated by the participation of volunteers from the other North Caucasus nations in the conflict and the oft-repeated Abkhaz and South Ossete demands to be included within the Russian Federation. As the Abkhaz crisis developed, Shevardnadze's suspicions of Russia's intentions increased and he became more forthright in his criticisms of Russia. The prospects for improved Russian-Georgian relations and bilateral cooperation on the North Caucasus have consequently plunged.

Shevardnadze faces a complex set of internal and external challenges for 1993. At the moment, he is still weak politically and the country is almost breaking apart, both socially and economically. It is perhaps not an exaggeration to say that without a just resolution of the Abkhaz and Ossete conflicts it would be difficult for the Georgian state to survive, let alone develop a successful market-orientated democracy. It is this critical question – the reconciliation of Georgian nationalism with defence of minority rights – which may overtax even Shevardnadze's considerable diplomatic skills.

Russia and the North Caucasus

The parts of the North Caucasus within the Russian Federation consist of seven autonomous republics with titular non-Russian nationalities: Adyghe, Karachayevo-Cherkessia, Kabardino-Balkaria, North Ossetia, Chechnia, Ingushetia and Daghestan. Nowhere has the Stalinist definition of nationality and the adherence to the principles of 'divide and rule' been so crazily and arbitrarily applied. Stalin deliberately fragmented this region to undercut the unifying force of Islam and the power of Muslim resistance which had consistently characterized the response of the North Caucasus to Russian and Soviet imperial expansion. That the Soviet system ultimately failed to quash this spirit of defiance became evident when, after the August 1991 coup, Chechnia elected Dzhokhar Dudayev President of the Republic and asserted its independence from Russia. Despite an economic embargo and constant military pressure, Chechnia refused to sign the Russian Federation Treaty. Dudayev has also been the leading force in the Confederation of the Caucasian Mountain Peoples, which brings together popular groups from 16 nations of the North Caucasus who seek independence from Russia. Although none of the other autonomous republics have yet followed Chechnia's example, the anti-Russian sentiment and desire for independence which Chechnia symbolizes represents a strong political current in the region.

As in other areas of the former Soviet Union where boundaries were arbitrarily drawn, the loss of central control and the increasing nationalist self-assertion has led to an upsurge in territorial disputes. The violent clashes between Ingush and North Ossetes in October 1992 was caused by a long-festering dispute over territory in North Ossetia claimed by the Ingush. These clashes were the first major instance of armed conflict in the Russian Federation and set alarm bells ringing in Moscow, seemingly confirming fears that multi-ethnic Russia might be destined to follow the disintegrative path of the Soviet Union. More directly, it raised concern that the North Caucasus might be on the verge of internal fragmentation, following the pattern of inter-ethnic conflict in Lebanon or Yugoslavia. It is salient to note that the Republic of Daghestan alone consists of over 30 different nationalities and any break-up of its multi-ethnic composition would necessarily result in endless territorial and inter-ethnic conflicts. The speediness of the response to the Ossete–Ingush fighting, the large numbers of forces sent to calm the region, and the high-level political figures sent to search for a political settlement testifies to the seriousness with which the Russian authorities responded to the crisis.

Despite this forceful intervention, Russian policy towards the region throughout 1992 has been essentially ad hoc and reactive. This reflects the unresolved debate in Moscow as to the correct strategic approach towards the North Caucasian problem. One radical option canvassed has been for Russia to withdraw from the Caucasus mountains and to redraw the Russian borders somewhere on the plains, allowing the indigenous North Caucasian peoples to determine their own future, whether violently or not. The other, perhaps more frequently expressed, option rests on the belief that Russia's natural defensive southern border lies at the Caucasus and that the consequences of withdrawal would be harmful to Russia's strategic defences. Advocates of this forward approach maintain that the Caucasian mountain range is an essential buffer against the spread of instability from the Transcaucasus and a defence against potential aggressors from the south, such as Iran or Turkey.

The speed and the extent of the military intervention to quell the Ingush–Ossete conflict obviously reflects the application of this second strategic concept. However, the reluctance to challenge militarily Chechnia's independence suggests the more cautious approach and the disinclination to become too involved in the region. Similarly, the statements in January 1993 indicating that Russia might withdraw its peacekeeping troops from South Ossetia and the remaining Russian troops from Abkhazia suggest that the will to remain as the external guarantor of stability for the region might be decreasing.

The fact that Russia appears to be oscillating between these two positions reflects the difficulty of its position in the North Caucasus. The anti-Russian hostility of the indigenous peoples, the inter-ethnic complications of the region, and the host of territorial disputes make continued Russian imperial control, however benignly administered, difficult to sustain. In the end, if Russia is determined to maintain its traditional presence, it will probably have to follow the Tsarist and Soviet practice of a combination of the use of force with the careful application of the 'divide and rule' principle. Such tactics, however, are difficult to justify if Russia truly wants to develop as a responsible and liberal democratic power.

Nevertheless, to withdraw completely would also have potentially dangerous implications, for it would leave the North Caucasus critically unstable with the certainty of continuing territorial and inter-ethnic disputes. It would be difficult for Russia to remain an indifferent bystander if such violent conflicts resulted in large refugee movements or attacks on ethnic Russians, such as the fiercely nationalistic Cossack groups. The prospect of Turkish or Iranian penetration into the Caucasus as a response to such developments would also be difficult for Russia to accept. There is also a strong feeling in Russia that instability in the Caucasus might extend further into Russia to the other Muslim nationalities, like the Tatars and the Bashkirs. The territorial integrity of the Russian state would then undeniably be at stake.

How Russia deals with the North Caucasus will, therefore, remain an immensely complicated issue. There is no obvious, nor easy, option to follow. Whilst there is certainly a strong domestic desire for Russia to be rid of its Caucasian problem, there is just as strong a belief that Russia's interests demand that it remain as the external guarantor for stability in the region. The future of Russia as a multi-ethnic entity and the hopes that it will develop on the path of a liberal and democratic state, which eschews the use of force so favoured by its Tsarist and Soviet forbears, may well founder in this area of intractable problems.

FEAR AND LOATHING IN THE BALKANS

When the European Community (EC) met at Maastricht in December 1991 and agreed to recognize the secessionist republics of Slovenia and Croatia, a chapter in the Yugoslav drama was closed. By mid-January 1992 Yugoslavia had ceased to exist. Efforts by the Serbian-dominated Yugoslav People's Army (JNA) to hold the two regions in a tight embrace had failed. Fighting had ended in Slovenia by the middle of 1991 and even the more serious conflict in Croatia had ceased early in 1992 as a result of a cease-fire plan brokered by United Nations' envoy Cyrus Vance. The Vance plan in effect froze the situation on the ground. It did not restore Croatian sovereignty in the Serbian enclaves, but it provided for an all-important element of UN troop deployment in the disputed areas of Croatia. It ushered in a period of peace during which, the international community hoped, Serbo-Croat negotiations could resolve the matter. Yet, even though the Vance plan provided the possibility for a final peaceful, negotiated settlement, it equally left open the possibility of renewed violence.

There had been some question about the wisdom of recognizing Croatia, with some arguing that recognition should follow rather than precede an overall Yugoslav settlement. Since the Serbs who lived in Croatia controlled at least 25% of its territory and had made it clear that they would resist being turned into a minority in a new state, pushing for recognition before assuring that Croats would fulfil all the necessary conditions for minority rights was risky. Even more risky was the precedent that was established: if Croatia, with its ethnic mix, could be recognized, what was to prevent other aspirants in the former Yugoslavia from requesting equivalent status?

Disaster in Bosnia-Herzegovina

Bosnia-Herzegovina was an ethnic potpourri made up of Muslim Slavs (44%), Serbs (33%) and Croats (17%). In the free elections that had been held in November 1991 the three most successful parties represented the national interests of the three groups. During the political struggles within the coalition government that was formed after the elections it was made clear that the interests of the groups was to prevent the domination by any one, or combination, over another. To assure this, an effort was made to operate on the basis of consensus regarding decisions of vital interest to any of the three groups. In a multinational republic this was the only meaningful hope for coexistence.

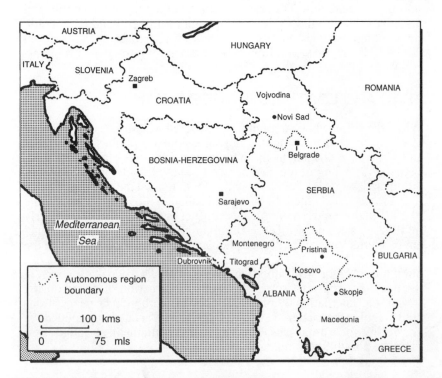

When the EC recognized Slovenia and Croatia it had invited applications for independence from any of the other republics to be submitted by 15 January 1992. Bosnia-Herzegovina duly applied – or rather, the Muslims and Croats in the government did. The Serbs wanted to stay in Yugoslavia. Life outside, separated from the bulk of their fellow Serbs appeared to them potentially dangerous. The Muslim-Croat coalition that pushed for independence created precisely the kind of minority status for the Serbs which they wished to avoid.

The Muslims and Croats were just as concerned not to stay in a rump Yugoslavia, which would inevitably become Serb-dominated. There was a vital difference between these two groups, however. The Croats did not look with favour on the prospect of living in an increasingly Muslim, independent Bosnia-Herzegovina, but they saw the Serbs as the immediate menace. For the moment, therefore, they were prepared to accept the idea of independence. Most Muslims were by now fully in favour of independence. Given the choice of coexistence with the Serbs in a truncated Yugoslavia, there could be no question of which course they would opt for.

The Bosnian Serbs left no one in doubt about their position. They said that they would not accept an independent state in which they would be a minority, and then went further to assert that independence would mean war. On 9 January 1992 they declared their own republic in protest against the decision by the Muslims and Croats to apply for EC recognition. Although it was clear that moves towards independence would provoke major internal opposition, the EC felt that it could not simply withdraw its previous offer. It opted for a quasi-legalistic approach. The Badinter Arbitration Commission, attached to Lord Carrington's Peace Conference, recommended recognition of the republic on condition that a referendum on independence be held.

A glimmer of hope for the future of the republic came during EC-brokered talks in February, in Lisbon, when the Serbs agreed on the preservation of the existing frontiers of Bosnia-Herzegovina. This was a change from their previous policy of seeking to remain in a rump Yugoslavia. In return, Muslim President Alija Izetbegovic agreed to the formation of several national territorial units within the republic. There was no agreement, however, on the degree of autonomy that the proposed units would exercise. Thus, when the independence referendum took place, the constitutional shape of the future Bosnia-Herzegovina was entirely unclear. The script for the two-day referendum, which began on 28 February, could have been written in advance. The Serbs boycotted it, and 99.7% of the remaining 64% of the population voted in favour of independence.

In a highly charged political atmosphere Izetbegovic proclaimed the republic independent from Yugoslavia. The Serbs reacted with great speed, putting up barricades and sealing off Sarajevo. This was a taste of things to come: the Serbs were evidently well organized, well armed and determined to support their cause.

The Muslims believed that the outcome of the referendum gave them the trump card in their drive for international recognition. Although the EC conditions were now fulfilled, the EC appeared hesitant. This was small surprise given the Serbs' grave reservations about independence. On 18 March, an EC-brokered agreement was reached in Sarajevo between the Muslims, Serbs and Croats: the Lisbon formula was reaffirmed, whereby Bosnia-Herzegovina would be 'a state in three parts formed on the basis of nationality and geographical and economic criteria'. Again, however, the relationship between central government and the three ethnic-based units was left undefined. Moreover, no sooner had Izetbegovic agreed on the so-called 'cantonization' of Bosnia-Herzegovina, he renounced it publicly much to the annoyance and anger of the Serbs, and the consternation of the EC. The Bosnian Serbs, led by Radovan Karadzic, announced the constitution of their own republic on 27 March.

Against this unpropitious background the EC extended recognition to Bosnia-Herzegovina on 7 April 1992. In the preceding days worsening armed clashes had spread across the republic. Izetbegovic's government controlled only a few cities. As the violence grew, Izetbegovic ordered the mobilization of the Territorial Defence force and the reserve police units. Clearly, given the chaotic conditions, normal criteria for recognition were hardly being met by Bosnia-Herzegovina. The EC decision to recognize it, however, must be seen against the background of the Croatian experience which had given rise to the view in some EC quarters that withholding recognition had merely prolonged conflict.

Upsurge in the Fighting

It was totally unrealistic, however, to assume that recognition would bring the fighting to an end. The Muslims were not prepared to negotiate over their now internationally recognized state; the Serbs, feeling trapped in this state, were determined to wreck it. Tension existed not only between the Serbs and the Muslim-Croat axis, but also between the latter and the federal army (JNA), which had regrouped in Bosnia-Herzegovina when it withdrew from Croatia. The Muslims (and the Croats) branded the 100,000 JNA personnel now stationed in the republic as an army of occupation. Except in two actions, against the Croats at Kupres and against the Muslims at Visegrad, the army stayed in barracks. Even Izetbegovic could only accuse it of 'passivity' as the Serbian forces occupied a string of towns in eastern Bosnia during the first fortnight in April. Serbian irregulars from Serbia proper played a prominent role in the fighting.

Militarily, the Serbs had the upper hand. When the JNA withdrew from Bosnia-Herzegovina in May more than half of it (over 50,000 men and officers, Serbs with local residence), stayed on to fight with much of the former JNA equipment. Politically, they were on the bottom rung of the popularity ladder. Three factors alarmed the international community about the Serbs: their military action in eastern Bosnia, coupled with the blockade and shelling of Sarajevo; the involvement of paramilitary groups from Serbia; and the emergence of the JNA as a Serbian force.

This alarm was increased in the following weeks and months by the enduring images of Sarajevo as a besieged city under indiscriminate fire from the Serbs. Lord Carrington, chairman of the EC-sponsored peace talks, initially took a somewhat different position, arguing that 'everybody is to blame for what is happening in Sarajevo', but his view was a minority one. Attempts by Lord Carrington to bring about cease-fires, either in the city or elsewhere in the republic, met with repeated failure.

Apart from Sarajevo, eastern Bosnia was the scene of the heaviest fighting which produced a stream of refugees, mostly Muslims. Media attention to the fighting and the plight of the Muslims put pressure on the international community which then felt it had to act. On 30 May the UN imposed comprehensive trade sanctions against the rump Yugoslavia (i.e., Serbia and Montenegro), reflecting the prevalent view that the Serbian regime of Slobodan Milosevic was responsible for the carnage in Bosnia-Herzegovina.

In July the UN authorized a 1,100-strong contingent to take control of Sarajevo airport in hopes of facilitating delivery of relief supplies. In mid-July, a serious diplomatic effort to halt the fighting began in London under the auspices of the EC Peace Conference on Yugoslavia, chaired by Lord Carrington. After two rounds of talks, however, the continuation of heavy fighting made nonsense of the cease-fire accords reached in London. In addition, the talks were complicated by the brutal displacement of civilians in Bosnia-Herzegovina that came to be known as 'ethnic cleansing'. The Bosnian Serbs claimed that the flow of refugees from ethnically mixed regions was a consequence of the war. Most other observers viewed the practice as a particularly obnoxious instrument of war. It called up comparisons with Nazi Germany.

This comparison was driven home by the discovery of what became known as 'concentration and extermination camps'. The Serbian claim that these were no more than collection points for refugees and prisoners of war, was belied by the evidence of widespread maltreatment and sporadic executions, and by the pictures of emaciated bodies behind barbed wire that appeared in the international press and on television. The camps were not 'concentration and extermination camps' in the Nazi sense, but they were close enough to drive the Serbian reputation even further down. The nadir was reached with press reports of widespread and protracted gang rape of Bosnian women, particularly Muslims. Rape is an inevitable concomitant of war, but this was so systematic that it strongly suggested a deliberate policy intended to dishonour Muslim women in order that they would be unacceptable to traditionalist husbands as marriage partners. There can be no doubt that the

Serbian forces, as a policy, were intent on erasing other Muslim identities: mosques were a particular target for Serb heavy gunners and, when they could get close enough, for Serb bulldozers.

The fighting in Bosnia-Herzegovina has been especially savage, with civilian suffering of an unusually high degree. The Croats have also been accused by the Muslims of 'ethnic cleansing' in their drive to acquire territory adjacent to Croatia, and mass graves of Serbs have been found in areas that were overrun by the Muslims. This is no conventional war, and there are no conventional armies, no front lines, no rules of war, merely an armed and radicalized set of ethnic groups. Yet the activities of the Bosnian Serbs and of freebooters from other Serbian areas appear particularly brutal.

Difficult Diplomacy

At the end of August the EC and the UN convened a Conference in London in an effort to address the problem in former Yugoslavia. By the eve of the conference, the Serbs had had considerable military success. They were in possession of some 65% of the territory of Bosnia-Herzegovina. The Croats had established themselves firmly in western Herzegovina, and had proclaimed a 'Herzeg-Bosnia' statelet. The Muslims enjoyed the overwhelming share of the world's sympathy, but had little or nothing to show for it on the ground.

The London Conference, co-chaired by British Prime Minister John Major and UN Secretary-General Boutros-Ghali, was attended by delegations from the UN, the EC and the CSCE, as well as by assorted Yugoslavs. With regard to Bosnia-Herzegovina, the Conference affirmed 'respect for the integrity of present frontiers, unless changed by mutual agreement', and it urged 'all parties immediately and without preconditions to resume negotiations on future constitutional arrangements'. The Conference also set up a Geneva-based negotiating forum, sponsored jointly by the UN and the EC, represented by Cyrus Vance and Lord Owen, who replaced Lord Carrington when he resigned just before the Conference convened. As the fighting in Bosnia-Herzegovina showed no signs of abating in the following days, a much enlarged UN presence to escort relief convoys was authorized by a Security Council resolution. The expanded UN effort was to be commanded by the French general Philippe Morillon.

The three sides assembled in Geneva for talks on 18 September, but the Muslims refused to sit in the same room with the Serbs, and no progress was registered. Early in October the Serbs scored a major victory in capturing Bosanski Brod on the northern border with Croatia. Amid continuing violence, the Security Council on 9 October adopted a resolution barring military flights over Bosnia-Herzegovina. It had no enforcement measures, however. In the meantime, the mediators had proposed a scheme for dividing Bosnia-Herzegovina into seven to ten regions.

Izetbegovic had in principle accepted this idea. He had little choice. On the battlefields, his problems were compounded by the fact that the Croats, nominally his allies, were increasingly turning against the Muslims in central Bosnia. The existence of a separate Croat agenda in the republic was confirmed as the Croat forces proceeded in late October with their own 'ethnic cleansing' against the Muslims.

During November and December, in a surprising twist to their seemingly hopeless military position, the Muslims began to fight back with a degree of success. In eastern Bosnia, they launched deep penetration raids from their besieged enclaves along the border with Serbia. Yet a much heralded Muslim offensive from the Sarajevo region failed to materialize. The likelihood of an external military intervention appeared to grow at this time, with much speculation, especially in the US, centring on the enforcement of the 'no fly zone', over which the Serbs were flying helicopters that they claimed were for humanitarian purposes, delivering medicine and evacuating wounded. They had not flown any clearly defined combat missions since November. In addition, the Organisation of the Islamic Conference had threatened to start delivering arms to the Muslims if no agreement on Bosnia-Herzegovina was reached by 15 January 1993.

It was in these circumstances that a major diplomatic effort to resolve the Bosnian question began in Geneva in early January 1993. All three factions were present, and the Muslims agreed to face the Serbs across the negotiating table. Cyrus Vance and Lord Owen, the co-chairmen of the Conference, presented the participants with a package containing three elements: proposals for constitutional principles for Bosnia-Herzegovina; a map dividing the republic into ten provinces; and a military paper on the cessation of hostilities and related measures. The co-chairmen insisted that the three elements were inextricably linked, and that changes would be incorporated only if all three parties agreed.

The thinking behind the proposed constitution was a combination of *Realpolitik* and high-minded principle. Bosnia-Herzegovina was to be 'a decentralized state with most governmental functions carried out by its provinces', but the provinces would not have 'any international legal personality' and could not 'enter into agreements with foreign states or with international organizations'. The annex to the proposed principles recognized that 'many of the provinces will have a considerable majority of one of the three major ethnic groups'.

On the table was an offer to break up Bosnia-Herzegovina, but in a way that would offer something to each of the contending parties. The express denial of international legal personality to the provinces and the stipulation that they could not enter into agreements with foreign countries was intended to ensure that no 'Greater Serbia' (or, for that matter, 'Greater Croatia') would emerge. The shell of Bosnia-Herzegovina would apparently survive, but internally the boundaries of the provinces were to reflect the ethnic-territorial principle. This

was in effect the 'cantonization' long demanded by the Serbs and
Croats, and so dreaded by the Muslims. Critically, moreover, the
Vance-Owen proposals revealed a largely impotent central government in charge of foreign affairs, customs duties and some taxation,
but practically everything else, including the 'police' (a euphemism for
armed forces) was to be controlled by the provinces.

The Vance-Owen plan reflected the political realities on the ground.
It could not save Bosnia-Herzegovina, and it was the maximum that the
international community could do for the Muslims short of military
intervention. The Croats readily embraced the plan in its entirety: they
saw the constitutional scheme as unworkable, while the map gave them
three provinces, two of them generously sized, and all contiguous to
the Republic of Croatia. The Muslims played for time in hopes of
international support. Thus Izetbegovic signed the constitutional principles, but refused to endorse the map which, he argued, required many
adjustments.

This turned the spotlight on the Serbs. They wished to have at least a
semblance of a state within Bosnia-Herzegovina, possibly within a
federal structure, and the Vance-Owen plan would not provide one.
The Serbs liked the maps even less: they reduced substantially the area
already under Serbian control, and the provinces were not connected to
each other, thus leaving the Serbian territories in western Bosnia and
the Krajina region of Serbian-occupied Croatia completely isolated.
This would frustrate any future plan to connect them to Serbia proper.

Radovan Karadzic, leader of the Bosnian Serbs, therefore refused to
sign anything and the Conference appeared on the verge of collapse.
Vance and Owen flew to Belgrade to see whether the good offices
of Slobodan Milosevic, the Serbian President, could save the day. On
10 January the Geneva Conference resumed, with Milosevic joining on
the following day. In private meetings, Karadzic came under enormous
pressure from Milosevic to sign the peace plan, and on 12 January he
signed a slightly modified version of the constitutional principles,
although on condition that the Bosnian Serb Assembly also endorse
them. The Serbs seemed to be playing for time as much as the Muslims
were.

The Bosnian peace process drifted on through the first three months
of 1993, but little substantive progress was made. The Bosnian Serb
Assembly voted to accept the constitutional principles set forth in
Geneva, while the question of the maps remained unresolved. Since
the maps and the principles were so interconnected, the action of the
Serb Assembly had little meaning. In early March the Serb forces
moved to solve the geographic problem by capturing and cleansing
areas in eastern Bosnia. Time after time they prevented the UN forces,
whose mandate would not allow them to use any force to move forward
in the face of opposition, from delivering humanitarian aid to the
beleaguered Muslim towns. The new US administration of Bill Clinton
mounted an air operation over Bosnia-Herzegovina, parachuting in

food and medical supplies. Neither this, nor the week-long effort by General Morillon to get ground convoys through the Serbian lines, seems likely to save the Muslims from being driven by the Serbs out of one of the areas that the Vance-Owen maps set aside for them. The Serbian obstruction throughout March 1993 cast considerable doubt on the willingness of the Serbs in Bosnia, if not the Serbs in Serbia, to take the agreement seriously.

The Rump of Yugoslavia

Legally, Yugoslavia did not cease to exist when Slovenia and Croatia were recognized as the EC did not at the same time 'de-recognise' the old country. In effect, however, Yugoslavia was now no more than Serbia plus Montenegro, given that Bosnia-Herzegovina and Macedonia were also seeking independence.

Many among the political elite in Serbia found it hard to give up the idea of Yugoslavia. They were the survivors from the days of the Tito regime, emotionally 'Yugoslavs' as well as communists. As early as January 1992 draft laws were being prepared in Belgrade to lay the foundations for a new Yugoslav federation for those republics that wished to be included.

The catalyst for the formal establishment of 'Yugoslavia Mark II' was the war in Bosnia-Herzegovina for which most of the rest of the world held Belgrade accountable. Against a background of the threat of sanctions and of measures against Yugoslavia in the CSCE, the new 'restructured' state was proclaimed in Belgrade on 27 April 1992. By establishing itself as Yugoslavia with borders which included only Serbia and Montenegro, the new entity in effect recognized the territorial integrity of the neighbouring republics of ex-Yugoslavia.

The international community, convinced that the fighting in Bosnia-Herzegovina was directed from outside, refused to recognize Serbia and Montenegro as the legal successor to the old Yugoslavia. Indeed, by June the UN had imposed punishing trade sanctions against the new Federal Republic of Yugoslavia (FRY) following events in Sarajevo, although there was not yet evidence of direct FRY complicity in Bosnia-Herzegovina. On 30 May, the day the Security Council voted for sanctions against Yugoslavia, a UN report cast doubts on Belgrade's control over Serbian irregulars fighting in Bosnia-Herzegovina, suggesting that General Ratko Mladic, the commander of the Serbian forces, was not being controlled by Yugoslavia.

The trade embargo was not likely either to stop the war in Bosnia-Herzegovina, or to dislodge Milosevic from power. One of Milosevic's political strengths was that the opposition in Serbia was divided between liberals, nationalists that included assorted conservatives and monarchists, and ultra-right radicals. For the time being, none of these forces posed a threat. The establishment of a revamped Yugoslavia, however, required the introduction of new federal administrative structures. Unexpectedly, certainly from Milosevic's point of view, these gradually developed into independent power centres.

The new federal president was Dobrica Cosic, an ageing novelist, ex-communist and ex-dissident, who was regarded as the spiritual father of Serbian nationalism in the Milosevic era. He was seen, wrongly, as Milosevic's mentor. The new federal prime minister, Milan Panic, a Serb who had become a US citizen and made a fortune in California, proved his own man.

Panic, a man combining good intentions, naïveté and a certain volatility, immediately declared that his mission was to bring peace. He condemned ethnic cleansing, ordered that no aid be provided for the war in Bosnia-Herzegovina, announced his support for the demilitarization of the entire region, and began talks with Croatia on the withdrawal of the remaining JNA forces from the strategic peninsula of Prevlaka south of Dubrovnik. During the London Conference at the end of August, Panic made moves towards Yugoslav recognition of Croatia, within internationally recognized frontiers. He was only stopped at the last moment by the Bosnian Serbs. Clearly, his pacifism, contempt for borders and his general ideas of national interest were somewhat removed from mainstream Serbian views.

The London Conference was a success for the Serbs and might therefore have been considered a success for Panic. It appeared to remove from the agenda the rumoured threat of intervention and, moreover, no new sanctions were imposed on Yugoslavia. However, a power feud erupted between Panic and Milosevic when, immediately on his return from London, Panic faced a no-confidence motion in the Yugoslav parliament. When this was dropped, Panic, on 10 September, dismissed Vladislav Jovanovic, the federal foreign minister identified with Milosevic, signalling the start of open warfare between the two camps. Significantly, President Cosic lined up behind Panic.

Panic was now being branded a 'CIA spy', and Milosevic boycotted the reconciliation talks with Croatia which Panic had instigated. Panic demanded Milosevic's resignation. Early in November, Panic again faced a no-confidence vote which he lost in the lower house of the parliament. He was only saved by the Montenegrin deputies in the upper house.

The embattled prime minister now announced that he would run against Milosevic in the Serbian presidential elections scheduled for 20 December. Milosevic won quite comfortably against his rival. Although there were allegations of fraudulent voting, it would have had to have been massive to affect the outcome. The truth was that most Serbs preferred to support their strongman. Driving the point home, the Serbs voted more than twice as many representatives of the ultra-nationalist Radical Party into parliament than had previously been there. With the whole world apparently against Serbia, the Serbs chose to defy it.

Prospects Elsewhere

During 1992 and early 1993 the war in Bosnia-Herzegovina was by far the bloodiest of any conflict in Europe since the Second World War. But two other areas of former Yugoslavia where violence had been widely predicted remained quiet: Kosovo and Macedonia. There was sporadic small-scale violence in Kosovo between the ethnic Albanians (who make up more than 90% of the population) and the Serbs. The Albanians were biding their time in the hope that they could achieve their political goal of self-determination and majority rule peacefully. At the minimum, they wish to recover their former autonomy, but only as a stepping stone to their real underlying goal – secession from Serbia and full independence for Kosovo. They recognize that the major impediments at the moment are the well-armed local Serbs, Montenegrins and Serbian security forces who have ruled the province since 1990. An inter-ethnic incident could easily get out of hand and result in a violent crackdown by these forces; the Albanians are trying to avoid such incidents.

The Albanian government, which supports the Kosovars, and would find it necessary to respond with force if fighting did break out in Kosovo and drive floods of refugees across the border, are encouraging the attempt to reach a peaceful, democratic solution. It is unlikely that Milosevic would be interested in provoking a conflict in Kosovo and risk bringing down on Serbia further international pressure and punishment. Certainly, while the fighting continues in Bosnia-Herzegovina the probability is that both sides will make every effort to keep the situation quiet.

Nor did the rump Yugoslavia wish to see trouble breaking out to its south, as part of the complex political and security situation in Macedonia. The JNA had left Macedonia, which had also applied for EC recognition as the Republic of Macedonia, in the first half of 1992. The major threat of internal conflict came more from the ethnic Albanians (some 30% of the population) who continue to be a separatist force much like their brethren in Kosovo. Although there were occasional clashes, the leaders of the Macedonian Albanians and the Slavs have tried to minimize the problems so that no third party would be able to exploit the differences which exist between them. There are external threats as well. Any fighting in Kosovo would probably spread to Macedonia. The Serbs might then find it necessary to move into Macedonia if the Albanians there were providing support for their brothers in Kosovo, and Greece might try to find an excuse to join with Serbia in partitioning the republic between them.

In hopes of preventing any such outside intervention the CSCE in the autumn of 1992 sent observers into Macedonia, and in January 1993 the UN decided to send 750 peacekeeping troops. This will not be very helpful if any conflagration which breaks out is caused internally rather than externally. The breaking point may come sooner rather than later, given that Macedonia, which had joined in the sanctions against Yugoslavia, was paying a heavy economic price for its gesture towards international solidarity. Not only had Macedonia lost its Serbian market, but Greece had mounted a blockade from the south.

In fact, Greece was causing more trouble for Macedonia than Serbia was. It had blocked recognition by the EC because it insisted that Macedonia was a Greek name for one of its own provinces and therefore could not be used by its northern neighbour. The standoff continued throughout the first three months of 1993, although in February 1993 the Greeks accepted a UN-sponsored arbitration process to decide on a name by which international recognition could be given.

Krajina, the Serbian-inhabited regions of Croatia, was potentially the most explosive of all, outside Bosnia-Herzegovina, but quiet in 1992. The Vance plan was gradually applied, with the UN Protection Force (UNPROFOR) of some 14,000 taking up its positions in the disputed areas. True, the cease-fire had been violated many times ahead of UNPROFOR deployment in April. Even after deployment violence was occurring, especially in the so-called 'pink areas' which were Serb-held territories outside the existing UN protected areas. For most of the period, however, in comparison with neighbouring areas in Bosnia-Herzegovina, a semblance of peace prevailed.

One of the little-noted developments in 1992 was the gradual coming together of the Serbs of Krajina and the Serbs of Bosnia-Herzegovina. Towards the end of October this culminated in a joint session of the parliaments of Krajina and the Serbian-Bosnian Republic. In the future, it is Karadzic rather than Milosevic who is likely to wield influence over the Serbs of Croatia.

This boded ill for the plans of the national government in Zagreb, which looked forward to the restoration of full Croatian sovereignty. In August, President Franjo Tudjman was solidly backed by the Croat electorate in the presidential election. He never made a secret of his intense dislike of UNPROFOR. The fact that the Serbs were practising 'ethnic cleansing' of the Croats in their areas under the noses of UNPROFOR only increased Tudjman's determination to recover these lands. He chose to strike in January, in the middle of the Geneva Conference on Bosnia-Herzegovina which he himself was attending. The Croatian army, now re-equipped, opened fire on the Serbian positions on a 100km-long front in northern Dalmatia. The initial assaults were successful, but the Serbs, who rearmed themselves by removing their heavy weapons from UN-monitored warehouses, fought back and the front soon stabilized. UNPROFOR was a helpless observer, and the UN protested in vain.

In Croatia, as in Bosnia-Herzegovina and Serbia, contempt for the international community was a characteristic which the inhabitants of former Yugoslavia were exhibiting with regularity and gusto. They saw confrontation, rather than cooperation as the only course of action when it came to the question of defending vital national interests. The limits of external influence on ethnic conflicts were thus on full view during 1992 and early 1993. Unless the international community is prepared to put some teeth into its efforts to provide humanitarian aid or to mediate these conflicts, it will be forced to face the horrors of continuing bloodshed.

THE TROUBLED EUROPEAN COMMUNITY

The theory of chaos, in natural science, explains how a butterfly beating its wings over the Amazon can lead to a hurricane in the Caribbean. Denmark's 50.7% rejection of the Maastricht treaty on 2 June demonstrates chaos theory at work in politics. Not all butterflies cause hurricanes. The Danes did because ominous clouds had already gathered over Europe. An economic depression was biting and many people were fed up with politicians in general and the EC in particular. To the east old nationalisms were reviving. Much was not well.

The Gathering Storm

The year began calmly enough. Everyone assumed that the Maastricht treaty would come into force at the end of the year, after ratification by referendum in Denmark and Ireland and by parliamentary vote in the other EC member countries. This optimism did not last long.

In February Jacques Delors, President of the European Commission, unveiled new budgetary proposals for the five years 1993–97. These would have increased the ceiling on the size of the EC's budget from its current level of 1.2% of Community GDP to 1.37%. When the governments began to debate Delors' plans it became clear that they were over-ambitious. Only the four poorer members – Spain, Ireland, Portugal and Greece – supported him; the other eight declared that they would not pay for such a big increase.

Also in February, the EC struck a deal with the seven countries of the European Free Trade Association (EFTA) to create a 'European Economic Area'. This would admit EFTA countries to the EC's single market, and, while they would have to follow Community rules, they would be consulted on new EC laws. The EEA should have come into force at the start of 1993, but did not because the Swiss voted it resoundingly down in a referendum in December 1992. Work then began on a new EEA agreement that would exclude Switzerland and, it was hoped, come into force during 1993.

In March the Community began to argue over whether it should take another step towards a federal Europe, beyond Maastricht. Delors argued that further reforms were needed lest decision-making seize up when Nordic and Alpine countries joined the EC. Britain disagreed, but France and Germany backed him and there was talk of a constitutional revision in 1993 while the EC negotiated the entry of new members.

The Danes, engrossed in their evenly-matched referendum campaign, followed this debate with keen interest. The Danish press reprinted 'Delors plan to rule Europe', an article from Britain's *Sunday Telegraph*, which said that Delors wanted the EC to be run by a European president instead of rotating national presidencies. This fed Danish fears that Maastricht was a step towards centralized rule from Brussels.

Mounting unemployment, which some Danes blamed on the EC, helped the campaign for a *Nej*. So did the 'June Movement', a well-organized group of non-party academics whose arguments made voting 'No' respectable. The campaign for a *Ja*, although supported by most political and business leaders, was desultory. The opposition Social Democrats, paralysed by a leadership contest, took little part. The government was silly enough to distribute copies of the unreadable treaty, without explanations or summaries, and some found it frightening. Danes do not hold their leaders in great esteem, and many of them admit to voting 'No' to teach the establishment a lesson.

Even before 2 June, there were signs of a West European *Fronde*. This was hardly surprising, for in every EC country, except Greece and Ireland, the same gang had been in charge for most of the previous ten years. President François Mitterrand changed prime ministers after France's Socialists won a miserable 16% in the March 1992 regional elections, but he and his party remained deeply unpopular. In their general election in April, the Italians shook their governing classes by voting for anti-establishment parties like the Lombard League. That month Britain's general election cut Prime Minister John Major's majority to 20 seats, giving Conservative backbenchers – many of them anti-EC – a hold on his government.

In Germany the popularity of Chancellor Helmut Kohl had slumped. Government borrowing of nearly 5% of GDP and inflation of the same figure highlighted the mismanagement of German reunification. Inflation made the Germans reluctant to sacrifice the Deutschemark for the ecu, which Bavaria's environment minister described as 'confetti money'. The huge cost of propping up the new *Länder* led to fears that a European economic and monetary union (EMU) would mean Germany supporting weaker economies like Italy.

Der Spiegel and the popular *Bild* railed against the Maastricht treaty and copied the British tabloids in attacking all that was 'Brussels'. Hans-Dietrich Genscher, the German foreign minister identified with European Union, resigned in May – with impeccable timing.

Opinion polls showed that most Germans opposed EMU (though a small majority favoured the Maastricht treaty). Germany's political elite, although loyal to the treaty, sought to reflect the new mood. In March the Social Democrats said that they would not support its ratification unless parliament could vote on the final phase of EMU before it began (the government was to agree to this demand before the end of the year). Volker Rühe, the defence minister, stressed that widening the EC was more important than deepening it.

In May Theo Waigel, the finance minister, proposed calling the single currency the 'frank' rather than the ecu (by September he had plumped for the Euro-mark). Helmut Schlesinger, President of the Bundesbank, reinterpreted the Maastricht treaty by saying that EMU's final phase would consist of 'phase 3a' and 'phase 3b'; only after a phase 3a of fixed exchange rates that would last for many years would the single currency of phase 3b commence.

Dane Action – Chain Reaction

In theory, the Danish referendum made the treaty of Maastricht void. But EC governments were loath to abandon the treaty they had so painstakingly crafted and which had given each of them prizes: France had won commitments to EMU and common defence; Germany more powers for the European Parliament; Spain a 'cohesion fund', and so on. Britain alone cherished little that was in the treaty, but Major was proud of his opt-outs on EMU and social policy. They all feared that any renegotiation could land them with a worse deal.

Thus, when EC foreign ministers met in Oslo on 5 June, they declared that they would press ahead with ratification and not renegotiate the treaty. Their implicit message was that Europe would not stop for Denmark and that the Danes should think again if they did not want to be left behind.

Neither this firmness nor Ireland's 67% vote for Maastricht on 18 June prevented the hurricane from gathering. British Conservatives who had sullenly accepted the treaty as inevitable saw that it could be stopped. On 3 June President Mitterrand had fed the uncertainty by announcing a referendum on the treaty. His intention, presumably, was to banish the doubts that the Danes had created, and to embarrass the French right, which was split on Europe. The risks seemed small since opinion polls showed that two-thirds of the French favoured the treaty.

Most of France's political establishment campaigned for a *Oui*, against the National Front, the communists, some Greens and some neo-Gaullists. But the people were fed up with their political leaders and they blamed the Socialists for unemployment of over 10%. Some remembered how a referendum defeat had made de Gaulle resign in 1969 and hoped for a repeat with another unpopular septuagenarian. As the summer wore on, the French began to turn against Maastricht – but not for the same reasons as the British and the Germans. Britons worried about losing sovereignty to over-mighty bureaucrats overseas, while Germans feared inflation and losing the D-mark. The principal theme uniting French critics of the treaty was that it stood for economic liberalism. Farmers who blamed the EC's farm policy for their shrinking incomes, industrial workers who feared foreign competition and *petits commerçants* who did not want a single market drove the *Non* campaign, rallying all those who felt unsuccessful. On 20 September there was to be a near-perfect match between areas of below-average wealth and areas voting against the treaty.

By the end of August some opinion polls pointed to a French *Non*. This shook Europe's currency markets, already unsettled by Denmark's referendum and by the Bundesbank raising its discount rate in July. There had been no realignment of the exchange-rate mechanism (ERM) since 1987, and the markets had assumed that the EC's political commitment to EMU meant that the parities were more or less fixed.

Doubts over Maastricht destroyed that assumption. The markets started to believe that the combination of high German interest rates and several fundamentally weak economies would force a realignment. Speculators sold lire, pounds and pesetas, and a weak dollar added to the strains by encouraging investors to buy D-marks.

When EC finance ministers met in Bath on 5 September they put heavy pressure on Helmut Schlesinger, the Bundesbank president, to cut interest rates. He ruled that out but hinted that a realignment would change the situation. Norman Lamont, the UK Chancellor of the Exchequer, had the support of Michel Sapin, his French colleague, in keeping that word off the agenda.

The markets forced a 7% devaluation of the lira on 14 September, but because Britain and Spain would not follow suit, the Bundesbank cut its Lombard rate by only 0.25%. Schlesinger did not help the pound when he told *Handelsblatt* that a further realignment would be in order. Two days later Lamont raised short-term interest rates by 5% in a bid to protect the pound; the Bundesbank and the Bank of England threw their reserves into the purchase of pounds; but a speculative hurricane, the likes of which the currency markets had never seen, forced the British government to suspend the pound from the ERM that evening. On the night of what has become known in Britain as 'Black Wednesday', after a meeting of the EC's monetary committee in Brussels, the lira left the ERM and the peseta devalued. Britons and Germans blamed each other for the pound's fate.

France's narrow *Oui* on 20 September did not restore calm. Thatcherite Conservatives, jubilant that the pound was floating (or rather sinking) free, argued that if 49% of the French – normally so *communautaire* – did not want the treaty, the British should ditch it. That evening John Major said on television that Britain would ratify Maastricht. But he set three conditions for doing so: popular concerns about EC bureaucracy would have to be addressed; the ERM would have to be reformed; and the EC would have to work out how to solve the Danish problem. In his role as holder of the EC's rotating presidency he announced a special summit to tackle these issues.

Britain's prevarication made EMU seem less likely and delighted currency speculators, who then picked on the franc. Only FFr160 billion of Franco-German intervention saved it from devaluation on 23 September. The foreign-exchange markets then calmed down, for nearly two months. Not enough currencies had devalued by enough, however, to convince money-managers that the ERM could remain stable with such high German rates. The markets doubted that the currencies of Spain, Denmark, Portugal, Ireland and France could stick to the D-mark when their economies were crying out for cheaper credit.

Speculators scented blood after the Swedish krona, which was pegged to the ERM, cut loose on 19 November. Central banks fought the markets with higher rates and intervention; the Danish krone, the Irish punt and the French franc survived, but the peseta and escudo had to devalue. A series of speeches by the Bundesbank president only added to the uncertainty in the currency markets. He attacked the convergence criteria of the Maastricht treaty for being lax and complained about the extent to which the Bundesbank had to intervene to help weak currencies in the ERM.

Meanwhile Britain had become increasingly isolated from its partners. When Prime Minister Major seemed to wobble over Maastricht in late September many French and German politicians spoke of a 'two-speed Europe'. They suggested that if Britain or Denmark blocked Maastricht an inner core should go ahead in certain areas such as EMU or defence. This talk was both sincere and tactical. The tactics seemed to work: before the Birmingham summit of 16 October Major promised that his government would get the treaty through the British parliament by the end of 1992 or early 1993.

Major's decision to allow British Coal to sack 30,000 miners overshadowed the Birmingham summit, which agreed to a lot of finesounding phrases about greater openness and subsidiarity - the idea that the EC should intervene only when strictly necessary. The Prime Minister's U-turn on the miners a few days later revealed the weakness of his government.

Major announced that a preliminary vote on the treaty would be held in the House of Commons on 4 November. His officials briefed journalists that he would resign if he lost. The opposition Labour Party reverted to its anti-EC past and joined the Thatcherites in voting against the motion. Major won by three votes – but only after promising waverers that Britain would not ratify until after a second Danish referendum.

That delay maddened EC governments, who knew that a Danish *Ja* was far from certain. They had just heard that the Danish parliament would not agree to another referendum unless Denmark had legallybinding opt-outs from the treaty's provisions on EMU, common defence policies, citizenship and cooperation on judicial affairs. Some

governments complained that this would amount to an effective renegotiation.

Deadlock in the GATT trade talks added acrimony to the arguments.
On the evening that Major scraped through his parliamentary vote, Ray
MacSharry resigned as the EC's chief agriculture negotiator. In Chicago he had come close to striking a deal with America on cuts to the
EC's farm exports and oilseed output. MacSharry claimed that Delors
had undermined his position by trying to stop a deal. The French
government, fearing its farmers' ire and a huge defeat in the elections
due in March 1993, threatened to veto any deal. Delors and France
claimed that a deal similar to that nearly reached in Chicago would
require the EC to cut its subsidies by more than the reform of the
common agricultural policy – agreed the previous May – would require. The Germans and the British were furious with the French.

November's GATT crisis marked a nadir in the EC's fortunes.
Pressure from the British government and other commissioners left
Delors with no choice but to reappoint MacSharry as farm negotiator.
The Irishman went to Washington and clinched a deal with the Americans which was slightly more favourable to the EC than that which had
been nearly agreed in Chicago: the value of the EC's subsidized farm
exports would fall by 21% over six years, starting in 1994.

French politicians huffed and puffed about using the 'Luxembourg
Compromise' (i.e., a veto) but other EC governments thought it unlikely that France would actually do so. In any case, there would be
nothing to veto until an overall GATT agreement was reached, and that
could not come about without several more months of hard negotiation.

The Edinburgh summit, in December, proved a striking success for
the British presidency, which managed to put together a whole series
of interlocking deals. The summit agreed to raise the ceiling on the EC
budget to 1.27% of Community GDP by 1999, which would allow a
doubling of regional aid for the four poorest members. The heads of
government also decided to start entry negotiations with Austria, Sweden, Finland and Norway early in 1993.

On Denmark, the summit agreed to a legally-binding 'decision' that
interpreted the Maastricht treaty to mean that the Danes would opt out
of monetary union and defence policy until 1996. This deal won the
backing of most of Denmark's opposition parties, making it more
likely, but far from certain, that the Danes would vote in favour of the
treaty in another referendum in the spring of 1993. That prospect, in
turn, made it seem more likely that Britain's parliament would ratify
the treaty some time in the summer (the other ten members had all
ratified by the end of 1992). The opt-outs won by Britain at Maastricht
and by Denmark at Edinburgh suggested that as the EC prepared to
admit new members to its table they would be offered less of a set
menu and more an *à la carte* one.

Bundesbank Blues

The coming into force of the Maastricht treaty, when and if it happens, will not bring back the optimistic mood which gave birth to it. And no wonder: the Community has always flourished during spurts of economic growth and festered during downturns. It gained a net seven million jobs in the three years 1988–90 when many of the most important single-market laws – such as that liberalizing capital movements – were agreed.

The rising unemployment of the past two years has increased pressure for protection and harmed the cause of economic liberalism. In countries where the EC symbolizes that cause, such as France, Switzerland and Sweden, its image has suffered. The downturn has weakened the governments of Germany, Spain, Britain, France and Italy and made them meaner; hence France's tough talk on GATT and Spain's on the size of the EC budget. Britain's shrinking economy could not stand the ERM while German interest rates were so high.

The Bundesbank maintained high interest rates to counteract the German government's inflationary fiscal policy. Having won the November 1990 election on the promise of no tax increases, Chancellor Kohl had to borrow heavily to support the new *Länder*. Yet the Bundesbank claimed that the roots of the ERM crises lay with the governments of weak economies (Britain, Italy and Spain) which treated currencies as virility symbols and rebuffed its calls for regular realignments. The Bundesbank pointed out that a core group of ERM economies, whose current accounts and inflation rates had converged to healthy levels, could weather German interest rates.

That may be true, but those rates made the difference between the pound sticking to the ERM and skidding out. And the French franc, which surely represents a healthy economy, hung on only with difficulty. In any case the Bundesbank has now got the flexible, pre-1987 sort of ERM that it wanted – one with regular realignments.

During 1990 and 1991, the unification of Germany had seemed to hurry along European integration. Many of its neighbours – and Germans such as Chancellor Kohl – argued that Germany should be bound into a political union to allay fears of its power. But having helped to inspire the Maastricht treaty, German unity then undermined it by slowing economic growth and by weakening the ERM, on which EMU depends.

The demise of communism has damaged the Community in other ways. From 1989 to 1992 Germany took about 600,000 immigrants a year from former communist countries (not including asylum-seekers, who numbered 400,000 in 1992). This influx revived the nationalist tendencies of Germany's right wing, while the EC's refusal to share the burden of Yugoslav refugees irked Germans. The failure of the EC to stop the war in the former Yugoslavia damaged its image not only in Germany, but also in France and in the world at large.

Can It Recover?

The EC's critics have attacked it – and by association the Maastricht treaty – for inaction on immigration, incoherence on foreign policy and instability in the ERM. Yet that treaty was designed to deal with those very problems.

The hostility to the Community appears to be part of a wider phenomenon. Those who voted against Canada's draft constitution, for America's Ross Perot or for Italy's Lombard League all showed contempt for established politicians. In parts of Europe this discontent focused on the remotest elite of all, the Brussels Eurocrats. That was to be expected, for since the mid-1980s the EC had touched the lives of more and more people. Community laws have opened markets and bankrupted firms, while Commission edicts have banned takeovers and curtailed state aid. Many people now believe that the Maastricht treaty would encroach further, establishing who defends Europeans and how, who votes in their elections and what banknotes they use.

An apparent lack of democratic legitimacy did nothing to help the Community's image. Ministers debated and voted behind closed doors and were at one remove from national parliaments, while the European Parliament had yet to win much credibility. The Commission's inclination to preach gave its critics ammunition. Some of its proposals, such as laws on the purity of drinking water, had been too detailed.

Governments had aggravated the EC's image problem by failing to explain how it works. Only those holding referendums on Maastricht bothered to inform their people of its contents. National politicians generally resented the EC's powers and found it a useful scapegoat for unpopular decisions. That most Europeans believed the Commission rather than the Council of Ministers takes decisions (when, competition policy excepted, the reverse is true) led few governments to shed tears.

The bug of Brussels-phobia was largely confined to Britain, France, Germany and Denmark, although after 2 June it was infecting countries outside the EC, such as Sweden, Norway, Finland and Switzerland. The inhabitants of the Benelux countries appeared to have been immunized by their faith in federalism. Many southern Europeans viewed the EC as a source of money and of modernization, and cared little about the sovereignty of their own (rather weak) parliaments. Some of the southerners' administrations are so inept that the one in Brussels may, by comparison, have appeared exemplary. Even the southerners, however, may yet catch the bug.

Governments have, it is to be hoped, learned a lesson while cleaning up the mess left by the hurricane of 1992. Next time they write a basic document to guide Europe's course they may try to create a public opinion in its favour, instead of moving too far ahead of the opinion which already exists.

THE CENTRAL EUROPEAN SEESAW

The Visegrad countries managed in 1992 to avoid any major instability resulting from continued domestic political squabbling and external disorder. The split between the Czech and Slovak republics became reality on 1 January 1993, despite serious public misgivings and Western concern. Yet it took place in an orderly and consensual manner that surprised those highly vocal pessimists who had predicted instant chaos and ethnic disturbances.

Poland's power struggle between the President, successive governments, and ever-changing parliamentary coalitions precluded any smooth functioning of the state. At one moment, the country was close to a classic *coup d'Etat* as a result of Prime Minister Jan Olszewski's government effort to blackmail MPs and President Lech Walesa with the alleged communist secret police files. Yet in the end Olszewski's government was removed in a constitutional manner, and relative stability returned to Poland in autumn 1992. Most importantly, there were signs of economic recovery by 1993. Hungary also managed to avoid major crisis despite the prolonged 'media war', renewed manifestations of the old Magyar irredentism and xenophobia, the Slovak–Hungarian conflict over the Gabcikovo power plant, and the damaging consequences of the civil war just across Hungary's borders in what used to be Yugoslavia.

The future of Central Europe is still uncertain, pregnant with potential instability and conflict. While all four countries remain committed to democratic and economic restructuring, the success of this restructuring should not be taken for granted. There are grounds for optimism, but there are equally strong reasons for pessimism in assessing the security prospects for this central part of the old continent.

From Hyphen to Separation

Early in 1992 it became increasingly evident that a single Czecho-Slovak Federal Republic was almost ungovernable. One constitutional crisis followed another, paralysing the decision-making process and bringing Czechoslovakia ever closer to economic and political catastrophe. The decision to split the country, made in the aftermath of the June 1992 parliamentary elections, thus seemed a way to end the deadlock, with potentially stabilizing benefits for both parts of the federation. Indeed, the new leaders of both republics swiftly managed to draft and sign 27 treaties designed to govern relations between the independent Czech and Slovak republics that would result from the dissolution of the 70-year old Czechoslovakia. On 1 January 1993 two new states came into being with only fireworks exploding in celebration of the event; a pleasant contrast with post-communist Yugoslavia.

That was the good news. The bad news was that the split solved some problems while creating new ones. The actual division of the country is a complicated process that will probably lead to years of uncertainty and conflict. The problems involved in the division of the Czechoslovak army in the planned 2:1 ratio illustrate this point.

Most Czechoslovak units were based in the Czech part of the country, and it is far from certain that all Slovaks previously serving in the Czech lands will go back to Slovakia where there is inadequate housing. Before the split, only 20% of Slovak officers serving in the Czech lands were willing to move back to Slovakia.

Dividing up military equipment may prove easier than dividing manpower, but Slovakia lacks sufficient storage facilities for its share of the equipment. To deploy its share of the air force Slovakia would have to construct its own airfields, an expensive project for the new country. Internal organization of the two new armies, their command structures, and their education and training systems are also in disarray as a result of the split, while new national security concepts and defence plans will still have to be created. Each country may acquire its own armed forces, but it is difficult to imagine that they will be made combat effective before 1994 at the earliest.

Coping with old and new problems will not necessarily be easier in the context of two separate states than in a single federation. Slovakia, in particular, will have severe economic difficulties stemming from its inefficient and polluting industries, the collapse of Eastern European markets for its products, a desperate shortage of domestic capital and foreign investment, rising unemployment, and rather ambiguous governmental programmes of economic restructuring.

The 600,000 Hungarians living in Slovakia (representing more than 10% of its population) could also cause problems. Before 1993 Slovak Hungarians could count on the support of the federal authorities in Prague when faced with manifestations of Slovak nationalism. Under the new dispensation Budapest will champion their rights; not a prospect to gladden their hearts. Slovakia might also find it difficult to handle its future relations with much larger Poland and Ukraine, especially if these countries are shaken by economic chaos or political instability.

The economic prospects of the Czech republic are much brighter than those of Slovakia. They may, however, fall short of existing expectations owing to residual partition problems, and insufficient Western investment. The Czech republic may also find itself under pressure from Moravians and Silesians demanding greater autonomy if not some kind of independence. Increased pressure from the Sudeten Germans might also be expected. The 1992 treaty between Germany and Czechoslovakia ignored the issue of property rights of the Sudeten Germans who had been expelled from Czechoslovakia in 1945.

The way in which the decision to divide the country was taken creates another potential problem. It was orchestrated behind closed doors by the two newly elected prime ministers and a small group of advisors. Calls for a referendum were ignored, as were public opinion polls which indicated a clear majority in both republics for a unitary Czechoslovak state. In fact, during the June 1992 electoral campaign none of the leading parties in Bohemia or Slovakia openly advocated the split of the federation.

There was nothing unconstitutional in the procedure, and it can be argued that holding a referendum on the breakup would have been a pointless, if not destabilizing, exercise. Even if the voters had plumped for preserving the common state, Czechoslovakia would still have been torn by the diverging political, economic and national ambitions of both republics and paralysed by continuing decision-making palsy. But that a referendum was not held creates a spectre of legitimacy which may haunt the division of the country for years to come. If things get tough in one or both of the new republics the people might find it easiest to blame the politicians for 'inflicting' problems upon them. Such a development could lead to chaos and anarchy, with serious security implications for the entire Central European region.

Poland and Hungary: Uncertain Progress

In early 1993 the Western media announced that Poland was coming along nicely, a degree of optimism not shared by Poland's major political actors. As Adam Michnik put it in *Gazeta Wyborcza*: 'This was a year of wasted opportunities, of many unneccessary conflicts, of many destructive actions, of much unwanted wrongdoing'. Michnik and other commentators acknowledge that major disasters were luckily avoided, but they all conclude that Poland's democracy is still fragile.

The greatest threat to the young democracy came in June 1992 when Poland's interior minister confronted parliament with a list of 64 alleged communist secret police collaborators, many of them the country's top political figures. The list, which included not only active collaborators but those whom the secret police had merely tried to recruit, was instantly leaked to the press. The whole affair was part of the power struggle between President Lech Walesa and Prime Minister Jan Olszewski over political control, particularly of the military. Time and again, the government failed to consult with the president on military and security matters over which the constitution gave him nominal jurisdiction. For example, the minister of defence authorized purges within the army and the military intelligence leadership without consulting the president or the National Security Bureau. He later accused Walesa of courting unhappy army generals behind his back, and of drawing up a contingency plan for martial law.

In the end, Olszewski's government was dissolved by parliament, and after several months of political squabbling a new coalition government led by Hanna Suchocka was formed. Her ability to provide a consensus platform for Poland's many divergent parties has been severely tested. Fortunately, she has proved a skilful and highly popular politician. She helped adopt the so-called 'small constitution' that clarified the division of power within the state. She also managed to bring together Poland's trade unions and employers' associations who signed the 'Pact on Enterprises' regulating their industrial relations.

Economic statistics were also generous to Suchocka: industrial production was rising, inflation was dropping, and the private sector was growing ever stronger. By 1993, Poland had the only Eastern European economy about which observers felt considerable optimism. At the same time, however, Suchocka was confronted with successive waves of strikes that forced her to make some damaging economic concessions. Several times her government lost important votes in parliament, which further undermined trust in the ruling coalition. In addition, the country was engulfed in moral scandals involving leading politicians, a prolonged decommunization struggle, and a heated ideological debate about the abortion law and state–church relations.

Poland's record in foreign affairs was more positive, helped, perhaps, by the fact that the Foreign Minister, Krzysztof Skubiszewski, had been retained throughout the many government changes. Suchocka made successful visits to Minsk and Kiev, helped to maintain the Visegrad cooperation framework after the division of Czechoslovakia, and signed a treaty on defence cooperation with Germany. Yet these successes must be qualified. Russia openly complained about Suchocka's alleged efforts to court Belarus and Ukraine behind Moscow's back. The Czech Prime Minister, Vaclav Klaus, repeatedly cast doubt on the usefulness of the Visegrad framework of cooperation. And nasty incidents involving ethnic Poles and Germans in Silesia in western Poland gave cause for concern in Bonn and Warsaw.

Hungary enjoyed a more stable coalition government than Poland, but its politics were also marked by dirty tricks campaigns and ideological infighting which did little to enhance either the market economy or democracy. Like Poland, Hungary had its prolonged constitutional struggle over the exact powers of the president, prime minister and the constitutional court. In Poland it was the abortion law that paralysed the work of the legislature. In Hungary similar endless battles were fought over the controversial law on the media. Like Poland, Hungary chalked up economic progress during the last year, although in Hungary improvements were made in the field of foreign trade rather than in industrial production. Unlike Poland, Hungary faced increased nationalist pressure created by the worsening situation of fellow Magyars living outside its borders.

The disintegration of neighbouring Yugoslavia and the division of Czechoslovakia threatened the moderate conservative line of Hungary's Prime Minister, Joszef Antall. The war in former Yugoslavia forced thousands of Magyars to seek refuge in Hungary; those Magyars who stayed in the Serb-dominated province of Vojvodina (about 350,000) were subjected to various forms of repression. The

Slovak Hungarians began demanding increased autonomy as soon as they learned about the forthcoming division of the Czechoslovak federation. In Transylvania, the situation of the Magyar minority of around two million did not improve, thus prolonging the diplomatic war between Budapest and Bucharest.

These developments stimulated nationalist, if not revisionist, tendencies in Hungary itself, producing mounting pressure on Prime Minister Antall, even from within his own party's rank and file. Nationalists, led by a bombastic leader, Istvan Csurka, set out on the political warpath. They criticized not only Antall's cautious policy towards Hungary's neighbours, but also the government's desire for integration with Western Europe, foreign capital investment in Hungary, and its policy of benign neglect towards former communists and Jews. In a highly controversial pamphlet, Csurka warned fellow Hungarians to beware of 'a Paris, New York, Tel Aviv' plot.

Jozsef Antall has for the moment managed to resist Csurka's challenge to his leadership, but only by acting suspiciously tough with Slovakia on such issues as the Gabcikovo dam and by curbing the editorial freedom of state-controlled TV and radio. The situation of ethnic Magyars in Slovakia, Romania and Serbia appears to be worsening, and this will further encourage revisionist trends in Hungarian politics. Antall has openly spoken of the need to protect all Hungarians no matter where they might live. Forthcoming parliamentary elections will open the doors to demagogy and xenophobia. Hungary might soon become preoccupied with a national, rather than democratic, agenda, giving rise to a new threat of destabilizing the Central European region.

Western policies

During 1992 the West by and large neglected Central Europe. Violent crises erupting in other parts of post-communist Europe naturally demanded more Western attention than a relatively stable Central Europe. Moreover, for most of the year Western countries were preoccupied with themselves: Western Europe was torn apart by the Maastricht controversy, while the United States was busy with its presidential election and transition. Perhaps most significantly the West, and the EC in particular, suffered from what the *Financial Times* called a 'lack of eastern vision'. The West was unable to work out a coherent policy for post-communist Europe, and thus could not choose any consistent set of options to put into practice.

That said, some small progress has been made, especially in the economic and diplomatic field. The Association Agreements which the EC signed with the Visegrad countries are being acted upon, despite the angry reaction of Western producers of steel and aluminium. Responding to Hungary's request, the United Nations sent several observers to the Pecs and Seged areas bordering with Serbia, and NATO

AWACS surveillance aircraft have been using Hungarian airspace to monitor the UN-imposed flight ban over Bosnia-Herzegovina. Both actions clearly served Hungary's security aims, the latter significantly because in the past Yugoslav army aircraft repeatedly violated Hungarian airspace and even bombed a Hungarian village. The EC Commission also mediated the Slovak-Hungarian dispute over the Gabcikovo dam. Its efforts and subsequent offer to evaluate the entire project persuaded the Slovaks to stop work on the dam thus helping to diffuse the conflict.

None of these actions, nor all of them together, came close to meeting Central European expectations. But criticism was not limited to the Central Europeans. Western actions were described as insufficient, if not counter-productive, by many Western observers. Jacques Attali, the president of the European Bank for Reconstruction and Development, for example, argued that the EC Association Agreements restrict Central European access to key Western markets rather than integrating them. Germany's plans to change its asylum law were also criticized for putting too much strain on Central Europe. A draft of the new German law envisages sending asylum seekers to the first foreign country they entered which is usually Poland and the Czech Republic. Neither of these countries has sufficient means to cope with a new flow of refugees.

The Western policy of benign neglect towards Central Europe has already stimulated anti-Western sentiments, not only in Hungary but also in Poland and Slovakia. The West is under fire for exploiting rather than helping Central European economies, for promoting liberal, if not decadent culture, and for its egoistic attitude towards the problems of Europe's security. Economic policies allegedly 'imposed' by the International Monetary Fund and the EC were blamed for causing deep recessions, excessive unemployment, and the collapse of national industries. Westerners were accused of taking over all profitable firms, of flooding Central European markets with their subsidized agricultural products, and of daylight robbery in its credit policy. Military specialists in Central Europe accused the West of not enhancing pan-European collective security structures such as the CSCE, while simultaneously denying membership of NATO to the Visegrad states.

These anti-Western sentiments have not yet become anti-Western policies. Despite the growing influence of populist figures, the governments of Central European countries are still in the hands of pro-Western liberal politicians committed to genuine economic reforms and democratization. But the region's problems should not be underestimated. The prospect for considerable chaos, if not violence, just across Germany's eastern borders is very real and very disturbing. The West would be guilty of strategic negligence were it not to give Central Europe in 1993–94 the attention it deserves.

The Middle East

TALKING WHILE FIGHTING

For more than a year after the Madrid Conference of October 1991, Israel and its Arab neighbours were engaged in an unprecedented multi-track peace effort. Much of its significance lies in its persistence. Despite efforts from both sides to sabotage the talks, the interests that each saw in their continuation proved strong enough to keep them moving. As the talks entered a third phase in 1993, hopes were rising for significant gains along one or another of the tracks.

The principal effort prior to 1993 – a series of bilateral meetings between Israel and Syria, Jordan, Lebanon and the Palestinians – may be divided into two distinct phases. The first began with the Madrid Conference of October 1991 and ended with the change of government in Israel as a result of the June 1992 elections. That change facilitated progress, particularly on the Syrian–Israeli track, where negotiations now appeared to offer the prospect of a new strategic departure, and in Jordanian–Israeli talks, where the first anniversary of Madrid produced an agreed outline for a future peace agreement. Progress was less evident on the Israeli–Palestinian track, where a considerable perceptual gap continued to separate the two sides, although by late 1992 small informal working groups were moving ahead. A secondary but, in the long term, equally significant effort – five multilateral forums for discussing regional issues – developed more slowly, its progress essentially linked to the bilateral track.

The second phase of negotiations was interrupted by the US presidential elections of November 1992. President Bush's defeat could have threatened the success of the talks since it meant the removal of James Baker, who had successfully conceived, implemented and guided an extremely complex international structure for Middle East negotiations. The negotiations, however historic their impact, could still falter if Washington did not retain a high-profile role in shepherding them. It was thus no surprise that the second phase ground to a halt with Bush's defeat. The Arabs, and particularly the Syrians, wished to take the measure of the Clinton administration before proceeding. The crisis that developed over Israel's subsequent expulsion of over 400 Palestinian Islamic militants in December 1992 exacerbated and prolonged the stalemate.

The Early Moves

The first phase of the peace process (see *Strategic Survey 1991-1992* for details) was ostensibly largely a procedural triumph. Arabs and Israelis met together, face to face, and without preconditions, but little of substance was achieved. In retrospect, however, it became clear that it represented a far-reaching political breakthrough. Essentially, the United States had managed to put in place an impressive, multidimensional process reminiscent, in its complexity, of the 1919 Versailles Peace Conference. Israelis were at last speaking directly to Syrians and Palestinians on political issues; it would be difficult to backtrack on this important precedent. By and large, the key actors had persevered at the conference table. Certain apparently unavoidable rituals of mutual accusation (who started the 1967 war, the meaning of UN Resolution 242) were acted out. The parties began to get to know one another. The international community was engaged. Of particular importance were those who would ultimately be called upon to finance Middle East peace settlements: Japan, the EC and the Gulf states.

Yet progress in the two main bilateral sets of negotiations, Israel–Syria and Israel–Palestinians, was minimal. The Shamir government refused to discuss territorial issues, and insisted that the Palestinians be content for now with measures that improved their quality of life, but little more. Syria refused to offer a peace settlement or even to define the nature of peace. The Palestinians, having agreed (largely out of post-Gulf War weakness) to discuss an open-ended interim arrangement, now demanded that the yardstick for approval of interim measures be their compatibility with a Palestinian state.

The talks in general were characterized by a total lack of confidence in both directions. The Israel–Syria negotiations, in particular, featured a tendency by both sides to define negotiating goals in ultimate terms, rather than seeking to identify feasible intermediate goals. Meaningful Israeli suggestions for reciprocal confidence-building measures and informal behind-the-scenes discussions were rejected by the Arabs, while the US refused even to contemplate active intervention until such measures were tried, and had failed. At the same time, the Shamir government's policy of massive settlement was day by day eroding any conceivable territorial basis for peace with the Palestinians.

New Faces, New Views

The 23 June 1992 Knesset elections in Israel significantly affected the tenor of the negotiations. The peace effort was the stimulus for the elections, and the talks, and attendant issues, were very much at the centre of the election debate. The results – a clear Labour plurality and mandate to form a government, but perpetuation of the broad divide in Israeli politics between territorial hawks and doves – mirrored the Israeli political dilemma regarding the peace process, yet generated a dramatic new departure towards a settlement.

The outcome – a Centre–Left majority (with key ultra-orthodox assistance) of 62 out of 120 Knesset seats, with Labour winning 44 seats and Likud only 32 – was seen in the Likud (and in the Tehiya

Party, which lost its Knesset representation entirely) as a failure for the Right. Prime Minister Yitzhak Shamir announced he would resign from the Likud Party leadership and from the Knesset as soon as a successor had been chosen. Defence Minister Moshe Arens announced his immediate departure from politics. Post-election soul-searching offered many reasons for the loss of voter confidence in the Likud after 15 years' domination of Israeli politics: widespread corruption, highlighted by the State Controller's reports; constant bickering and infighting among the leadership; acquiescence to political demands by the ultra-orthodox; economic setbacks; a sharp decline in Russian Jewish immigration; and the crisis in relations with the United States. Even a rise in Arab violence against Israelis in the months preceding the elections (stabbings inside Israel, *Hizbollah* attacks in southern Lebanon, a terrorist attack in Eilat) failed to produce the 'classic' effect of moving voters towards the Right. On the contrary, the reaction in Bat Yam to a particularly brutal stabbing of a young girl in late May was heightened electoral support for the Left.

The Likud's loss was a direct spin-off of its insistence on giving budgetary and ideological priority to settling Judea, Samaria and Gaza, whatever the strategic and economic cost to Israel. After the election both Shamir and Arens conceded that voters, particularly the young and Russian immigrants, had rejected the Likud's ideological insistence on the Greater Land of Israel. Arens even declared that this was not his priority either, and suggested that, at a minimum, the Gaza Strip was dispensable. Shamir remained adamant, suggesting that a revitalized Likud would eventually win back the Israeli voter, and declaring that he would have 'conducted autonomy negotiations for ten years, and meanwhile we would have reached half a million Israelis in Judea and Samaria'.

Correspondingly, a central aspect of Rabin's electoral strategy focused on linking the peace issues – the stalemated talks, the Likud's territorial intransigence and the issue of Israel's settlements in the West Bank – with Israel's troubled economy, plummeting Russian immigration, and the deterioration in relations with the United States. Whatever else may have motivated the Israeli electorate, Rabin emerged from the elections believing he had been given a clear mandate to enforce a new order of priorities in Israeli policy-making. He could downgrade the effort to construct settlements in the West Bank and Gaza in favour of urgent domestic social and economic needs, and he could advance a territories-for-peace policy in negotiations with the Arabs. In a dramatic inaugural address to the Knesset on 13 July, Rabin offered Israelis the option of changing both their priorities and their world view:

> We are no longer an isolated nation and it is no longer true that the entire world is against us. We must rid ourselves of the feeling of isolation that has afflicted us for almost 50 years. We

must join the campaign of peace, reconciliation and international cooperation that is currently engulfing the entire globe, lest we miss the train and be left alone at the station.

On With The Talks

Immediately after the quick formation of a government, Israel appeared to take on the role of catalyst, or protagonist, in the resumed talks, even though not always in ways entirely consistent with Rabin's earlier plans. Before the vote, Yitzhak Rabin had signalled clearly the ways in which he intended to alter Israel's approach to the Arab–Israeli peace process. He would base it on the territories-for-peace principle, accelerate autonomy talks, and search for ways to grease the creaking process through confidence-building measures and, where possible, a more liberal attitude towards the Palestinians' day-to-day problems. Rabin's position also reflected a view he had often voiced in criticism of the negotiating structure that James Baker had put in place during 1991. Only by negotiating sequentially with its Arab neighbours, Rabin believed, could Israel make progress towards peace; parallel and multilateral meetings were bound to escalate Arab demands and complicate negotiations. Consequently he hinted that he would give priority to what appeared to him, and, he believed, to Israelis in general, to be the most urgent issue, an interim autonomy settlement with the Palestinians. The Syrian track would become a siding.

Even before Israel returned to the negotiating table in Washington in late August 1992 for a month of intensive talks, Rabin was obliged to revise his strategy. In talks held in July with Baker and with President Mubarak of Egypt, he was warned of the emphasis they placed on the talks with Syria in order to maintain both the inter-Arab acceptability of the process, and the American commitment to the Syrians to produce a positive Israeli approach to the territorial issue. This was supported by an increasingly open Israeli intelligence assessment that Syria's reappraisal of its strategic situation was indeed wide ranging. The changes in the global, inter-Arab and economic scene that had brought the Syrians into face-to-face negotiations with Israel in the first place, also informed a readiness on the part of President Assad to end the conflict with Israel.

New Approaches

The new chief Israeli negotiator, Professor Itamar Rabinovich, opened the resumed talks in late August 1992 with a new offer: a declaration that Israel agreed to apply UN Security Council Resolution 242, with its territories-for-peace element, to its negotiations with Syria. Israel was prepared to include the territorial element on the Golan Heights as part of the discussion of peace and security. Rabinovich also improved the atmosphere of the talks, for example by avoiding a rancorous catalogue of Syria's transgressions against human rights.

The tenor of the negotiations was immediately altered. The leader of the Syrian delegation, Ambassador Muaffaq al-Allaf, abandoned his tight-lipped approach and replied in kind. Syria, he said, was prepared to offer Israel full peace in return for full territory. Damascus recognized that both sides had legitimate security interests to be taken into account. It could envisage a Syrian–Israeli peace achieved prior to a final settlement of the Palestinian issue. Peace could be 'delivered' by the Syrians in parallel with Israel's withdrawal and once the principle was agreed that withdrawal could be implemented in stages. Syria presented many of these positions in writing: the first written document it had ever offered Israel.

These developments led to a carefully orchestrated series of conciliatory statements for home consumption by both Syrian and Israeli leaders. Assad spoke publicly of a 'peace of the brave'. Rabin told Israeli audiences that Israel should prepare to offer Syria part of the Golan Heights, and even to remove some settlements from there. This provoked a controversy within Israel over the Golan settlements issue that reminded many Israelis of the debate over the fate of the Sinai peninsula that accompanied the Begin–Sadat peace initiative in 1977–78.

Yet a number of points of contention remained. Israel agreed in principle to discuss the territorial dimension, but only after the Syrians clarified what they meant by 'peace'. Israel also signalled its intention that withdrawal would be partial and would involve mainly Israel's military deployment rather than settlements. Rabin's reiterated statements regarding partial withdrawal ('withdrawal on the Golan, not from the Golan') were clearly unacceptable to Damascus, which wanted Israel to commit itself to a complete withdrawal. Israel also rejected Syria's traditional demand for some linkage between a bilateral settlement and progress on the Palestinian and Lebanese fronts.

At the same time, Syria's references to peace remained vague. It talked of a peace agreement, not a treaty, and rejected the notion of 'normalization' in the short term. Nor had Syria yet offered any explicit recognition of Israel and its right to exist. It continued to hold the Israel–Lebanon talks hostage to progress in its own negotiations with Israel, and to condone Iranian-sponsored terrorism from Lebanon against Israel. Syria also continued to boycott the multilateral talks on arms control and other issues, insisting that progress should first be registered at the bilateral level. Perhaps most significantly, Assad indicated that he would settle for no less than the total withdrawal Sadat had achieved 15 years earlier on the Egyptian front. Yet the Syrian leader seemed unable, or uninterested for the present, in developing the atmosphere of reconciliation that had characterized the earlier talks, and had helped to persuade Israelis that it was in their interest to give up all of Sinai.

The Syrian position was undoubtedly affected by the impending US presidential elections. Syria had managed major changes in its global orientation, joining both the anti-Iraq coalition and the peace process, in close coordination with Bush and Baker. Assad attributed to these men not only credibility, but a relatively congenial position, one that offered the prospect of eventual total Israeli withdrawal on the Golan issue. Clinton, on the other hand, seemed likely to de-emphasize the substantive aspects of the process, re-emphasize inconvenient human rights issues, and be more responsive to pressures by the organized American Jewish community. The looming prospect of a Bush defeat appeared to trigger a possible change of approach.

Despite all this, the talks made progress. The negotiators persevered even when tensions flared on the Lebanese–Israeli border in November. Both parties declared that most of the differences were negotiable. By November–December 1992, more than one year after Madrid, an agreed 'statement of principles' that would provide an outline for substantive talks appeared achievable. Statements by the Syrian leadership appeared to reaffirm its commitment to the process, and hinted at Syrian readiness to entertain the possibility of an interim agreement and to 'go it alone' if the Palestinians held up progress.

Chugging down the Israeli–Palestinian Track

The Israeli–Palestinian talks on an interim autonomy settlement in the West Bank and Gaza also made progress in Washington. It was more modest, however, and was often obfuscated by the conceptual gap that continued to overshadow the talks.

Rabin had retained the defence ministry in his new government, and tried to encourage a change in the security sphere by the use of unilateral Israeli CBMs. He organized the release of some detainees, cancelled deportation orders, relaxed travel restrictions, and dismantled barricaded streets and houses. These measures were met by indifference or derision from the Palestinians, and were not reciprocated (e.g., by reducing the violent aspects of the *intifada*). Nor did Rabin's principal new departure – a partial settlement freeze – elicit great enthusiasm. The Palestinians pointed out that some 10,000 buildings already started would continue to be constructed, and accused Rabin of packaging the freeze more for American consumption to obtain the long-delayed loan guarantees than for the Palestinians.

Indeed, Rabin's initial confidence-building moves, while unilateral and therefore an innovation, were generally guarded. Thus much of the building that would continue in the Territories was in so-called 'security regions' (the Jordan Valley, Maaleh Adumim, Gush Etzion), destined by Rabin to remain part of Israel under any solution. This tended to placate many of the settlers, while the US government insisted on discounting huge loan sums against the ongoing construction.

Nor did Israel replace its chief negotiator, Dr Elyakim Rubinstein, whom the Palestinians consider to be a hawk, or offer any dramatic new breakthrough with regard to autonomy. Rather, Rubinstein emphasized that Israel now sought to maintain a continuous dialogue, in a more flexible mode than previously, aimed at producing rapid progress: an outline agreement on the authority of an administrative council by February 1993, and elections to that council in April or May. This was intended to be viewed within the strategic backdrop of Rabin's overall readiness eventually to invoke territorial compromise on all fronts, and his emphasis on the need for Israel to disengage from direct rule over the Palestinians.

Thus, upon resumption of negotiations in late August 1992, Rubinstein produced a detailed document describing the functions to be attributed to the council, including a Palestinian police force, tax collecting, education, health and even a standards institute. The document indicated that Israel saw itself as the source of authority for autonomy, although some issues, such as disposition of water and land resources, might be referred to a joint Israeli–Palestinian authority, and others to a joint Israeli–Palestinian–Jordanian liaison unit. By dint of omission, security issues were still to be left in Israel's hands during the five-year autonomy period.

The Palestinians acknowledged that these Israeli positions were a step forward. Yet they still insisted that agreement be reached first on the broad outlines of the Palestinian Interim Self-Government Authority which contained institutions of far more extensive authority. In particular, the Palestinians demanded that the autonomy agreement itself be the source of authority, and that, rather than the small administrative council that Israel proposed, they elect a 180-member legislative council.

Moreover, the Palestinians continued to reject Israel's suggestion, embodied in its new proposals, that the parties begin by discussing non-controversial issues, such as transfer of authority over health facilities, on a non-conditional basis, in order to build confidence. They saw this Israeli approach as designed to entrap them in inconsequential details, thus avoiding discussion of the broad principles and framework of autonomy. In the words of delegation leader Dr Haider Abd al-Shafi, the Palestinians would not agree to 'make it easier for Israel to rule' by taking over administrative functions alone. Indeed, the Palestinians countered by demanding that Israel register its commitment to eventual territorial withdrawal in accordance with UN Resolution 242, despite the interim nature of the settlement being discussed. They also insisted that Israel agree to discuss the status of Jerusalem, a partial withdrawal of Israeli forces and the transfer of some initial security authority.

One hopeful sign by October 1992 was an indication of implicit Palestinian readiness to coordinate directly with Israel on security issues. Another was a readiness to meet in informal three-person working groups to discuss the definition of the interim period, and the status of state lands. The two sides finally agreed in October to move to a discussion of a detailed negotiating agenda, after Israel reportedly undertook to drop the adjective 'administrative' from its definition of the Palestinian autonomous council, and to acknowledge Palestinian self-rule over Arab-populated lands rather than the Arab population alone. But the Palestinians now complained that by offering them autonomy only over Palestinian-populated lands in the Territories, Israel was implicitly granting a parallel 'autonomy' to its settlements in the Territories, thereby laying the groundwork for large-scale annexations.

Thus the basic Palestinian insistence on defining in advance the far limits of autonomy in all spheres, continued to run headlong into the gradualistic Israeli approach. It would be difficult to bridge this critical substantive gap unless both Israel and the Palestine Liberation Organization (PLO) showed greater flexibility. Progress was also being hampered by basic faults in the procedural approach of both sides. On the Palestinian side, this appeared to reflect difficulties in leadership and the command-structure; their delegation was stymied in its decision-making on all sides. Back home, in the West Bank and Gaza, Islamic extremists whipped up opposition to Palestinian concessions. In Tunis, the part of the PLO leadership led by Chairman Yasser Arafat seemed bent on obstructing any progress that appeared to award the peace negotiators with a leadership status that might challenge its own mantle, while other members of the leadership circle were more accommodating towards the needs and status of the negotiators.

This highlighted the inherent weakness of any Palestinian peace delegation not openly led by the PLO. The Madrid procedural formula that excluded the PLO had, in a way, locked the process in a vicious circle. True, Rabin did agree, in a new departure, not to obstruct consultations by the 'insider' leadership with the Tunis 'outsiders', in the hope that this might facilitate Palestinian deliberations. He also agreed, under pressure from Foreign Minister Peres, to the participation of non-PLO 'outsiders' in the multilateral talks. His steadfast refusal, motivated at least in part by a reluctance to alienate parts of the Israeli body politic, to negotiate directly even with Faisal Husseini (a resident of East Jerusalem), not to mention the official PLO, appeared to exacerbate the Palestinians' negotiating and decision-making problems, to the detriment of the entire process.

Israel could hardly claim to be 'putting the Palestinians to the test', unless and until it allowed them to field their strongest team – one that it had, in any event, already implicitly recognized. This contention received support from virtually half of Rabin's cabinet in the aftermath of the December 1992 mass expulsion of Palestinian Islamic militants. In effect, large parts of the Israeli Left now argued that the use of a strong 'stick' against extremists, which they had reluctantly supported, required that a tastier 'carrot' also be proffered.

Yet it was not clear that even an overt PLO negotiating team could overcome the Palestinians' many internal rifts and contradictions. The gains made in the West Bank and Gaza by Islamic fundamentalist movements opposed to the peace process, appeared to signal that the long-term effects of the 1991 Gulf War were particularly salient among the Palestinians: the PLO was discredited on the inter-Arab scene, and its coffers were empty. Meanwhile, *Hamas* and the Islamic *Jihad* were riding the wave of Islamic fundamentalism generated by Iraq's humiliation at the hands of the West. And Iran, freed from the Iraqi threat, was becoming increasingly active in leading the anti-peace, pro-Islamic camp.

More Speed on the Israel–Jordan Track

The most dramatic advance prior to the American elections came in the Jordanian–Israeli sphere. The bilateral issues separating the two countries as they entered the process were minor, and centred on peripheral border and water disputes. Early in the talks in Washington, however, Amman also signalled that it would not, indeed could not, move ahead of the inter-Arab consensus. Israel would have to register progress with the Palestinians, perhaps with Syria too, before King Hussein could sign a peace treaty with Israel.

What remained ambiguous was the degree of flexibility this stand granted Jordanian and Israeli negotiators. This was clarified at the close of the seventh round of negotiations, in late October 1992, when Jordan itself leaked the contents of an 'agenda' for negotiations that had been agreed, and that awaited King Hussein's approval. Although it left much for future negotiation (indeed the Jordanians, under inter-Arab pressure, soon insisted on renegotiating parts of it), the agenda appeared to lay out the boundaries for an eventual peace. Thus it placed Jordan at the vanguard of the peace process, yet without committing it to a formal step that might draw excessive inter-Arab (especially Syrian) ire. At the same time it created an incentive for Syria to finalize its own agenda with Israel.

The Israeli–Jordanian document appeared also to reflect internal political pressures on both Rabin and Hussein to produce a recognizable sign of progress in the otherwise sluggish talks. Perhaps both leaders also sought to provide President Bush with a final election boost.

The contents of the agreed agenda were remarkable on several counts. All the mandatory elements – economic and human contacts, water and refugee issues – were there. Yet Jordan could also claim to fellow Arabs that it had extracted Israel's first formal commitment to divest itself, 'as a matter of priority and as soon as possible', of weapons of mass destruction. For its part Israel could argue that this arms-control goal was to be achieved only 'in the context of a comprehensive. . . peace', that is, at the end of the entire process. This formula indeed presaged a new Israeli departure on nuclear arms control in the region. Israel had also succeeded in reducing the two countries' border disputes to the issue of 'demarcation of the international boundary' established under the British mandate, rather than one of returning conquered territory. In addition, it obtained from Jordan a commitment to a peace treaty and not merely an 'agreement' as Syria had hitherto insisted. In return, Israel granted that the objective of the talks was indeed 'comprehensive peace', the inter-Arab catch phrase that Syria has championed.

Hanging In The Balance

In the short and medium term, the peace process was liable to be most affected by a number of domestic issues among the key actors, and by developing regional trends. By early 1993 it was not clear to what extent the removal of James Baker and his team might cause a delay, or reformulation, of the elaborate mechanism he had wrought. There was, after all, no official 'architecture' to this process; by and large, Baker had been coordinating it intuitively, and with admirable success. Could Warren Christopher be as successful? Would President Clinton provide the same forceful White House backing that Bush had offered Baker? The initial activity of the new administration appeared to suggest that it intended to try to keep the momentum up with regard to the peace talks. Whether this would be enough to produce steady progress was yet to be seen.

Inside Israel, Rabin faced extensive potential political problems. Rabin's original plan had been to produce a quick autonomy agreement, for which he felt he had a clear mandate from Israel's voters, and then, presumably, to reassess his options. He had defined his timeframe, which roughly corresponded with the four years of his maximum term of office, to correspond with a regional post-Gulf War 'window of opportunity' in which Israel could negotiate from a position of relative strength. Within a few years that window was likely to be closed by the emergence of Iran and/or Iraq as much strengthened, if not nuclear, powers and by the threat of increasingly militant Islamic movements in the region. Yet more immediate dangers – the rise of a Palestinian 'refusal' front, a possible new American approach to the peace process – could shorten his timeframe considerably. Now, the prospect of compromise agreements with Jordan, the Palestinians and Syria, coupled with the shaky nature of his coalition, threatened to arouse enough domestic dissent to precipitate early elections. Certainly it was not clear how Rabin intended to neutralize the opposition to any interim agreement on the part of the 110,000 Israelis settled in the Territories by previous Israeli governments. Rabin might opt to give priority to a deal with Syria and to place the more troublesome dialogue with the Palestinians on the back burner. There were indications that he might find a sympathetic hearing for this position in the new administration in Washington.

By late 1992 the possibility had emerged that despite (or perhaps because of) the pending Israeli–Jordanian agreement, dramatic progress between Syria and Israel, possibly coupled with stalemate or a waiting game on other fronts, might give Damascus a power of veto over the entire process. Whether this would hinder or enhance flexibility and progress was not clear. Certainly Palestinian fears of a separate Israeli–Syrian deal that essentially ignored their dilemma, explained some of the erratic behaviour of the Palestinian delegation. Moreover, in one of those paradoxes that frequently characterize events in the Middle East, Syria's 'strategic ally', Iran, together with a number of extremist Palestinian and Lebanese Shi'ite organizations under the Syrian or Iranian wing, were whipping up opposition to the peace process in Lebanon, Jordan and the Territories. Israel appeared to be resigned to talking to Syria, even as the latter winked at terrorism against it – this being seen as Damascus' tried-and-tested *modus operandi*.

But this delicate balancing act could easily begin to wobble. Indeed, it came to a head with Israel's mass deportation, on 18 December 1992, of some 414 *Hamas* and Islamic *Jihad* activists. Public reaction to a series of brutal killings of Israeli security personnel forced this move. Prime Minister Rabin intended to traumatize the Muslim militant movements, save the peace process from their aggressive intentions, and save his own government.

He may have achieved these goals. But the immediate result in the region was to stoke the ire of all Arabs, and particularly Palestinians, at what appeared to them to be a dangerous precedent of mass 'transfer'. The deportation provoked an unexpected display of toughness by the new Lebanese prime minister, Rafiq al-Hariri. And it generated an Arab refusal to return to the peace process even after the delay generated by the inauguration of a new American president. It also created an unexpected challenge to US–Israel relations at a time when the nurturing of a positive Rabin–Clinton relationship was judged by both to be critical to the continuation of the process. Thus early contacts between the new administration and the Israeli and Arab governments were devoted largely to working out acceptance of a series of compromises whereby Rabin softened various aspects of the deportation in order to enable the Arab–Israeli peace talks to reconvene.

There were regional and global dangers to the process as well: militant Islam, a rampant Middle East arms race, the potential spillover effect of new tensions in the Gulf, and instability in nearby areas of the former Soviet Union and Yugoslavia, to name but a few. Yet for the time being, Israel, most of the Arabs and the US shared two strong and complementary emotions that would continue to spur on the peace process: cumulative fatigue with Arab–Israeli wars; and growing fear of what the next war might be like. With these feelings pushing, and the US tugging, the Israelis and Arabs might be able to overcome enough of their reservations to achieve a historic settlement.

IRAN: SEEKING STABILITY

Iran has reawakened international concern about its military and foreign ambitions. For the past two years it has been engaged in a programme of weapons acquisition that has raised questions about its intentions. The continued strategic instability and uncertainty in the Gulf region in the aftermath of the 1991 allied war against Iraq provides a background against which these concerns have been heightened.

At the same time, President Hashemi Rafsanjani, who had struck Western observers as a more moderate and pragmatic Iranian leader, has run into considerable trouble. Although theoretically bolstered by successful parliamentary elections in April and May 1992, he still has to contend with more ideologically minded members of the Iranian hierarchy led by Ayatollah Ali Khamenei, the successor to Ayatollah Khomeini as *Wali Faqih* of the Islamic Republic of Iran who doubles as supreme Islamic juriconsult and commander-in-chief of the armed forces. Furthermore, Rafsanjani faced difficulties in trying to implement a policy of liberalization which has increasingly become open to accusations that it has caused the Revolution to lose its way.

Political Background

When the Iranian government was dominated by the single voice of its spiritual leader, Ayatollah Khomeini, it maintained a clear line of policy. This was bequeathed to his successor governments, but is now at times supplemented and at times drowned by a host of contradictory ones. These serve to diminish considerably, if not to negate, the main thrust of policy. To use a cliché, for every step forward, the government is more than likely to take two steps back.

One reason for the apparent contradictions in Iranian politics is that the government is continually trying to reconcile ideology with political necessity. This was also the case when Ayatollah Khomeini was alive, but Khomeini maintained a consistency of vision even when political realities intruded. The best example was his reluctant decision to accept a cease-fire to end the eight-year Iran–Iraq War without making any attempt at ideological revisionism to help explain away the political necessity of stopping the fight.

By contrast, those who have succeeded him have neither the same ideological imperative nor the same single-minded mission to impose such a vision on the country. Most importantly, none can claim the religious authority which allowed Khomeini's ideology to remain unchallenged. Instead, the government is fragmented. There is no single individual at the political helm with supreme religious authority and, while President Rafsanjani is politically the most important person in the country, he does not rule those around him with the same unchallenged power as his neighbour Saddam Hussein in Iraq.

The death of Khomeini in June 1989, the isolation caused by years of fundamentalist rhetoric and behaviour, the sponsorship of the *Hizbollah* in the Lebanon, all served to push Iran into a corner. It has only recently begun to emerge and there are many directions it can now take. As forces try to pull the country in one direction, others pull it in another.

Having learned a bitter lesson from the extreme political isolationism suffered by the country during its war against Iraq from 1980–88, President Rafsanjani has made clear his aim to reintegrate Iran into the international system. The demands of the economy have also pushed the government towards seeking foreign investment which has entailed introducing a freer-market economic system. At each point, however, he must contend with still strong religious forces which wish to push Iran in an opposite direction.

President Rafsanjani was preoccupied during 1992 with domestic problems, including the election of a new parliament in April and the continuation of sporadic political and economic disruption. Externally, security concerns remained focused on the Persian Gulf region and the north where the emergence of the new republics of the former Soviet Union created a risk of instability.

Strategy in the Gulf

Iran's aims in the Gulf can be divided into three interlinked objectives. It wishes to become the dominant power in the area and to have the greatest say in regional affairs through a regional security structure; it seeks to achieve this through a process of normalization of relations with the Arab states of the Persian Gulf; and it wishes to nullify, or at least neutralize, the influence of Western powers, particularly the United States, in the region.

Any hope of attaining these aims suffered severely when Arab distrust of Iran was reinforced by Iranian actions regarding Abu Musa. Abu Musa is one of three strategically important islands in the Persian Gulf seized by the Shah in November 1971 when the British were withdrawing from the region. However, in contrast to the seizure of the two other islands, the Greater and the Lesser Tunbs, the landing of Iranian troops on Abu Musa was carried out in accordance with an agreement on joint sovereignty between the Shah of Iran and the ruling Sheikh of Sharjah. The settlement was reached through British mediation between Iran and Sharjah, which later became one of the constituents of the United Arab Emirates (UAE) when it was formed in December 1971.

The present dispute began in April 1992 but intensified in September when Iran refused a ship carrying passengers from the UAE entry to Abu Musa. Iranian officials demanded that non-Sharjan residents produce Iranian permits and that all passengers intending to land on Abu Musa tell the Iranian authorities in advance. Iran claimed that it had forewarned the UAE of these measures.

The incident caused an immediate outcry. The Gulf Cooperation Council, meeting in Qatar on 9 September, issued 'strong condemnation of the measures taken by Iran on Abu Musa, which are a violation of the sovereignty and territorial integrity' of the UAE. Even Syria, Iran's only ally in the Arab world, supported the Arabs and condemned Iran for its behaviour.

President Rafsanjani, forced on the defensive, first claimed that Iran's action was a function of increased security measures made necessary by an incident in which armed strangers had landed on the island. At another time he blamed over-zealous Iranian officials, while Ayatollah Khamenei, the spiritual leader, conveniently blamed the West for trying to create divisions between Iran and its neighbours. The Foreign Ministry referred to the 'misunderstanding' which had arisen between Iran and the UAE. A measure of Iran's desire to mend fences can be discerned in its concurring to Syrian mediation in the dispute even though Syria, because of its support for the UAE's position, could no longer by regarded as an 'honest broker'.

While Iran tried to play down the incident, the UAE played it up. It filed a complaint against Iran with the United Nations and took the opportunity of widening the agenda to resuscitate the question of sovereignty of the islands at bilateral talks with Iran in Abu Dhabi.

Whatever the immediate cause of the incident, it is unlikely to have been the result of an overt policy move by Tehran to annex the island. This would have run counter to its main aim of trying to win the trust of its neighbours as a way of isolating Iraq and playing off the anxieties of the Gulf states against Iraq and Saudi Arabia. Indeed, the incident was a setback for Iran since it revived an old territorial dispute and led to regional talks being dominated by the issue rather than the question of collective security.

Although Iran tried hard to limit the damage that flowed from the incident, President Rafsanjani's subsequent and provocative reference to Abu Musa as an Iranian island belied Iran's own stance. The original fracas may have been an over-zealous mistake that got out of hand, but Iran's later positions make it clear that while it would like good relations with its neighbours, it seeks them on its own terms.

Forcing the Military Procurement Pace

It was against this background that the Gulf states and the West expressed their fears concerning Iran's intentions in building up its military capabilities. That Iran would want to build up its military forces after the Iran–Iraq War is no surprise. It was the shortage of arms and ammunition which had forced the government to accept a cease-fire. A few months after the end of the war, Mohsen Rezai, the commander of the Revolutionary Guards said: 'They had armour and we did not . . . We were unarmed infantrymen against the enemy's cavalry'.

Nor is it surprising that Iran would spend more on rearmament than it did during the war. An arms embargo on both sides during the war prevented substantial purchases, while damage to Iran's oil installations meant that exports of oil and therefore of foreign exchange were low during much of the eight-year war. The return to oil production and the rise in oil prices allowed it considerable leeway in purchases.

The Iranian government could point to a number of developments that would serve to justify its military procurement programme. The continued presence of 22 US ships in the area did nothing to alleviate its fears about long-term US interests in the region. Most of the littoral Arab states signed bilateral defence agreements with the US during the year, and the announcement at the end of January 1993 that Saudi Arabia was to purchase 48 *Tornado* aircraft from the UK, and in early February that the UAE has ordered 436 *Leclerc* tanks (including armoured recovery vehicles) from France, will have reinforced Iranian apprehension and a sense that it was once again isolated.

Estimates of Iran's defence expenditure differ considerably. A figure released last year by the CIA put Iran's annual expenditure on arms at $2bn. Akbar Torkan, Iran's Defence Minister, claimed in December that the military budget for 1992–93 was $750m in hard currency and another $1bn in rials. However, the Iranian navy chief, said in December 1992 that Iran had spent over $600m on the purchase of two submarines from the former Soviet Union, which suggests that its defence expenditure is well above the level quoted by Torkan. Even so, it is doubtful that it would come anywhere near the $8.5bn a year spent by the Shah during the last four years of his rule.

Iran has taken advantage of the former Soviet Union's need for hard currency to acquire Soviet armaments. In February 1992, air force commander Brigadier-General Mansour Sattari said that Iran had deployed MiG-29 fighters, Su-24 attack aircraft and Chinese F-7 fighter planes in its air force. Iran was known to have taken delivery of a first batch of MiG-29s in 1990 under a ten-year economic and defence agreement with the Soviet Union, but Sattari's statement was the first time that an Iranian official had acknowledged the acquisition of the other planes.

In November, Iran took delivery from the former Soviet Union of one *Kilo*-class diesel-powered submarine, armed with 18 torpedoes and possibly a surface-to-air missile capability. A second such submarine is under construction for Iran, who may have an option on a third. The submarine purchase greatly alarmed the Arab states of the Persian Gulf, already in dispute with Iran over Abu Musa, and that alarm spread to the West. Acting US Secretary of State, Lawrence Eagleburger, told his Russian counterpart, Andrei Kozyrev, that the sale was 'a matter of concern'. However, Vladimir Godev, the Russian ambassador to Tehran, said in early November that the sale was aimed at 'preserving the balance of power in the region' and cited the need for Russia to have good relations with Iran.

Other armaments acquired by Iran include T-72 tanks from the Soviet Union and *Scud* B and C missiles from North Korea, as well as a host of 'dual technology' equipment from predominantly Western countries, including radar-testing devices, navigation and avionics equipment, fibre-optic cables, high-speed computers and remote sensors. Despite the increased diversification of its arms sources, Iran has reiterated that its overwhelming preference is for US armaments. Torkan said early in 1993 that Iran's first priority was to buy US spare parts for the country's F-4, F-5 and F-14 fighter jets and for its mainly American transport aircraft.

The chances that the United States will soon again export arms to Iran are hardly propitious. On the contrary, it has been emphasizing its fears that Iran is attempting to acquire a nuclear capability. The US said that it had blocked transfers of equipment from China and Argentina to Iran earlier in the year, which it claimed would have given Iran the ability to begin its own nuclear manufacturing capability.

The country suffers from serious power shortages and the government has said one way in which it seeks to address this is through nuclear power generation. Under the Shah, Iran had an extensive nuclear power generation programme which was halted during the Iran–Iraq War. Iran's efforts since then to persuade Germany to complete the Bushehr nuclear power plant – the largest plant under construction – have not been successful.

Opinion regarding Iran's nuclear potential differs both within the US intelligence community and outside. The International Atomic Energy Agency (IAEA), which had made a number of satisfactory visits to Iran, called upon the US to share its intelligence so that IAEA officials could visit those areas in Iran which might harbour a covert operation. Until more substantial evidence emerges, there will continue to be suspicions that US fears regarding Iran's nuclear potential may be exaggerated for political purposes.

Neither the Bush nor Clinton administrations welcome an increase in Iranian power which could result from the demise of Iraq as a force in the region. Iran's aggressive foreign policy and its support for activist Muslim groups, particularly in the Sudan, are viewed with alarm. The US also attributes the continued existence of Muslim fundamentalism in Egypt and Algeria in part to Iran, although Saudi Arabia is known to have been the main external source of funds for the *Front Islamique du Salut* in Algeria and the Muslim Brotherhood for several decades before the establishment of Iran's Islamic Republic.

Although Iran's capacity to be a global menace is often exaggerated, there are valid reasons for international concern at some of its activities. So long as Iran continues to sponsor terrorist activities abroad, insists on calling for the assassination of Salman Rushdie, and violates its own citizens' human rights, it will have difficulty moving back into the good graces of the international community.

A Schizophrenic State

The domestic situation continued to be dominated by the weakened state of the economy and the lack of agreement on what measures were needed to revive it. The high rate of inflation and increasing unemployment have made life difficult for ordinary Iranians, and moves to devalue the rial are certain to add to the problem. Instead of being anti-inflationary, the 1992 budget doubled subsidies and raised salaries for public-sector employees. The governor of the Central Bank was brought to the brink of resignation over the issue, but the government was only too aware of the dangers of economic discontent and dared not remove the cushion of subsidies. The dangers could be seen in the sporadic disturbances that continued during 1992. In one of the most serious, in late May, a number of people were executed by the government in Mashhad, following rioting sparked off by municipal action against squatters.

Expectations of an improved standard of living after the Iran–Iraq War have been dangerously thwarted, partly due to the difficulties of reforming the economy. Rafsanjani's opponents have criticized him for moving ahead too quickly with privatization and ending price controls. An increase in oil prices and exports allowed Iran to embark on a spending boom which has now resulted in delays on payment of letters of credit, damaging the country's excellent payments record.

Failure to deliver on the economy leaves Rafsanjani vulnerable to political challenge. The parliamentary elections in the spring resulted in the defeat of many hardline candidates, but this has not been enough to ensure a smooth passage for his reforms because of the continuing unresolved struggles for power. In the summer the Minister of Culture and Islamic Guidance, Mohammad Khatami, was forced to resign as a result of pressure from radical factions opposed to his relaxation of controls on the media. His departure was a considerable setback for Rafsanjani.

As Iran struggles to establish an identity and to reconcile the ideology of the Islamic Republic with practical realities, its schizophrenic behaviour will continue, with the government at times making conciliatory noises and at others reviving its fiery rhetoric as witnessed by the eruption of the Rushdie affair again earlier this year. The economy will also continue to pose a challenge for Rafsanjani as he presses ahead with economic reform while trying to deflect the political discontent that will result from his efforts. Iran is in a period of 'disequilibrium'and it is too early to foresee an end to the seemingly contradictory behaviour which has so characterized its politics since the death of Khomeini.

East Asia

Post-Cold War politics are beginning to take shape in East Asia, and it is not quite what people forsaw. Some trends remain as expected – the retreat of Russian power and a drawing-down of the American military presence. It remains true also that economic issues seem to dominate the agenda more than military ones. But important differences are also beginning to emerge.

None is more important than the rise of China alongside an apparent slowing of Japan. China's impressive and sustained economic growth is not only reshaping the politics of this looming power, but it is also reshaping the way East Asians are beginning to look at their future. As China rushes along its course towards becoming the world's largest economy in the second decade of the twenty-first century, even the Japanese are adjusting to it. The task is all the more difficult for Japan because it comes at a time of increasing self-doubt about its ability to sustain the post-war economic miracle. While Japanese politics may appear to be business-as-usual, the backroom debates are now more far-reaching in their reassessment of Japan's role in the world.

Post-Cold War confidence has also been punctured on the Korean peninsula. Despite a smooth transition to a civilian government in South Korea, hope of détente and a speedy reunification of the two Koreas is fading fast. Squabbles over *Team Spirit* exercises and the inspection of North Korea's nuclear facilities are only the most obvious manifestations of what is a drift back to old-style stalemate. As optimism dies, so worry increases about managing the post-Kim Il Sung succession and eventual reunification. In a similar vein, but of much less importance, is concern that Hong Kong will not be as smoothly integrated with China as was once thought.

Confidence in ending regional conflict in Cambodia has also slipped. Despite superficial progress, the parties have made few important concessions that make for a viable compromise. Whatever optimism exists depends on broader trends in Association of South East Asian Nations (ASEAN) states focusing on economic growth, and Vietnam's determination to join them. But just as China's economic growth poses challenges to the old balance of power, so the rapid development in South-east Asia can also be destabilizing. The absence of any serious form of arms control, and the rapidly escalating arms race, especially in South-east Asia, makes East Asians worry about their ability to control their own future.

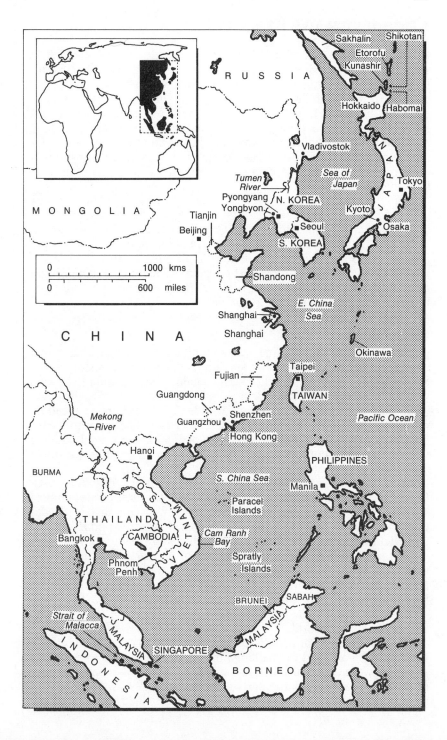

AS CHINA GROWS STRONG

While the economies of most of the great powers were sluggish in 1992, China powered ahead with 12% growth. Increases of this magnitude are generally not sustainable, but even with a somewhat slower growth China might well come close to being the world's largest economy by the year 2010. But by what year will it have the world's largest defence expenditure, and by when will it be too late to meet a possible Chinese challenge? And yet, the question of what kind of a challenge it will be remains moot, for the flourishing is bringing with it fundamental changes in China's economy, political system and perhaps even its frontiers.

Coping with China's growth is as much a problem for China's rulers as it is for the outside world. In 1992, the contest for the fate of China was waged in the run-up to the 14th Communist Party Congress as well as in negotiations with the outside world about trade, arms transfers and Hong Kong. No decisions were final, if only because the succession to Deng Xiaoping has yet to take place. One thing is increasingly clear, however, for the world as a whole China is becoming both more important and more difficult to handle.

Party Politics

For those who thought China was a totalitarian communist state that would inevitably be dumped on the same rubbish heap of history as the Soviet Union, 1992 was a year to think again. Deng Xiaoping, the man who calls the shots in China, decided that the best reaction to the death of the Soviet Union and its communist ideology would be to speed up reform of the Chinese economy in order to buy greater legitimacy for the ruling party. In the first few months of 1992 Deng waged political war on his more conservative colleagues who wanted to slow down both the economy and its reform.

Deng Xiaoping has always been the most pragmatic of pragmatists. He realized that if the party were to rule with at least a minimum of socialist principles, there would have to be real and sustained economic growth. In order to achieve such growth, there would have to be a modicum of political reform, although for Deng that merely meant a greater separation between the functions of the party and the state. If managers were to manage more efficiently, they would have to be allowed greater freedom from rigid party dictat. If intellectuals were to help modernize China, they would have to be freer to think. The effect of this was that by the summer there was even some liberalization within the artistic world.

Despite these reforms, it was always clear that political reform would not be allowed to challenge the right of the party to rule. The struggles were essentially within the party, and mainly about the pace of reform. They were particularly acute because 1992 was the year of the 14th Party Congress, and by the time it took place between 12 and

18 October there was no longer any question that Deng was going to get most of his way. Party Congress time is beloved of the tea-leaf-reading sinologists, but most still managed to agree that Deng had put in place the kinds of successors he wanted. Yet it was also clear that there was sufficient diversity among the successors to make it difficult to be sure who would end up on top. What is more, because none of the successors would have anything like the authority of the dying elders, power would be diffused.

Chart 1: Party Leadership

POLITICAL BUREAU (PB)
Standing Committee Members (7)

Jiang Zemin	1926	1989
Li Peng	1928	1987
Qiao Shi	1924	1987
Li Ruihuan	1934	1989
Zhu Rongji	1928	1992
Liu Huaqing (m)	1916	1992
Hu Jintao	1942	1992

Regular Members (20)

Chen Xitong	1930	1992
Ding Guangen	1929	1992
Hu Jintao	1942	1992
Jiang Chunyun	1930	1992
Jiang Zemin	1926	1987
Li Lanqing	1932	1992
Li Peng	1928	1992
Li Ruihuan	1934	1987
Li Tieying	1936	1987
Liu Huaqing (m)	1916	1992
Qian Qichen	1928	1992
Qiao Shi	1924	1985
Tan Shaowen (**93)	1929	1992
Tian Jiyun	1929	1985
Wei Jianxing	1931	1992
Wu Bangguo	1941	1992
Xie Fei	1932	1992
Zhu Rongji	1928	1992
Zou Jiahua	1926	1992
Yang Baibing	1920	1992

Alternate members (2)

Wen Jiabao	1942	1992
Wang Hanbin	1925	1992

In 1987 PB, not in 1992 PB

Hu Qili (*)	1929	1985
Hu Yaobang (**89)	1915	1978
Li Ximing	1926	1987
Qin Qiwei (m)	1914	1987
Song Ping	1917	1987
Wan Li	1916	1982
Wu Xueqian	1921	1985
Yang Rudai	1926	1987
Yang Shangkun (m)	1907	1982
Yao Yilin	1917	1982
Zhao Ziyang (*)	1919	1979

CENTRAL COMMITTEE SECRETARIAT (5)

Hu Jintao	1942	1992
Wei Jianxing	1931	1992
Ren Jianxin	1925	1992
Ding Guangen	1929	1992
Wen Jiabao	1942	1992

Secretaries in 1989, not in 1992

Qiao Shi	1924	1985
Li Ruihuan	1934	1989
Ding Guangen	1929	1989
Yang Baibing	1920	1989
Wen Jiabao (Alt.)	1942	1987

CENTRAL COMMISSION FOR DISCIPLINE INSPECTION (108 members. 13 Standing Committee members)

Sec.:	Wei Jianxing	1931	1992
DS:	Hou Zongbin	1929	1992
	Chen Zuolin	1923	1985
	Cao Qingze	1932	1992
	Wang Deying	1931	1991
	Xu Qing	1926	1992

The first date is the year of birth and the second that of appointment to the relevant position.
Abbreviations: (m): military; *: dismissed in 1989; Alt.: Alternate; Sec.: Secretary; DS: Deputy Secretary; **: died.
Source: *China News Analysis* No. 1471.

The new 20-man Politburo (increased from 14) was headed by a seven-man standing committee. Apart from party leader Jiang Zemin, Premier Li Peng, Qiao Shi (the chief of internal security) and Li Ruihuan (the former Mayor of Tianjin in charge of recent liberalization of propaganda), three new entrants represented different dimensions of the Dengist agenda. Zhu Rongji, who was catapulted to the top without even having been a member of the Central Committee, was formerly in charge of Shanghai. He was now the standard-bearer of those wishing the fastest pace of reform, which saddled him with the burdensome tag of 'China's Gorbachev'. Hu Jintao, formerly in charge of Tibet, was a surprise entry, and represented a conservative voice on political issues. The final, and by far the most elderly, entrant was General Liu Huaqing, China's most senior military leader, with a reputation for championing greater professionalism within the People's Liberation Army (PLA). It is from this 'gang of seven' that Deng's successor will probably be chosen.

Given the role of the PLA in keeping the party in power in 1989, it was perhaps not surprising that the largest category of new members to the 14th Central Committee came from the PLA – 24 of the PLA's 43 full members and 16 of its 21 alternate members. In total there were 83 new members of the Central Committee, whose overall size increased by 34 to 189. Total PLA representation on the Central Committee rose from 19.6% to 21.7% (14.9% in 1982). The PLA had only two people on the Politburo (Liu Huaqing and Yang Baibing), but a number of the key civilians had strong PLA connections (most notably Qiao Shi and Zou Jiahua). Regional party leaders also joined in larger numbers. The most notable of these changes was the elevation to the Politburo of the party bosses from coastal China including Jiang Chunyun from Shandong, Tan Shaowen from Tianjin, Wu Bangguo of Shanghai and Xie Fei from Guangdong. One of the surprises of the selections was that the 'red princes' – the children of the elderly leadership – failed to be chosen for high office, suggesting that at least some heed was being taken of concerns about corruption in government.

By far the most startling personnel changes only became fully apparent in the weeks after the Congress. Yang Baibing, the half-brother of President Yang Shangkun and a noted conservative, had been expected to take control of the PLA after Deng's death. Instead, it became clear that he had been booted up to the Politburo to make it easier to remove him from any control of the PLA. Following the Congress, his acolytes in the PLA were cleansed from leading positions as the largest purge of the armed forces since the defeat of Lin Biao in 1971 got under way. In almost every major central and regional command senior officers were replaced in a campaign led by an old PLA stalwart and Deng intimate, General Zhang Zhen. The Beijing Military Region and the General Political Department, where Yang Baibing had been most influential, were special targets of the purge (See Chart 2).

Chart 2: PLA Leadership (January 1993)

DEFENCE MINISTER	Gen. Qin Jiwei (retiring April 1993)

CENTRAL MILITARY COMMISSION

CHAIRMAN	Jiang Zemin
VICE-CHAIRMEN	**Gen. Liu Huaqing**
	Gen. Zhang Zhen
MEMBERS	**Lt Gen. Zhang Wannian**
	Lt Gen. Yu Yongbo
	Lt Gen. Fu Quanyou
	Gen. Chi Haotian

GENERAL HEADQUARTERS

General Staff Department

CHIEF	**Lt Gen. Zhang Wannian**
DEPUTIES	Lt Gen. Xu Huizi
	Lt Gen. Li Jing
	Maj Gen. Cao Gangchuan

General Political Department

DIRECTOR	**Lt Gen. Yu Yongbo**
DEPUTY	**Gen. Wang Ruilin**

General Logistics Department

DIRECTOR	**Lt Gen. Fu Quanyou**
DEPUTIES	Maj Gen. Wang Tailan
	Lt Gen. Liu Mingpu
	Lt Gen. Zhang Bin
	Lt Gen. Li Lun

MILITARY REGIONS

	Commander	Political Commissar
Beijing	Lt Gen. Wang Chengbin	**Lt Gen. Gu Shanqing**
Chengdu	Lt Gen. Li Jiulong	**Lt Gen. Zhang Gong**
Jinan	**Lt Gen. Zhang Taiheng**	Lt Gen. Song Qingwen
Lanzhou	**Lt Gen. Liu Jingsong**	Lt Gen. Cao Pengsheng
Nanjing	Lt Gen. Gu Mui	**Lt Gen. Liu Anyuan**
Shenyang	**Lt Gen. Wang Ke**	Lt Gen. Song Keda
Guangzhou	**Lt Gen. Li Xilin**	**Lt Gen. Shi Yuxiao**

Names in **bold** are new appointments.
Source: *Jane's Defence Weekly*, 2 January 1993.

The main explanation for the clear-out was that Deng had won a struggle against those who opposed his vision of reform. He was supported by much of the rest of the PLA, who resented Yang's neglect of professionalism and worried about his rapid promotion of cronies. By cutting Yang down, the armed forces began to purge themselves of some of the guilt for the 1989 Tiananmen Square massacre in January and set themselves up for a less active political part in the succession to Deng. Nevertheless, whoever follows Deng will have to build a coalition of support within the PLA as Deng has done, if he is to succeed. The Party Congress marked an impressive shift in the players, but the rules of the game were basically unchanged. Depending on the timing and the state of the economy, it would be foolish to write the conservatives out of the succession.

The Economy: Growth and Diversity

A gross domestic product (GDP) growth rate of 12.8% in 1992 is remarkable, especially compared with 4% in 1990 and 7% in 1991. China's conservatives wanted growth at about half this rate, while Deng Xiaoping wanted, and achieved, faster growth. But even these impressive figures hide the scale of China's success. Using more accurate figures based on purchasing power parities, the chief economist of the World Bank estimates that the real size of the Chinese economy is much larger than the dollar exchange rate values suggest. China may now have become the world's third largest economy, some 45% the size of the United States. Given only a 6.5% difference between American and Chinese future GDP growth rates, China is on course to give the EC Single Market (if it ever comes into being) competition for the number one spot by the year 2010.

This success has been spearheaded by the phenomenal growth in China's non-state sector and coastal regions. In 1978, before the reforms began, the state accounted for 78% of industrial output. By the end of 1992 its share had dropped to just over 50%, and if agriculture and services are taken into account the state's share of total output is now no more than 25%. Rather than creating a socialist economy, China has been building capitalism with Chinese characteristics.

The largest part of this shift took place when township and village enterprises were created by local government, mainly in coastal China. During the last five years provincial government statistics indicate that there the GDP increased by 14% annually. Trickle-down economics and a central government with some ability to redistribute tax revenues have ensured that the hinterland provinces have also grown, but obviously not at such startling rates.

Because the economy of the hinterland was larger than that of the coast until the 1980s, the boom on China's gold coast – at least initially and to a certain extent – provided greater equality among the regions. But disparities are now being magnified as the coastal regions continue to power ahead. As they do so, they link into what Professor Robert Scalapino has termed Natural Economic Territories (NETs) outside China's formal borders, zones where the naturally developing trade, financial and personal links create a tight web of interdependence. Nowhere is this more vividly apparent than in the NET that links Guangdong and Fujian provinces with Hong Kong, Taiwan and the wider overseas Chinese community.

Growing regional disparities is the price central government seems willing to pay for overall growth. It is a high-risk strategy in the long term, for richer regions develop both a desire and a capacity to ignore central economic directives. Where economics lead, politics are likely to follow. There are also worries about inflation in an over-heated economy, although this has been less of a problem than in the past because the reforms have also meant a shrinkage in the most inefficient, state sector of the economy. An unbalanced investment structure and hectic growth also lead to a waste of resources. Imports are again growing a bit faster than exports, but vastly increased foreign trade has meant the size of the debt is not a serious problem.

When compared with the reform path followed in the former Soviet Union, there can be no doubt that China has chosen the better route. But there are risks in success as well as in failure. The logic of the Chinese reforms is to decentralize power: the party surrenders power to the market and the centre surrenders to the region. What is more, the fact that some 17% of China's GDP now depends on foreign trade, means that China, like all advanced economies, is also forced to surrender some state sovereignty to the international market economy and China's major trade partners.

Between Irredentism and Interdependence

The clash between the needs of the ruling party for legitimacy and pressures from the outside world have been felt most acutely in relations with that unique entrepôt for China's trade – Hong Kong. Beijing thought it had the Hong Kong problem settled after the 1984 accord with the UK, but the events of 1989 – the Beijing massacre, the death of communism in Europe and the ending of the Cold War – re-set the agenda for Western relations with China. While Hong Kong grew more economically interconnected with coastal China, coastal China pulled further away from Beijing. When UK Prime Minister John Major appointed a new Governor for Hong Kong (Chris Patten arrived in July 1992), it was at a time when the West was far less willing to tolerate China setting the agenda for relations.

Chris Patten's proposals for slightly more democracy in Hong Kong, announced on 7 October 1992, were rejected by China more because they were made without prior agreement with Beijing, than because they constituted a real threat to Chinese rule after 1997. China's acute sensitivity to its new position in relations with the West, and its deep concern that Hong Kong would be used to democratize all of China, were key factors behind China's rapid escalation of the crisis with Britain over Hong Kong in late 1992. China issued threats to let the 1984 accord be 'cast to the wind' and for a time the Hong Kong people and stock market shuddered. In March 1993 China began setting up what it called a 'second kitchen' for Hong Kong, suggesting that Chris Patten might be bypassed if he cannot be bludgeoned into surrender.

No one could doubt that China held most of the cards in the negotiations over Hong Kong. If it so chose, China could force Britain to retreat, but it would damage Hong Kong (and southern China) in the process. Thus the struggle over Hong Kong was increasingly about how much interdependence China would have to accept with the outside world, carrying with it, as it does, the threat of growing pressures for democracy at home.

Similar calculations were also apparent in relations with Taiwan in 1992. As the West, and the United States in particular, recognized that it could get tough with China in the post-Cold War world, and the US even forced China to back down on a trade dispute in 1992, the West was more willing to deal with Taiwan. The American and French decisions to sell advanced fighter aircraft (F-16s and *Mirage* 2000-5s) and a general Western policy of sending higher-ranking ministers on official visits to Taiwan, made China worry that previous agreements which were intended to let Taiwan wither on the international diplomatic vine were being undone. Indeed they were. In part because China itself was increasing its economic and cultural links with Taiwan, so the West felt it could do the same. The problem was that China was under the illusion that such contacts would lead to the unification of China, while almost everyone else recognized that in the modern, interdependent world, we were seeing the emergence of *de facto* independence for Taiwan.

China was far less constrained in pursuit of its irredentist agenda in 1992 when it came to the South China Sea. In July China seized yet more atolls from Vietnam (the Da Lac coral reef), provoking virtually no reaction from ASEAN states, which may be next in line for the attention of Chinese marines, or from the United States, which might have issued more robust messages of deterrence. On 4 September China positioned an oil rig in Vietnamese waters having sent in seismic survey teams in August. Vietnam and China, despite a prime-ministerial summit in 1992 (30 November to 4 December), continued to have cool relations, with territorial disputes being only the most obvious area of disagreement. Both sides also looked on warily as the Cambodian peace process sputtered, for they knew that the last time there was a civil war in Cambodia, Vietnam and China went to war. In the 1990s Vietnam was in no shape for a re-run of the 1979 war, which only made Hanoi even more frustrated that China could continue to treat Vietnam as an inferior to be humiliated.

China's jittery behaviour regarding irredentist issues was in part the result of uncertainty about its main international adversary, the United States. China had regarded President Bush as a 'friend' because he resisted Congressional efforts to link the renewal of China's Most Favoured Nation trading status to a more acceptable human rights record. As a result, as President Bush grew weaker at home, China grew more inclined to make concessions on everything from human rights, trade and the response to the F-16 sale to Taiwan. The election of Bill Clinton, and the ensuing uncertainty about whether he would take a less critical line on China than he did during the election campaign, meant that China remained cautious. Should the new American president continue to sell arms to China's adversaries, provide support for greater democracy in Hong Kong, and take a tough line on trade and human rights disputes, a deterioration in Sino-American relations is inevitable.

China has hinted at what it might do in response. The F-16 sale provoked China to withdraw from the process whereby the five permanent members of the United Nations Security Council were trying to limit conventional arms transfers. China also sold M-11 missiles to Pakistan in violation of a previous agreement to abide by the Missile Technology Control Regime (MTCR). China could go further and withdraw support for UN peacekeeping everywhere from Cambodia to Central America. It could veto Security Council action against everyone from Iraq to Serbia. And it might even step up support for North Korea or be more aggressive in pursuing its territorial claims in the South China Sea.

The use of such blatant instruments is doubtful, however. China is restrained for a number of reasons, including the fact that even in the current mood the US announced in December 1992 the transfer of jet engine technology, radars, torpedoes and avionics to China. China is mainly restrained by its growing interdependence with the international economy and the impact that any crisis might have on its domestic economy. The Chinese will try to be more subtle, in part by encouraging other states to stand up to what it perceives as a Western attempt to re-order the post-Cold War world. This sentiment is an important part of the rationale for much closer Sino-Russian relations in 1992, despite the adverse impact of the death of communist-party rule in Europe.

President Yeltsin visited China in December 1992 after a year when the extent of Sino-Russian military cooperation emerged more clearly. There had been flourishing rumours about China acquiring an aircraft carrier from Ukraine and sophisticated weapons from Russia, but the reality was a more cautious and long-term strategy. Russia did begin providing 24 Su-27s, and negotiations continued for long-term cooperation between the defence industries of both countries for follow-on models. China was more interested in technology transfer and only wanted hardware if it was at rock-bottom prices. Earlier in 1992, it had obtained in-flight refuelling technology from Iran.

China and Russia also discussed shared concerns about instability in Central Asia. Although China had established official relations with these former parts of the Soviet Union, there was little warmth in these contacts. Russia could emerge as a strategic counter both in Central Asia as well as in the east with Japan. China (like South Korea) quietly gloated when President Yeltsin managed to visit China in 1992 while having to cancel a trip to Japan in September. Japanese Emperor Akihito visited China in October and Sino-Japanese trade relations remained stable, but there are undoubted long-term uncertainties in Sino-Japanese relations.

The tacit Chinese concern about Japan in the post-Cold War world was also part of the reason why China agreed to establish full diplomatic relations with South Korea on 24 August 1992. Sino-South Korean trade relations had been booming for years, but China had held back on full relations for fear of losing influence in North Korea. The end of the Cold War meant Pyongyang was friendless and as China's strategy of regional economic growth moved into high gear, Beijing realized that it was useful to have successful NETs in the north (as well as in Shanghai), in order to counter the influence of the southern NET in Guangdong and Fujian. Once again, domestic affairs were helping set a foreign policy agenda.

China also established diplomatic relations with 14 other states in 1992, most notably Israel. But most of its new partners were the residue of the former Soviet Union and Yugoslavia, and were more of a burden for the cash-strapped foreign ministry than a benefit in the diplomatic arena. China certainly worried that the trend in 1992 seemed to be towards the dissolution of states, thereby leaving its vast empire to look more out of step and encouraging those who would hope for change.

A State in Transition

China was evidently oscillating between confidence and insecurity. The confidence derived from the fact that the death of the Soviet Union meant China was more secure from external threat than at any time in several centuries. Longer-term confidence could be derived from the superb performance of its economy and the real prospect of overtaking Japan and then the United States. With this state of mind, why should China worry about minor setbacks on the way?

Yet the logic of developing trends suggests that a very different China could emerge from the intervening years. Hence the insecurity. Rapid growth might require so much regional diversity that China might not be recognizable as a centre-driven, single state by early in the next century. Under such circumstances, China's pursuit of irredentism in Hong Kong, Taiwan or even the South China Sea, might only help split China. Rapid growth might also demand so much international interdependence that China would not be free to punish those in the outside world who have a different agenda for China. If interdependence leads to greater fragmentation at home, less ability to hold democratic forces at bay, and less ability to wage effective trade war or counter Western influence around the world, China's remaining hardline leaders may wonder what the rush to growth was all about.

The events of 1992 suggest that, certainly until the death of Deng Xiaoping, China will settle for a compromise with the demands of international interdependence. Deng's successors, whoever they may be from the 14th Party Congress line-up, will find that, even if they want to, it will be hard to undo the basic features of his reforms – capitalism with Chinese characteristics and openness to international interdependence. East Asians and the wider world have only a decade or so in which to plan for a region that will face new challenges from a vastly stronger China.

JAPAN: LOSING CONTROL

Prime Minister Kiichi Miyazawa, who cast himself in the role of the captain best able to steer the *Nippon Maru* (Japan's ship of state), has proved a disappointment in navigating through some very choppy waters. Despite the Liberal Democratic Party's (LPD) better-than-expected results in the July 1992 Upper House elections, he has appeared half-hearted over political reform, disengaged from the economy's problems and hesitant in dealing with a major political corruption scandal, involving gangsters, businessmen and loads of money, which claimed the scalp of Shin Kanemaru, one of the most influential politicians of the last decade. The political demise of the LDP's kingmaker shattered the largest faction supporting Miyazawa and infighting surged once again. Miyazawa's ratings plummeted as the Japanese public became increasingly disillusioned with the leadership vacuum and the mounting economic difficulties.

The economy continued to slow down and has drifted into the worst recession in Japan since the 1973–74 oil shock. As domestic demand slumped, Japanese manufacturers turned once again to what they know best – exporting – and, assisted by exchange rate movements, the trade surplus in dollar terms rose to record levels. The aftershock of the bursting of Japan's asset-inflated 'bubbles' was felt keenly in the stock market, where prices in August 1992 reached their lowest level for six years. The announcement of a ¥10 trillion pump-priming economic package, the largest ever, helped a partial recovery, but lost much of its real stimulative effect by being delayed for five months by parliamentary wrangling over political scandals. Miyazawa's introduction of a five-year programme to turn Japan into a 'lifestyle superpower' fell flat. The Japanese grumbled more than ever not only about the quality of their life, but also the quality of their democracy.

After a prolonged parliamentary struggle, Miyazawa managed to pass legislation enabling the Self-Defense Forces (SDF) to take part in UN peacekeeping operations, and a small number of troops have arrived in Cambodia. In other respects, however, the Japanese still seemed confounded by the rapid pace of change in international affairs and unable to establish new approaches to foreign and defence policy.

Faction wars

During the first half of 1992, Miyazawa's popularity was steadily eroded by his inability to provide strong leadership for either political reform or economic resuscitation. In the run-up to the July Upper House elections, however, his fortunes began to recover. The controversial UN peacekeeping legislation finally made its way through the Diet and his chief rival, Michio Watanabe, the Deputy Prime Minister and Foreign Minister, fell ill. Despite dissatisfaction within the LDP, faction leaders were fearful of dumping Miyazawa for they could see no real alternative.

Over the past two decades, periods of recession have, ironically, actually sustained support for the LDP, as voters have been scared to plump for the uncertainties of an inexperienced opposition coalition. Such was to be the case again in the July elections. The LDP recovered strongly from the setbacks of the 1989 Upper House elections; it took 69 seats, more than its initial predictions, and although it failed to regain its overall majority, it may well do so in the elections in 1995 (only half the seats come up for re-election each time). On the other hand, the opposition Social Democratic Party of Japan (SDPJ) (which had had such a success in 1989) failed to gain any new seats and its share of the vote almost halved. The trade union-backed grouping, Rengo, which had also done well in 1989, failed to win any seats at all. The newest force in Japanese politics, the Japan New Party, gained four seats but has yet to achieve a power base strong enough to carry forward its political reform ideas. It had been formed only two months before by Morihiro Hosokawa, the previously LDP-backed former governor of Kumamoto prefecture.

The biggest winner, however, was not the LDP itself, but rather the faction named after former prime minister Noboru Takeshita, although actually led by Kanemaru. It expanded its membership amongst the Upper House LDP members, while other factions either shrank or remained the same. Miyazawa had had to rely heavily on the Takeshita faction during 1991–92 to coax two opposition parties, the Komeito and the Democratic Socialist Party (DSP), into supporting the UN peacekeeping bill (PKO). In recognition of his crucial role, Kanemaru had been made vice-president of the LDP in January.

The triumph of Kanemaru and the Takeshita faction was shortlived. At the end of August 1992 Kanemaru was forced to resign as LDP vice-president after admitting that he had received ¥500 million ($4m) from an express delivery company, Tokyo Sagawa Kyubin, in 1990, precisely at the time when LDP politicians were pledging themselves to keep clean in the aftermath of the Recruit insider-share scandal. The money had been handed over as part of a complex deal which involved the Sagawa president using his contacts with a leading *yakuza* (gangster) to silence a right-wing gang's vociferous agitation against Takeshita, when he was trying to win the LDP presidency in 1987. The Sagawa money was distributed amongst 60 members of Kanemaru's faction, but only Kanemaru and the governor of Niigata prefecture, who had separately received ¥100m from Sagawa, were indicted for violations of political funding laws. Kanemaru, who was excused even from appearing in court, was fined a mere ¥200,000 ($1,600).

Public disillusionment with politicians, reflected in a turnout of only 50% in the July elections (the lowest in post-war history), turned to anger at the lenient treatment of Kanemaru. As a wave of criticism flooded in from local assemblies, business circles, and even from within the Cabinet, Kanemaru finally resigned from the Diet on 14 October. While the resignation step marked a decisive end to his pervasive influence on Japanese politics, it was not quite the end of the scandal. The outcry forced Kanemaru, who was questioned in hospital, and Takeshita to testify about the affair.

The impact on the Takeshita faction was nonetheless traumatic, as open feuding broke out. A Takeshita supporter, Keizo Obuchi, took over the leadership of the faction, but Kanemaru's own protégé, Ichiro Ozawa, linked up with the Finance Minister, Tsutomu Hata. By December the Hata–Ozawa faction was in operation and the Takeshita faction had suffered a fatal split, ending its long-standing position as the largest LDP faction. The disintegration of the Takeshita faction, ironically, pushed Miyazawa closer towards the factions headed by Watanabe and Hiroshi Mitsuzuka, his chief rivals for the prime ministership the previous autumn. This gave Miyazawa temporary political stability, and enabled him to carry out a cabinet reshuffle which displayed a more balanced line-up, in factional terms, than the previous one.

Miyazawa's record suggests some parallels with Takeshita's; both started with public opinion ratings in the high 30s (quite reasonable by Japanese standards), but these slumped, mainly due to corruption, to around half that level. However, unlike Takeshita who was deeply implicated in the Recruit scandal, Miyazawa has not yet been directly associated with the Sagawa scandal. He is likely, therefore, to survive until the end of his two-year period as LDP president (October 1993), but the factional in-fighting to be his successsor will only intensify. Another prolonged period of LDP introspection is unlikely to help the Japanese take decisive initiatives in other affairs.

Sending Forces Abroad

Miyazawa's main political achievement during the year was the passage of the law allowing the Self-Defense Forces to cooperate in UN peacekeeping operations. To do so, he had had to rely heavily on Kanemaru to ensure, through tortuously negotiated minor amendments to the text, that the Komeito and the DSP came on board in support. Lacking an overall majority in the Upper House, the LDP needed the support of these two parties to ensure the bill's passage. The SDPJ plumped for an all-or-nothing confrontation with this tripartite alliance. It adopted a time-honoured delaying tactic – the 'ox walk' – in the Upper House and, when the amended bill went back to the Lower House for final approval, it boycotted the session and proffered the resignation of all its members to force a dissolution of the Diet.

The SDPJ's tactics backfired, for its rigid approach did nothing to dispel doubts about its abilities to become a governing party. Indeed, criticisms about the party's tactics with regard to both the PKO bill and the Sagawa scandal forced the SDPJ's leader, Makoto Tanabe, to resign in December 1992. Public opinion polls throughout 1991–92, although inconsistent, generally reflected slowly growing public support for the SDF's limited participation in UN operations. The results of the July Upper House election did not support the SDPJ's call for a public rejection of the new law.

The appointment of a Japanese national, Yasushi Akashi, as head of the UN Transitional Authority in Cambodia (UNTAC) in January 1992 had increased the likelihood that Cambodia would be the first country to receive SDF troops, once the legislation was passed. In October, for the first time since the Second World War, Japanese ground troops left on an overseas mission; by the end of the year 600 SDF engineers were active in road repairs and other construction tasks in Cambodia.

The PKO law provoked widely differing views abroad: the United States and many Western countries welcomed it as a sign of Japanese efforts to contribute to the new international order, while some neighbouring Asian countries (China, South Korea and North Korea) expressed concern that this was the beginning of an inevitable resurgence of Japanese military might.

Although an important psychological first step, the PKO law is closely woven with restrictions. A maximum of 2,000 SDF troops can be sent in response to UN requests for deployment, they can carry light firearms but these can only be used for self-defence, and they are only allowed to conduct medical, refugee aid, transportation, infrastructural repair, election-monitoring and policing operations. As the price of their parliamentary support, the Komeito ensured that the SDF was not allowed to participate in any operations that might involve military action, and the DSP insisted on mandatory Diet authorization for each dispatch that might involve military activities. This has so far precluded Japanese participation in UN operations in the former Yugoslavia and Somalia. In addition, the law has to be reviewed after three years.

Given the problems involved in passing this law, it is unlikely that the LDP would attempt to introduce a strengthened bill even at that time. The government may even find it necessary to withdraw its troops from Cambodia if the UN attempts to use force to compel the *Khmer Rouge* to accede to the resolutions it is now flouting. Should an SDF soldier be killed while abroad, however accidentally, public opinion, now finely balanced, is likely to make it more rather than less difficult to revamp the legislation. Because of this, and the deep desire of the Japanese government to make this first Japanese peacekeeping operation a success, there have been reports of Japanese pressure on the UN to resist a more forceful role in Cambodia.

Return to the drawing-board

Despite its success in passing the PKO legislation, the Miyazawa government remained unsure about Japan's position in the post-Cold War world. Indeed, the annual Defense White Paper, issued in August 1992, admitted that not only the future of the SDF role, but also the medium-term basis of the Japanese defence build-up programme were still under re-evaluation.

The necessity for such a re-examination was driven by the Finance Ministry's determined efforts to reduce the defence budget. Its arguments, based on a combination of a probable tax revenue short-fall because of the recession and the disappearance of the Soviet threat, were strongly countered by the Defense Agency, which argued that the emerging arms race in East Asia, coupled with increasing US demands for burden-sharing, made an expenditure cut unrealistic. Lack of resources had already complicated US–Japanese negotiations over the purchase of four airborne warning and control system (AWACS) aircraft. President Bush, during his January 1992 visit to Japan, had pressed the Japanese to buy the AWACS, but the government balked at Boeing's asking price, almost double the Defense Agency's original estimate. Eventually the Americans compromised on the cost, but the new budgetary restraints made certain that the Japanese could go for no more than two aircraft in fiscal year 1993. The Finance Ministry's initial 1993–94 budget draft had actually proposed the first ever cut in the defence budget, but, after strong lobbying from the Defense Agency, the final version approved by the cabinet in late December 1992 allowed a mere 1.95% growth in the defence budget, still the lowest ever recorded.

The Defense White Paper did significantly tone down its presentation of the former Soviet Union's military power, describing it only as a 'factor of uncertainty' for the security of North-east Asia. But that did not mean that the Japanese were finding it any easier dealing with Russian President Boris Yeltsin than they did with Soviet President Mikhail Gorbachev. The run-up to Yeltsin's planned visit to Japan in September 1992 was a replay of the prelude to Gorbachev's April 1991 visit. The Japanese, while beginning to think a little more flexibly on separating the desired return of the four 'northern territories' into two stages, continued to be unimpressed by Western – and Russian – suggestions that economic assistance was vital to ensure Yeltsin's survival. Instead they called for Yeltsin to make a 'political decision' over the islands. Just as Gorbachev had, however, Yeltsin found that mounting domestic pressures made it increasingly difficult to consider territorial concessions, especially if no economic aid were forthcoming. At the last moment, Yeltsin aborted his trip to Japan and looked for consolation in South Korea. Whilst Russian domestic political difficulties were the primary reason for this cancellation, the obvious Japanese reluctance to provide economic aid also acted as a chiller. Russo-Japanese relations slipped back into a frozen state.

North Korea remained a serious concern to Japan. Cooperating closely with the South Koreans and the Americans, the Japanese insisted not only on IAEA inspections, but also South Korean inspections of the North Korean nuclear facilities. As a result of North Korean foot-dragging, the Japan–North Korea normalization negotiating process began to look weary and unproductive.

But, during 1992, the most notable change was the heightened Japanese worry about China's growing military capabilities. The Japanese were upset by the Chinese law of February 1992 which included the disputed Senkaku islands within Chinese territorial waters. Their anxieties were openly expressed when they went as far as to warn the Chinese against the rumoured purchase of an aircraft carrier under construction in the Ukraine. These concerns complicated the preparations for the October visit to China by Emperor Akihito, the first ever by a Japanese monarch. The Chinese had asked for such a visit several times, for they saw it as an important symbol of their rehabilitation into international society as well as a harbinger of greater Japanese investment in their economy. It required considerable political massaging for the Japanese government to overcome opposition from those who felt that the Emperor should have nothing to do with a blood-stained communist power and from those who objected to the Emperor being used for political purposes. In the end, the Emperor was allowed to make a relatively anodyne expression of regret for past Japanese actions in China and the trip went off incident-free.

The Japanese saw the visit as part of their campaign to gain Chinese acceptance for their attempts to adopt a higher profile in the Asia–Pacific region and, more specifically, for their objective of achieving a permanent seat on the UN Security Council within five years. A marked lack of enthusiasm amongst existing members of the Security Council, however, led the Japanese to consider possible new arrangements, such as initially, at least, *ad hoc* meetings of the UN Security Council and G-7 Summit members. The Japanese also became more receptive to ideas of regional security discussions and Miyazawa's speeches began to pick up this point, though remaining vague on specifics. In December a private advisory panel set up by Miyazawa to examine policies towards the Asia–Pacific region recommended that the CSCE could act as a model for similar discussions on security in the Asian region.

Aid and Trade

Overseas aid continued to be Japan's primary channel for contributing to the international order. Japan regained its ranking as the world's largest donor and was well on track to complete its pledged programme of $50bn over five years. Despite the fiasco of Miyazawa's non-appearance at the Rio Earth Summit in June 1992 (unable to leave the Diet because of the PKO bill deliberations, he failed even to get a video-recording of his message played to the conference), Japan made large commitments for environmentally related aid. It also produced guidelines to curtail its aid to countries which were guilty of excessive military spending, arms exporting or poor human rights records. The criteria for these categories remain ill-defined, which means a case-by-case process; doubtless some exceptions, such as aid to China, will continue.

After the anti-climax of the Bush visit, US–Japanese relations appeared to mark time, with mutual irritation the main characteristic. The Japanese, noting the winding down of the US presence in the Philippines, urged the United States to maintain its military presence in North-east Asia, but realized that much would depend on the incoming administration. They found themselves at variance with the Bush administration over the US decision to sell F-16s to Taiwan, which they judged to be destabilizing, and over the resumption in November, after a 14-year suspension, of Japanese aid to Vietnam. As the slump in domestic demand reduced imports and once again inflated Japan's export surpluses, the Strategic Impediments Initiative (SII) talks petered out. The Japanese became more wary of US protectionist sentiment (vividly encapsulated in the rhetoric of Ross Perot) and expressed concern about the formation of the North American Free Trade Agreement (NAFTA). Having succeeded in pushing the EC into a deal on farm products, the Americans began to see Japan's stated opposition to opening up its rice market as the main remaining obstacle to the conclusion of the Uruguay Round negotiations. Although the Japanese clearly would benefit from the overall General Agreement on Tariffs and Trade (GATT) package, domestic political sensitivities over rice threatened to sabotage progress.

Bill Clinton's success in the presidential elections was seen by the Japanese not just as a generational change, but as the start of a new US approach. Opinion was divided over exactly how Clinton's rhetoric would work out in practice. Some officials and observers expected him to be tougher on trade and market-opening issues and that differences over policies towards China and Russia would become more pronounced. Others interpreted Clinton's call for a revised industrial policy to enhance US competitiveness as belated recognition of US weakness; reinvigorating the US economy would, in the medium-term, stabilize bilateral economic relations and assist Japanese commercial activities. Whatever approach materializes, Japanese officials and politicians will have to get used to a new set of US counterparts; settling in will not be easy for either side.

Same Old Tune

Clinton's success in the US elections is just the kind of dramatic generational and political change which may be necessary, but is inconceivable in the current Japanese political scene. A growing number of younger politicians both outside and within the LDP feel the need for reform in a system clearly driven by dirty money, pork-barrel profligacy, and unsavoury underworld connections. Following on the Japan New Party's success in the July elections, a number of reform-oriented informal groupings have begun to emerge and even Kenichi Ohmae, the noted economist, has formed his own political study group.

Instead of a 'Mr Clean' at the top, however, there remains a vacuum. Toshiki Kaifu, Miyazawa's predecessor, lost office for trying too hard over political reform and is now out of the running. Miyazawa, despite including a couple of noted 'reformers' in his latest cabinet, shows no signs of measuring up to the challenge. As the next election could be postponed until February 1994, the elders of the LDP are no doubt hoping to muddle through as they always have, first by cosmetic tinkering to the constituency system, and then by relying on the reform movements to run out of steam. Although indignation is now high, Japan's voters have notoriously short memories and a disinclination for widespread change. The combination may once again prove strong enough to assure that reform is kept to a minimum.

THE KOREAN PENINSULA

Whatever optimism there had been in 1991 over the potential for an end to the enduring stalemate on the Korean peninsula evaporated in 1992. By autumn, efforts to implement the December 1991 agreements ground to a halt. To be sure, North Korea had finally agreed to inspection of its nuclear facilities by the International Atomic Energy Agency (IAEA), but the proposed North–South inspection regime foundered. Exasperated by the North's delaying tactics, the US–South Korean side announced the resumption of the joint *Team Spirit* military exercises in 1993. The North's inevitable response to increasing pressure was to cancel all planned contacts with the South and in mid-March to end cooperation with the IAEA and threaten withdrawal from the Nuclear Non-Proliferation Treaty (NPT).

In contrast, optimism about the course of developing democracy in South Korea proved to be well founded. In 1992 it elected its first civilian president for over 30 years. The victor, Kim Young Sam, is indeed a civilian and has been a leading member of the opposition for many years, but he is essentially a conservative politician and few dramatic changes can be expected. Against a background of constant electioneering, President Roh Tae Woo concentrated on foreign affairs which yielded several successes. But there was much domestic criticism of the government's comparative economic failings, a theme which featured prominently in the election campaign. Roh's attempts to distance himself from the political jockeying offended some of his friends and failed to satisfy his enemies.

In North Korea the government's economic failings were far from imagined, but they were not yet serious enough to force a change in its dealings with the South. The need to assess political developments in the South and the consequences of Clinton's election account in part for North Korea's more rigid stand on North–South issues in 1992. Otherwise, there was little change in the North's condition. Kim Jong Il's slow plod towards power labours on. Energy problems and food shortages continue to be reported, but claims of the imminent 'collapse' of the economy seem exaggerated. Whatever the North's difficulties, they do not appear sufficient to induce rapid changes in its self-defeating approach.

South Korea: The Last Of The Old Politics?

The presidential election was not held until 18 December, yet it loomed over the whole year. Officially, electioneering was not permitted before 20 November, but this was a prohibition little honoured. The governing Democratic Liberal Party (DLP) had failed to win an overall majority in the National Assembly elections in March and had to resort quickly to traditional horse-trading to restore its majority.

This failure rebounded against the DLP's executive chairman and expected presidential candidate, Kim Young Sam, who had been saddled with the difficult task of running the party's campaign; he found himself challenged by those who blamed him for the March setback. One of these, Lee Jong Chan, mounted a strong campaign against him. Lee has good nationalist family connections and a background which includes the Korean Military Academy, the Korean CIA, diplomacy and a mildly radical approach to social issues, thus neatly combining orthodoxy and a new image. Before the DLP's nominating convention in May, however, he dropped out of the race, claiming that President Roh Tae Woo was unfairly supporting Kim Young Sam.

Kim duly received the DLP's nomination, with some 66% of the votes. Even though Lee Jong Chan did not appear at the convention and was officially not a candidate, he still received the support of about a third of the party. Lee must have been encouraged by this showing. After some months of indecision, he left the DLP in August to launch his own party and presidential campaign.

The opposition Democratic Party, as expected, put forward Kim Dae Jung, the veteran whose first try at the presidency had probably been stolen from him by corrupt politics in 1971. Like Kim Young Sam, Kim Dae Jung undoubtedly thought that this, his third campaign, would be his last shot at the presidency, and he deliberately distanced himself from his 'radical' past.

The list of candidates was rounded out by Chung Ju Yung, founder of the Hyundai business group and leader of the recently formed United People's Party. The government showed its acute concern over his candidacy, both before and during the campaign, by instigating police inquiries into his alleged illegal Hyundai support and a series of tax investigations directed against both the Chung family and the Hyundai group. There were also allegations of a government smear campaign; Kim Young Sam apologized for some of the wilder attacks. Lee Jong Chan, too, complained of harassment. In an attempt to distance the government from party politics, Roh announced in September that he would leave the DLP and would form a neutral cabinet. The message about government neutrality, however, failed to reach everybody and several officials were caught helping Kim Young Sam.

Showbiz razzamatazz and vague promises marked the actual campaign. Despite some predictions of a close-run result, most commenta-

tors thought that the government machine would ensure victory for
Kim Young Sam but with a low percentage of the vote. Prediction
became even more difficult towards the end with defections from the
DLP and a surprise decision by Lee Jong Chan to withdraw his own
candidacy and to throw his weight behind Chung Ju Yung.

In the event, Kim Young Sam won relatively handsomely, with
41.4% of the vote. Kim Dae Jung came second, with 33.4%, similar to
his share in the 1987 election. Chung Ju Yung trailed a poor third, with
16.1%. Four minor candidates accounted for the rest. Kim Dae Jung
promptly announced his 'retirement' from politics. Chung Ju Yung
also retired and fell out with his party over promised funds. Since most
of the parliamentary members of the party have deserted, the party has
in effect collapsed. Lee Jong Chan's political future is also uncertain.
By the time of the next presidential election, he will be in his sixties
and less able to represent a younger generation. More damaging is the
widespread belief that his frequent changes of position showed poor
political judgement.

Despite the election of a civilian president, there are not likely to be
major changes of policy. Kim Young Sam is essentially a conservative
politician and his association with the government in the last two years
has done nothing to modify this assessment. Hopes that the new
president might introduce an era of reconciliation were quickly dashed
by his insistence that all alleged election violations by the opposition
should be relentlessly pursued. He has promised early action on the
economy and the 'Korean disease', a vaguely defined shorthand for
higher wages, conspicuous consumption and an unwillingness to work
long hours, but so far has done little to translate this into action. Even
his wish to bring new faces into the administration has been less
successful than expected. His first ministerial team drew on new
talents from the universities and journalism, but he suffered a setback
when a number of his choices for cabinet posts were strongly criticized
for corruption, and were forced to resign during the first ten days of his
administration.

In foreign affairs, Roh's 'Nordpolitik' – to establish relations with
communist countries, especially South Korea's neighbours – came to a
triumphant conclusion with the establishment of diplomatic relations
with China in August. Roh visited China in September, when trade,
investment, and science and technology agreements were signed. The
South Koreans were also pleased that China supported their position
on the denuclearization of the Korean peninsula.

Some tensions remain, however. The PRC's first ambassador to
Seoul, for example, caused offence by saying firmly that China had
nothing to apologize for over its part in the Korean War. Yet the new
legal framework should help trade and investment. Bilateral trade is
expected to total US$10 billion in 1992. There are now over 300 South
Korean investment projects in China, and a few small-scale Chinese
investments in South Korea. Both categories are certain to grow, and
other ties will develop. In December, for example, Yonhap news

agency sent the first ever resident South Korean correspondent to China.

Relations with Russia, though less important than in the past, received a boost from President Yeltsin's visit to Seoul in November. The South Koreans welcomed his statements about stopping military sales to North Korea and the 'abrogation or revision' of the 1961 defence treaty between the Soviet Union and North Korea. Yet it was not easy to be sure what he had pledged since both the North Koreans and the Russians later said that the treaty remained in force, though it needed revision. They also welcomed his apology for the shooting-down of Korean Airlines flight KAL 007 in 1983 and his agreement to hand over the aircraft's black box. Some of the positive effect of the gesture was lost when it was discovered that the material handed over was not the original tapes but copies. The Russians later gave the 'original' tapes to the International Civil Aviation Organisation. Fortunately for the Russians, most South Korean anger was directed at their government for failing to realize what had happened, rather than at Yeltsin for deception. In the margins of the Yeltsin visit agreement was reached in theory for the formal resumption of South Korean loans to Russia, but there was some speculation that this might be affected by the dispute over the KAL tapes.

In December South Korea also formalized its relations with Vietnam. South Korean companies have wasted no time in establishing themselves there and will be further helped by an economic and technological cooperation agreement signed in February 1993.

Nordpolitik apart, South Korea's foreign relations moved along familiar grooves. Relations with the United States continued to be strained over trade, with Seoul continuing to resist a true opening of its markets. As expected, further moves took place to increase the role of the South Korean military in the US–South Korean Combined Forces Command, with South Korean generals taking over both the Ground Component Command and the newly established Combined Marine Forces Command in December. While planned US troop withdrawals remain suspended for the present because of North Korea's intransigence over nuclear inspections, many South Koreans fear that President Clinton will in due course resume a programme which is likely to be popular at home, whatever unease it causes in Seoul. Suspicions about US intentions might have been enhanced by the unease felt in South Korea over the anti-Korean feelings displayed in the Los Angeles riots in May 1992.

Roh's concentration on foreign affairs led to some domestic criticism. With hindsight, it is easy to argue that the cost of Nordpolitik has been too great, expecially since Russia now has little influence over North Korea. The president's foreign travels were also scrutinized. A one-day visit to Japan in November, in particular, aroused much domestic hostility. Now that the worldwide recession has begun to be felt, many South Koreans argue that the time the President spent on foreign affairs should have been devoted to the country's economic woes. Growth in 1992 was estimated at 6%, good by world standards but well below that to which South Koreans have grown accustomed. For the last quarter of 1992, it was only 3.1%, the lowest since 1981, with a trade deficit for the third year running. South Koreans noted ruefully that the growth of the country's external trade was lagging well behind rivals such as Taiwan and the PRC. The government has set out plans for a 7% growth in 1993, but attaining this level depends heavily on factors well outside Korean reach.

North Korea: On a Hiding to Nowhere

North Korea has been marching backwards for many years. There was no indication during the past year that the calcification of leadership or policies, which are the chief cause of North Korean malaise, would soon crack. Clearly, until the 80-year-old Kim Il Sung becomes incapacitated or dies, significant change is doubtful. In preparation, some further steps in the steady consolidation of Kim Jong Il's position as his father's successor were taken. In April, he became a marshal, his first military rank, while his father became 'grand marshal'. The South Koreans claimed that a new constitution was adopted in April 1992, and a 'full version' appeared in Seoul in November. The changes reflect Kim Jong Il's elevation to Armed Forces Commander-in-Chief in 1991, the continued emphasis on self-reliance, and provided for economic links with South Korea and other countries. South Korean speculation that Kim Jong Il might be given full power at the December 1992 Supreme People's Assembly (SPA) meeting proved as unfounded as all such previous prophecies.

In the absence of any new thinking, North Korea's economic problems showed no sign of abating. South Korean sources claimed that, after the negative growth that was the hallmark of 1990 and 1991, the economy contracted even further in 1992. There were persistent reports of food and energy shortages. A currency reform in July, probably also connected with economic difficulties, may have amounted to a major devaluation; Japanese and South Korean press reports said it had led to rioting. The North's media routinely denied such reports, but appeals to eat less and to produce more energy seemed to bear them out. Despite the periodic claims that North Korea is on the verge of economic collapse, however, the evidence is inconclusive.

At the same time, there are growing signs that some of North Korea's leaders accept the need for economic reform but remain wary of the threat this would pose to the regime. One sign of change was a partial ministerial reshuffle at the December SPA meeting. Kang Song San, who had been prime minister in the mid-1980s and is particularly associated with the limited economic opening that was attempted during this time, regained the post, and several relatively reform-minded ministers were left in place. Other factors point in the same direction: the emphasis on economic cooperation in the new constitution; the visit by Deputy Prime Minister Kim Dal Hyon to Seoul in July (when he admitted some economic problems existed); and the new and more extensive Joint Venture Law passed in October. There were also efforts to build trade links with Western Europe, the Middle East and South-east Asia, and to re-establish links with the new republics of the former Soviet Union.

The dilemma facing North Korea is highlighted by the Tumen River development project. This brings together China, Russia, the two Koreas, Mongolia and Japan in a scheme to exploit the economic potential of the Tumen River delta, where the Chinese, Russian and North Korean borders meet. It has some United Nations Development Program (UNDP) support. North Korea's enthusiasm for the project, evident at discussion meetings in Vladivostok in August and Beijing in October, is partly economic and partly political. It wants to tap into the economic success of South Korea and Japan, and to apply China's experience of Special Economic Zones, while at the same time keeping potentially disruptive influences far away from Pyongyang and other important cities. North Korea's enthusiasm is not echoed in the other countries, however.

Internationally, it was a difficult year for North Korea: traditional friends began to desert and its attempts to broaden its contacts with the rest of the world were frustrated. The Chinese decision to establish diplomatic relations with South Korea was a major blow, even if long-anticipated. The public reaction was mild, reflecting an awareness that North Korea has few friends left. Privately, the North Koreans were furious. Continued Chinese professions of support and friendship have a hollow ring, for the Chinese have made it clear that 'friendship prices' are over. From January 1993, the Chinese will only trade with North Korea on a cash basis.

There was no progress in the talks with Japan. The 'comfort women' issue (revolving around the mostly Asian, and particularly Korean, women forced to provide sexual services for Japanese troops during the Second World War), the alleged kidnapping of a Japanese woman for terrorist training, and nuclear questions dominated acrimonious exchanges until the North Koreans walked out of the negotiations in November. The Japanese Defense Agency expressed concern over North Korea's long-range missile capability, indicating a possible further obstacle on the road to normalization. The North Koreans responded with allegations of a Japanese nuclear build-up. The departure from the Japanese political scene of the veteran Liberal Democratic Party vice-president Shin Kanemaru has not helped the North Korean cause. Kanemaru's visit to Pyongyang in September 1990 led to the opening of negotiations, and the North Koreans have few friends of such standing in Japan.

Low-key talks with the United States continued in Beijing. There was no progress despite conciliatory moves such as the return in May of the remains of US soldiers killed in the Korean War. Senator Robert

Smith went to Pyongyang in December 1992 to discuss the emotive subject of Missing In Action (MIA), with a team that included the first US State Department official to visit North Korea since the Korean War. However, although the North Koreans have returned some bones they claim are American remains, thus far they have been unable to exploit the MIA issue. They reacted angrily to US allegations that they were developing a chemical and biological warfare capacity and to various joint South Korean–US military exercises.

Pyongyang has also protested at US Treasury measures which froze North Korean assets in the United States. The relevant regulations date from 1959 but there were no assets to be affected until the collapse of North Korea's traditional trade relations with the USSR and China. The technicality of the argument was not one to impress the North Koreans. In addition, hopes that President Clinton might take a more flexible attitude than Bush were dashed when the new administration refused visas to a North Korean parliamentary delegation in early February 1993.

What Are They Up To?

A major impediment to any improvement in North Korea's international relations is the still unresolved question of its nuclear intentions. Despite much discussion and five IAEA inspection visits to North Korea, the issue continues to poison the atmosphere. Frustration at the North's refusal to allow North–South mutual inspection, as agreed in December 1991, led the US and South Korea to announce the resumption of the *Team Spirit* exercise in 1993. The North promptly called off scheduled talks with the South on the nuclear question, arguing that the exercise was 'nuclear blackmail' and would increase the danger of nuclear conflict on the peninsula. Although the 12th meeting of the Joint Nuclear Control Committee took place at Panmunjom on 10 December 1992, the two sides discussed nothing but the proposed exercise.

The IAEA inspections sent mixed signals. The Supreme People's Assembly ratified the inspection agreement on 9 April 1992, and the North began cooperating with the IAEA immediately. An initial 100-page North Korean report giving details of nuclear installations was submitted on 14 April, but rather than quieting speculation it raised further questions, for it disclosed hitherto unsuspected installations. The first inspection began in May. The teams reported a high degree of cooperation from the North Korean authorities, but this impression was spoiled by their certainty that some of the facilities at Yongbyon were originally for purposes other than those stated. What the North Koreans termed a 'radiochemical laboratory', for example, was probably a reprocessing plant.

According to the IAEA, what evidence it could see indicated that whatever the original plans, most nuclear experiments seemed to have been small-scale and the projects had been abandoned. The last inspection visit of 1992, from 14–19 December, produced a list of further work, but when the IAEA asked to inspect certain sealed sites at Yongbyon in January 1993, the North Koreans refused. This led to renewed international demands that the North Koreans comply with IAEA requirements.

The lack of precision of the IAEA findings had led to unconfirmed speculation that the North Koreans had hidden some aspects of their nuclear programme. North Koreans at all levels regularly denied that they had been or were in the process of developing nuclear weapons, and the Director of the US Arms Control and Disarmament Agency said in November that he now thought that there was little likelihood of the North Koreans developing nuclear weapons. Less sanguine comments continued to come from other sections of the US government, however, and from Japan. Such doubts are likely to be re-enforced if the North Koreans do not resume cooperation with the IAEA. Despite continued IAEA demands to inspect the sealed sites at Yongbyon, the North Koreans remained firm. When the IAEA issued a demand for compliance by 25 March, North Korea announced its withdrawal from the NPT. Although the IAEA extended its deadline to 31 March, North Korea still refused all further cooperation with the IAEA, giving US–South Korean nuclear war threats and the alleged US manipulation of the IAEA as reasons for its actions. Although some commentators in the West called for drastic action to force North Korea to reconsider, calmer voices have so far prevailed. The US resumed talks with the North Koreans in Beijing on 17 March, while even in South Korea there were warnings about the danger of pushing the North too far.

The Fading Relationship

The dialogue between North and South Korea, which had generated some hope in 1991, came to a halt in the autumn of 1992. A seventh round of prime ministers' talks had been held in Seoul in May and an eighth in Pyongyang in September. But the ninth, which was due to take place in Seoul in December, was cancelled by the North once the outcome of the South Korean election was known. Pyongyang was obviously disappointed in the results and this, coupled with the need to assess the position the new American administration might take, seems to have given them pause.

Although they were constantly overshadowed by the nuclear question, the talks which did take place were outwardly cordial. At the seventh meeting, the two sides reached agreement on the establishment of liaison offices at Panmunjom, three joint commissions for the promotion of non-aggression and reconciliation, and an exchange of visits between people over 50 to mark National Liberation Day on 15 August. The exchange groups were to be accompanied by 70 performing artists and 70 journalists. Like so many similar proposals in recent years, this one quickly sank into a bog of detail and mutual recriminations.

What were seen as North Korea's delaying tactics led to increasing exasperation in some quarters in the South. Those favouring a harder line towards the North had their position strengthened by two incidents. In May, three North Korean soldiers, apparently on a reconnaissance patrol, were killed in an exchange of fire when they crossed into the southern part of the Demilitarized Zone. Although the signs were that this was probably a local initiative, and those killed were not equipped for a serious penetration exercise, it was portrayed in the South as a deliberate undermining of the North–South dialogue. The North's refusal to attend a Military Armistice Committee meeting called to discuss the incident did not lighten the atmosphere.

Despite this incident, the September prime ministerial talks went well, and a number of important subsidiary agreements were signed. Then in early October the South Korean Agency for National Security Planning – the former Korean CIA – announced the arrest of 62 people connected with what it described as a long-established North Korean spy ring. Some of those involved were said to have links with South Korean opposition groups. The South promptly cancelled a planned visit to the North by its deputy prime minister and the dialogue stopped. Suspicions about the North's intentions, and continued uncertainty over the nuclear issue, may account for a downturn in intra-Korean trade, which only increased by 1.4% to $194.92m in the period January to November. The same suspicions bolstered the South Korean defence ministry's case that there should be no cuts in the defence budget.

Once Again Around the Ginseng Bush

Despite the complications created by North Korea's threatened withdrawal from the NPT, there is a widespread belief in South Korea that the North will propose a resumption of the dialogue in late April or May, once *Team Spirit* is out of the way. By then, the North will have had time to assess the policies of both Kim Young Sam and Bill Clinton, and its own new ministerial team will have settled in. As well as international pressure over nuclear issues, the North's need for economic assistance is seen as a powerful factor in bringing it back to the negotiating table.

South Korea is likely to accept such a proposal, but the North may find the going tougher than it has been recently. In addition, Kim Young Sam is not under the same constraints as Roh Tae Woo. He has five years in which to make his mark and feels no need to rush. Dialogue with the North was not high on his election agenda and is unlikely to be a first priority. His first statements on the North, made before he took over as president, were an uncompromising demand that it improve its human rights' record and implement the mutual nuclear inspection agreement, or else risk UN Security Council involvement. The South Koreans will try to persuade the North to rejoin the NPT and to resume nuclear inspections, with economic assistance as the carrot. The Clinton administration, which otherwise has little interest in North Korea, will attempt to strengthen South Korean resolve and maintain international solidarity on the nuclear issue.

There are ways out of the current difficulties. The 1991–92 agreements are still in place and can be reactivated. If the IAEA inspections are resumed, it should be possible to find a face-saving formula for the North–South joint nuclear inspection. Alternatively, the North–South nuclear agreement might provide an initial way around the IAEA/NPT impasse. Without a basic change in the troglodyte North Korean regime, however, the Korean peninsula looks set for a period of further insecurity.

SECURITY DILEMMAS IN SOUTH-EAST ASIA

An appropriate regional slogan for post-Cold War South-east Asia could well be that for every solution there is a problem. The Cambodian conflict has been settled as an issue among global and regional powers, even if the attempt by the United Nations to implement the peace agreement reached in Paris in October 1991 has run into acute local difficulty. Cambodia has been replaced as the most foreboding regional issue by the rumbling and potentially explosive contention over conflicting claims in the South China Sea.

Moreover, the regional pattern of power has begun to change significantly from that which existed during the Cambodian conflict, when it was possible to mobilize a countervailing alignment of states against a forcible challenge to the territorial status quo. By itself the Association of South-East Asian Nations (ASEAN), which engages in political cooperation for common security, is not capable of responding collectively to such a challenge, but no alternative structure involving external states is available. The Five Power Defence Arrangements between Malaysia, Singapore, the UK, Australia and New Zealand have endured more than two decades, but this limited consultative provision for security is not a basis for wider regional association.

During the Cold War, regional and global conflicts had been coupled together and fed off one another. With the Cold War's end, Southeast Asia has not been detached from global rivalry; rather global rivalry has ceased to exist as a point of reference for regional conflict. During the 1980s, the Cambodian conflict attracted a pattern of competing alignments which had formed logically from concurrent Sino-Soviet antagonism and Sino-American reconciliation in the early 1970s, as well as from the failure of Soviet–American détente. With the formal settlement of the Cambodian conflict as one result of the end of the Cold War, and, importantly, Vietnam's accommodation to China, that distinctive and complex interwoven pattern no longer exists.

The disintegration of the USSR has removed one external makeweight from the regional balance of power. This was pointed up by the withdrawal of all but a vestige of the Soviet military presence from Cam Ranh Bay in Vietnam. The United States was unable to negotiate acceptable terms for the continuing use of military bases in the Philippines and, with some alacrity because it fitted with the revision of strategic priorities as the Cold War ended, the last of its troops were withdrawn in November 1992. Although limited access to forward military and repair facilities has been agreed with Singapore, Indonesia, Malaysia and Brunei, the American commitment to the projection of military power in East Asia has been cast into further doubt.

Japan has broken with long-standing practice by sending a military contingent to participate in United Nations peacekeeping in Cambodia, but not to engage in military duties. The domestic and regional controversy over that initiative militates against an active Japanese regional security role beyond economic and diplomatic engagement. By contrast, China has displayed in the South China Sea a creeping assertiveness at the expense of an enfeebled Vietnam, underpinned by a programme of rearmament for its air and naval forces. What is most worrying is that the rearmament has been undertaken at a time when the People's Republic is more secure against external threat than at any time since its formation in 1949.

Although Vietnam and Laos have been accepted as virtual candidate members of ASEAN, the potential expansion of the Association does not portend a new regional order. ASEAN has always lacked the common strategic perspective required to ensure any deployment of collective countervailing power as a basis for managing regional security. Nor does it enjoy the prospect of access to acceptable external sources of such power which might engender confidence in an evolving regional order with external actors in a constructive role.

Impasse in Cambodia

In Paris in October 1991, the Cambodian conflict was settled formally under the auspices of the United Nations Security Council. By finessing an intractable problem of internal power-sharing the UN acquired a mandate to engage in law-and-order peacekeeping preliminary to elections which it would conduct to determine the political future of the country. The vehicle for overcoming the problem of power-sharing was a Supreme National Council (SNC) on which all four warring Cambodian factions (the communist Cambodian government; the *Khmer Rouge*; the forces under Son Sann; and Sihanouk's forces) were to be represented under the chairmanship of Prince Norodom Sihanouk. In the Paris Agreement, the SNC was defined as the unique legitimate body and source of authority in which, throughout the transitional period before elections for a constituent assembly, the sovereignty, independence and unity of Cambodia would be enshrined. It was carefully not defined as a government.

The United Nations Transitional Authority in Cambodia (UNTAC) acquired its mandate by having the SNC delegate to it all powers necessary for implementing the Paris Agreement, especially to ensure a neutral political environment conducive to so-called free and fair general elections. To that end, five key ministries of the Phnom Penh government were specifically put under the 'direct supervision or control' of the UN so that the elections planned for May 1993 would take place in such an environment.

The operation, involving around 22,000 military and civilian personnel at a cost in the first instance of some US$1.8 billion, is the most ambitious and expensive ever undertaken by the UN. UNTAC began the first substantive phase of its operation, that of policing the cease-fire which the Paris Agreement had established, from March 1992. However, the second, and equally critical, military phase of the operation which should have begun in June 1992 has not been effectively implemented.

This difficult phase was to have seen to the regroupment, cantonment and disarmament of least 70% of the forces of each of the warring factions once the cease-fire was stabilized, with the remaining 30% to be incorporated eventually into a new national army. The Phnom Penh government and the two non-communist factions did cooperate to a limited extent in this exercise, but this was not matched by the *Khmer Rouge* which refused to regroup and disarm its forces. The *Khmer Rouge* also denied UN personnel entry into its enclaves to register electors. These enclaves have been expanded in violation of the cease-fire to some 15–20% of Cambodia's territory, containing around 10% of the population of some eight million.

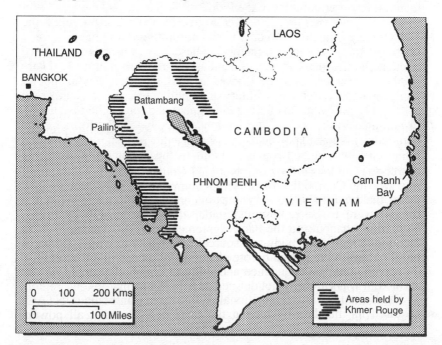

By November 1992, on the grounds that the UN had not addressed the issue of the Vietnamese presence in Cambodia and had not replaced the Phnom Penh administration with the SNC, the *Khmer Rouge* refused also to participate in the elections deemed the ultimate key to a political solution. It had not registered for those elections by the closing date of 27 January 1993.

The charge that UNTAC was collaborating with the Phnom Penh regime in serving the interests of Vietnamese aggressors indicated that *Khmer Rouge* expectations of the peace process had been misplaced. It had consistently sought not only to remove Vietnam's military presence from Cambodia, but also its political legacy in the form of the government implanted in Phnom Penh in January 1979. The United Nations operation has not dismantled the Phnom Penh government. On the contrary, UNTAC has been obliged to cooperate with it and thereby has bolstered its position. This infuriated the *Khmer Rouge* which, like all the other factions, has participated in the Paris Agreement only in order to exercise power exclusively, not to share it with hated adversaries.

By its conduct, the Khmer Rouge has made it quite clear that it is determined to frustrate the peace settlement. It almost certainly does not have the capability to effect a direct military seizure of power, but seems to hope to gain power again through a strategy of attrition. It has tested the mettle of UN peacekeeping efforts to its satisfaction without suffering any tangible penalty. It intends to wear down the will of the contributors to UNTAC so that they tire of expending human and material resources and leave the field.

On 30 November 1992, *Khmer Rouge* recalcitrance provoked the UN Security Council (with only China abstaining) into imposing trade sanctions from the end of December. These, however, could only have a token significance because of Thailand's ambivalent attitude. There had been considerable political violence in Bangkok in May in another confrontation between the military and civilian forces over democratization. The intervention of King Phumiphol had forced the resignation of non-elected Prime Minister Suchinda Krapayoon, the former army commander who had played a central role in the military coup of 1991. Fresh elections in September resulted in the appointment as prime minister of Chuan Leekpai, leader of the Democrat Party.

Even though this change of regime in Bangkok brought an evident downgrading of the role of the military, it did not make a fundamental difference to Thailand's strategic perspective. Newly appointed Foreign Minister, Prasong Soonsiri, had been Secretary-General of the National Security Council during the 1980s when Thailand pursued a hardline policy against the Cambodian government in an attempt to redress the balance of power in Indochina. That policy, informed by competition with Vietnam for influence in the trans-Mekong region, has not changed. It explains in large part the studied equivocal response of the Thai government to the decision by the United Nations

Prince Sihanouk's complaint drew attention to growing suspicions that the *Khmer Rouge* were not the only Cambodian party seeking to pervert the peace process. In addition, it may be construed as part of a lobbying exercise to revise UNTAC's mandate in his interest. Should Prince Sihanouk stand in a presidential election, he would not be opposed by any other candidate, while the *Khmer Rouge* would find it difficult to repudiate the outcome. Support for such an election has come from the foreign ministers of Australia and the ASEAN states who, in some desperation, see it as the only way to promote a legitimate government in Cambodia.

Although Sihanouk is the only solution at the moment, paradoxically he is no real solution. Even if he were successful, at best he would only give Cambodia and the UN a political breathing space. Prince Sihanouk's temperament and record do not provide any guarantee of a stable order. He turned 70 at the end of October 1992 and has been in mixed health. His election as president would not solve the critical problem of political institutionalization which the UN role was intended to address.

A Security Role for ASEAN?

The formal settlement of the Cambodian conflict in Paris in October 1991 demonstrated the marginal diplomatic role of ASEAN, which during the 1980s had taken the lead in keeping an international spotlight on the issue. ASEAN had been effective in appearing to lead a strategy of attrition against Vietnam because it had been a complementary party to an alignment (including China and the US) which had been able to impose military and economic sanctions. ASEAN's diplomatic role was only able to serve a regional security purpose in the context of that alignment. The end of the Cold War and the settlement of the Cambodian conflict under the aegis of the UN Security Council has changed that context and exposed ASEAN's intrinsic limitations as a security organization.

In January 1992, the fourth meeting of ASEAN's heads of government convened in Singapore. In the concluding declaration a request by Vietnam and Laos to accede to the Treaty of Amity and Cooperation which had founded the Association in February 1976 was warmly welcomed as a way of providing 'a common framework for wider regional cooperation embracing the whole of Southeast Asia'. The original treaty includes a code of conduct for orderly regional relationships and incorporates provisions for dispute settlement, but they have never been invoked.

The six heads of government instead addressed other possible ways of promoting common security. Above all, it was suggested that annual post-ministerial conferences with external dialogue partners among industrialized states should be used to discuss regional security issues. In addition, declaratory goals of a Zone of Peace, Freedom and Neutrality, and of a South-East Asian Nuclear Weapons-Free Zone were reaffirmed, but pointedly 'in consultation with friendly countries, taking into account changing circumstances'. The six also made a commitment to an ASEAN Free Trade Area to be established progressively over 15 years from January 1993 in order to overcome a problem of credibility arising from the contrast between its declaratory goals and operational experience.

By the time the Foreign Ministers of ASEAN convened in Manila in July 1992 for their annual meeting, President Corazon Aquino had been succeeded by her nominee and former Defence Minister, Fidel Ramos. In elections in May he had defeated six other candidates with only 23.6% of the vote. Despite obtaining the narrowest electoral margin ever and being the first Protestant president, Fidel Ramos' assumption of executive office did not lead to any notable discontinuity in policies.

The legalizing of the Philippine Communist Party at the beginning of September indicated an improved state of internal security. In the middle of the month, President Ramos affirmed that he would not pursue the long-standing claim of the Philippines to Sabah which is part of Malaysia, a fellow member of ASEAN. On 30 September, the American Navy decommissioned the Subic Bay naval base which had long been the major supply and repair centre for its Seventh Fleet. Cubi Point Naval Air Station was returned to Filipino jurisdiction on 24 November, bringing the American military presence to a complete end.

In Manila, ASEAN's foreign ministers addressed a major issue of regional security which had arisen in the South China Sea. For many years, China has asserted its sovereignty over the Spratly islands. Although the Chinese claims are in contention with Vietnam in particular, claims to some of the islands are also advanced by three members of ASEAN – Brunei, Malaysia and the Philippines. China had begun physically to challenge Vietnam's measure of control in March 1988, when it saw off Vietnamese forces in a short, sharp battle.

In February 1992, the Standing Committee of China's National People's Congress adopted a new law on territorial waters and their contiguous areas which reaffirmed China's claim to various islands in the South China Sea. The promulgation of that new maritime law was followed by China's occupation of additional islands in the Spratly archipelago, but not any of those claimed by ASEAN states. In addition, China appeared to act to exploit the persisting alienation in American–Vietnamese relations which remained when President Clinton took office in January 1993. In May 1992, the Chinese authorities entered into a contract with the Denver-based Crestone Energy Corporation for it to explore for oil and natural gas in some 25,000 square kilometres of what the Vietnamese claimed was the Tu Chinh Bank, 80 nautical miles off their southern coast within the country's continental shelf.

Although Li Peng's visit to Vietnam at the end of November 1992, the first by a Chinese prime minister in 21 years, was said to have taken place 'in an atmosphere of friendship, sincerity, frankness and mutual respect and understanding', basic differences over jurisdiction in the South China Sea were not resolved. Moreover, his attempt to allay fears that China was engaged in trying to fill a regional power vacuum failed to stop the defence ministers of Indonesia and Singapore from openly voicing suspicions of China's intentions.

When ASEAN's foreign ministers sought to address the tangled issue of the Spratly Islands, they did so in the full knowledge that the Association had never aspired to the role of an alliance. Its members have neither shared nor demonstrated a common strategic perspective, even during the course of the Cambodian conflict. ASEAN's role as a security organization has always been confined to conflict-avoidance and management among member governments, and to corporate diplomatic initiative beyond its walls.

Following time-honoured custom and practice, the six Foreign Ministers issued a declaration on the South China Sea which called on contending claimants to settle their disputes in a peaceful manner. That declaration demonstrated that ASEAN had rediscovered its collective diplomatic voice in the wake of the settlement of the Cambodian conflict. It met with Vietnam's approval, but with studied reserve on China's part and in no way indicated the emergence of a new regional security regime which might cope with violent challenges to the status quo corresponding to the experience of Cambodia. Moreover, the concerns which led to the promulgation of the declaration did not appear to attract any shared interest on the part of the Bush administration.

In Manila, in July 1992, the Association also formally approved the accession of Vietnam and Laos to its Treaty of Amity and Cooperation and accorded both countries observer status, but without adding more than form to provision for regional security. Discussions on regional security did take place for the first time at the post-ministerial meeting with the Association's dialogue partners, but only on a serial bilateral basis, not as the embryo of an evolving multilateral structure. In a speech in Bangkok in January 1993, Japan's Prime Minister, Kiichi Miyazawa, called on Asian and Pacific nations to 'develop a long-term vision' for regional security. He called for a regional dialogue in which Japan would be prepared to play an active part as opposed to a policeman's role. By way of regional vision, however, ASEAN remains committed to the declaratory goal of a Zone of Peace, Freedom and Neutrality which commands general support because there is not the slightest chance of its operational application.

The Continuing Barriers

ASEAN's role as a manager of regional order is limited because of the very nature of the Association. This limitation has been exposed in Cambodia where members' participation in the UN peacekeeping operation has taken place on an individual and not on a corporate basis. It has been exposed also in the new regional strategic context by developments in the South China Sea. There the question is very much one of a balance of power which ASEAN cannot affect collectively through military means. Several countries, including members of ASEAN as well as China, have acted independently and have employed military force, partly through display and partly through confrontation, to create facts of possession in the Spratlys with which to underpin their position in international law. What distinguishes China's assertiveness is that it has taken place at a distance of some 800 miles from its mainland in the very mediterranean of South-east Asia.

ASEAN faces an acute dilemma with respect to its regional security role. Unless members transform their mixed strategic perspectives into a more homogeneous outlook, buttressed by corporate military capability, it cannot be more than a mechanism for avoiding and managing intramural conflict and for expressing a collective diplomatic voice on regional issues. The very nature and experience of the Association means not only that such change is exceedingly difficult to realize, but also that the kind of change required to enable ASEAN to address new threats to regional security would almost certainly challenge its very identity and viability as a security community with a limited role. Indeed, should any member of ASEAN seek to cause the Association to overreach itself in order to change its regional security role, then the evident success which it has enjoyed over more than a quarter of a century would be jeopardized by intramural discord.

The present distribution of power in South-east Asia has left China as the principal beneficiary of the ending of the Cold War. The change in the nature of conflict in Cambodia has eliminated Vietnam as the dominant power in Indochina. China's assertiveness in the South China Sea has not given rise to a countervailing combination of states which might arrest its drive. In the absence of such a combination, in which the United States would be expected, and required, to play a critical role, regional order will almost certainly be based on an accommodation to Chinese interests.

South and Central Asia

THREATS TO MODERNISM IN SOUTH ASIA

With the ending of the Cold War, it was widely believed that global realignment would ease the diplomatic log-jams that since independence have bedevilled South Asia. More than a year after the Moscow coup and the disintegration of the Soviet Union, however, it is clear that this was at best a pious hope. Indo-Pakistani relations remain hostage to domestic issues, especially Kashmir, while Sino-Indian relations are stalled because of historical mistrust and indifference. More pointedly, the ending of bipolarity has not yet resulted in the much talked about Indo-US *rapprochement*, despite the opening up of India's protected markets to the world economy.

In 1992 national politics in India and Pakistan continued to suffer the extraordinary degrees of social and religious violence that have been the curse of both countries since the mid-1980s. But important differences remained, both in the structure of their political institutions and in the flexibility their elite groups showed in responding to illegitimate and violent pressure. Of the two, it was always thought to be Pakistan, not India, that was the most friable of states, and given the uncertain nature of its Islamic identity, the most likely to crumble.

By contrast, India was strong, democratic and above all secular. While the division of powers between centre and states was an issue – and resulted in endemic violence in most of India's states – the principles of nationalism, the commitment of the Congress Party to secularism and the concepts of a liberal, democratic order were never contested. In a country where over 80% of the population are Hindu, secularism may have been doubted, at times even questioned, but it was never seriously challenged. Even as the Punjab crisis flared, the majority of Sikh opinion still favoured some compromise within the Indian constitution. All this is now in grave doubt.

Indian Politics and the Ayodhya Crisis

In December 1992, the party of revivalist Hinduism, the *Bharatiya Janata Party* (BJP), and its affiliated organization, the *Vishwa Hindhu Parishad* (VHP), shattered India's political system by demolishing a mosque at Ayodhya in the northern state of Uttar Pradesh. The BJP had long claimed that the mosque was on the site of a temple forcibly converted at the time of Emperor Babar, and sacred to the Hindu deity Lord Rama who was born in, and originally ruled, Ayodhya. The demolition of the mosque contravened several edicts of India's Supreme Court, and was the most serious challenge to India's commitment to a secular constitution since Independence in 1947.

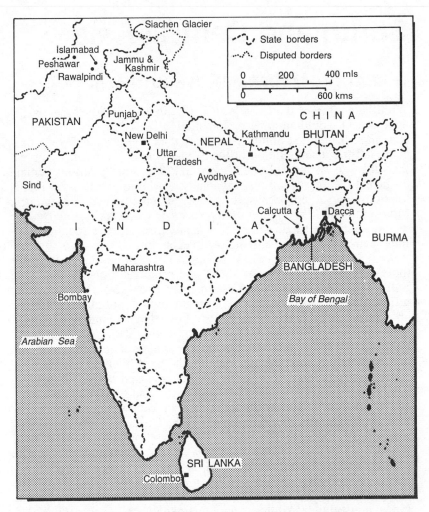

During the summer of 1992 the Supreme Court ordered all construction work around the mosque to stop. Indeed, after widespread violence in July, the VHP undertook to halt construction 'around' the site
until the findings of an all-party committee were published early in
1993. The demolition of the building also ran counter to a similar
undertaking by the VHP to a delegation from India's National Integration Council (NIC) who visited the site in August. Yet attempts by the
NIC to set up all-party talks on the mosque dispute failed in November,
when the BJP and the VHP refused to take part.

The chief minister of Uttar Pradesh's BJP government, Kalyan
Singh, was warned on several occasions by the central government to
comply with the court rulings or to face dismissal. His response was to
outline the difficulties the state authorities would face if and when they

were required by New Delhi to break up crowds of Hindus congregating at Ayodhya. In mid-November, despite the withdrawal of the BJP from the NIC-sponsored multiparty talks, Kalyan Singh promised the central government that the BJP's call for 'volunteers' to assemble at Ayodhya on 6 December was 'purely symbolic', that it would not constitute a threat to the mosque and that construction of the temple would not be resumed.

There is still some dispute about the actual sequence of events which led to the sacking of the mosque on the evening of 6 December. Clearly the state government failed to protect the site adequately and was culpably negligent in allowing the 'volunteers' to destroy a historic building of great value to Hindus and Muslims alike. Disturbing evidence also emerged that the BJP lost control over the 'volunteers', and is currently losing control over the wider movement of Hindu fundamentalism that it has so deliberately fostered. There is some feeling that, far from furthering their electoral aims to take national power from the Congress, the destruction of the mosque at Ayodhya may actually lead to a reaction against the BJP. Yet there was a clear mood of triumphalism among some influential Hindus following the events, and a sense of near-panic amongst middle-class Muslims.

Belatedly, the government of P. V. Narasimha Rao rushed to close the door to conflict. With the damage already done, it sent in the Central Reserve Police to recapture the site, and deployed the army on the streets of most of the towns and cities in north India. Disclosing the degree of panic that had struck New Delhi, the central government rounded on the BJP and on 7 December arrested its national parliamentary leader, R. K. Advani (his arrest in 1990 had brought down the V. P. Singh government). Advani had already accepted responsibility for the incident and had made public his remorse before his arrest: a curious response given the centrality of the Ayodhya dispute to the BJP's image as a Hindu party.

The government then banned several 'extremist' Hindu and Muslim parties. Following the resignation of the Uttar Pradesh government, the centre dismissed the three remaining BJP state governments. These measures were hardly enough to prevent sustained communal rioting throughout northern India, in the western state of Maharashtra and in the city of Bombay. Although the deployment of the army restored a semblance of order, the government appeared confused over its general policy. To the Muslims of India, such diffidence – especially over the rebuilding of the mosque – could prove fatal to their confidence in the government's ability and willingness to defend secularism.

The tragedy of the demolition of the Ayodhya mosque was that it came at the end of a year in which the national government, on the whole, had been exhibiting a calmer and more responsible mood. The government's grip on national power was given a significant boost in February 1992 with the Punjab elections. Either in spite of, or because of, the low turnout (officially put at 28%) and an extensive boycott by all but one of the factions of the *Akali Dal* (the Sikhs' political organization), the Congress-I took 12 of the Punjab's 13 national parliamentary seats. The Congress-I also won the state government, with 87 of the 117 assembly seats.

Before December, Prime Minister Rao was praised as a skilled, consensual politician, conscious of the limitations to Congress power, but aware of the numerous divisions amongst the opposition parties. Unlike the hapless Rajiv Gandhi, he appeared more than capable of exploiting these divisions to achieve his desired policy objectives. The national parliament voted through a radical budget (approved by the International Monetary Fund) in February, successfully elected Shankar Dal Sharma, the candidate sponsored by Congress-I, to the office of Union President in July, and survived two no-confidence motions: one in March over economic strategy, and another in July.

The prime minister even appeared capable of weathering the continuing dramas associated with corruption. When External Affairs Minister Madhavsinh Solanki was involved in an apparent attempt to encourage Swiss agents to 'go slow' in investigating the Bofors scandal, the Rao government resisted parliamentary pressure to resign and satisfied internal opposition by accepting Solanki's offer of resignation. On 9 July, the Finance Minister Palaniappan Chidambaram resigned over a Bombay stock-exchange scandal, which involved irregular fundraising for private companies without adequate securities. The minister had invested savings in a company under investigation. The Reserve Bank of India found in August that the scandal had lost the country around $1,200 million, and had seriously undermined confidence in India's banking and financial institutions. Yet Rao was able to use this to push forward with reform of the banking and financial system on the grounds that liberalization would make them more accountable.

Yet these qualities of leadership, caution and calculation, were the very ones that Rao was denounced for after December, when such an approach appeared to many as diffident and indecisive. The national government's miscalculation over the significance of the 6 December demonstration brought its judgement and commitment to the minorities into question. Many pointed to the proven record of brinkmanship by the BJP as evidence that the government should have reacted firmly to their plans for Ayodhya.

Provincial Passions

The Ayodhya incident sent severe shock waves through the Indian federal system, threatening to disturb the existing political fault-lines in Kashmir, Punjab and the north-east. Kashmir has been a headache for many national governments and it is one which only seems to get more painful. The basis of India's rule in Jammu and Kashmir now depends wholly on the presence of the military, and seems to lack any popular support or even legitimacy. In July, the Indian parliament granted the Union President the law-making powers of the state assembly and cancelled a planned update of the state's electoral register. Such a move implied that the government was still pessimistic about how long it would take to restore elected government in Srinagar, or worse, fatalistic about ever receiving a popular mandate to rule.

Muslim opinion within the province continues to be divided among the Jammu and Kashmir Liberation Front (JKLF), which is separatist and secular in orientation, the Islamic organizations that favour the integration of Jammu and Kashmir into Pakistan, and the pro-Indian factions of the National Conference party. The threat of Hindu fundamentalism in India weakened the government's hold on the state further, since the BJP's position on Kashmir is against Article 370 (which grants 'special status' to the state), and for the large settlement of Hindus in the valley area.

In Punjab and Assam, the Indian government continued to grapple with the problems of ethnic resurgence and acts of terrorism in a seriously deteriorating national situation. In India's troubled northeast, a much proclaimed deal between the United Liberation Front of Assam (ULFA) and the Indian government in January was undermined in March, when extremists within ULFA denounced the organization for striking a deal with the 'genocidal' regime in New Delhi. Even so, the prospects for a settlement between the Assamese and the Indian government, despite continuing realignments within the Assamese themselves and problems of Muslim immigration from Bangladesh, had appeared tantalisingly close until overshadowed by the larger national identity crisis of 6 December.

Although it had been possible to hold elections in the Punjab in mid-February 1992, the state continued to be rent by violence and terrorism. Throughout 1991–92, an average of 600 people were killed a year. In an attempt to demoralize further the machinery of law and order, Sikh terrorists during 1992 expanded their targets from Hindus in general to attack families of Sikh individuals identified as working with the Indian police force or with the army. At the end of the year Amnesty International pinpointed the widespread torture and brutality by India's police force in Punjab, and Jammu and Kashmir. In particular, the report condemned the large number of people detained without trial and the scope of national preventive detention legislation.

As with Kashmir, a national groundswell in favour of the BJP would further alienate Punjab from mainstream politics. The attitude of the various Hindu parties to factions of the *Akali Dal*, and to Sikhism in general, is extraordinary in that they claim Sikhism to be a mere variant of Hindu culture. The official position of the BJP is to reject Sikh calls for greater autonomy in Punjab on the grounds that, as a religion at least, Sikhs are Hindus.

The Threat of Disintegration

After Independence, India adopted a secular constitution to accommodate the minorities, and to fashion a form of statecraft that would give the Congress Party a legitimate claim to the territorial dimensions of the old Raj. If Hindu fundamentalism continues to rise, and more mosques are destroyed, political order in India will disintegrate. To reiterate the agenda of a secular state, secular political parties must be in a position to make common cause against an eclectic, obscurantist appeal to Hindu sentiment. Yet the Congress-I, the parties of the Left Front, and the weakening party of the *Janata Dal*, are divided over economic and foreign policy, making it difficult to reach consensus on other issues.

The record of alliance politics in India is a poor one, given the weak institutional structure of many of the centrist political parties. The temptation for political parties to score political points over the Ayodhya incident against the government is great. At the same time, within the Congress-I itself a potential for division over the extent to which Hindu revivalism should be condemned, and whether or not the BJP should be banned as a communal party, is also great.

The Ayodhya crisis came at a critical stage in India's economic reform programme, when the country was moving towards a greater degree of integration with the world economy, and reform of the public sector generally. Although India's economy appeared to be stabilizing in the summer (with an expected annual growth-rate of 3.5% GNP, up from 2.5% in 1991–92, and a dramatic improvement in India's balance of payments), such growth was threatened by the serious instability and violence that follows from widespread communal violence. 1992 was the worst year for Muslim–Hindu violence in India since Independence, with over 1,400 being killed by the end of the year. India's need to attract important foreign investment requires confidence in India's stability and future performance. The Rao government managed to survive another no-confidence motion on 15 December, but its continued weakness was manifest and deeply worrying.

Pakistan: A Weakening Coalition and Provincial Unrest

Although democracy seemed to have been restored in Pakistan in the elections of 1988, it was in truth only a partial restoration. Endorsement of popular elections remains weakened by the existence of a large and diverse number of parties which are in themselves unable to form a government. The constituent parties of the inevitable national coalitions are often in violent competition with each other for power at the state level. Furthermore political parties must co-exist and compete with a powerful and autonomous military, a powerful bureaucracy, and a national president whose powers of office work independently of the prime minister.

Party politics is further complicated by the ongoing dispute over whether an Islamic Pakistan can be a pluralistic, federal and capitalist state. This unresolved question has haunted Pakistan since its creation. How is an Islamic state to represent those groups who are not Muslims, or whose Islamic interests are subordinate to interests of language or local culture? All of these factors interact in certain policy fields to weaken decision-making or the implementation of policy. The resulting discord makes the Pakistani political process uneven and volatile, and blights any attempts to institutionalize a particular system.

Throughout 1992, the coalition government of Nawaz Sharif was shaken by a sustained political crisis in Sind, its apparent failure to implement meaningful Islamic reform, and popular agitations led by Benazir Bhutto, the leader of the Pakistan People's Party (PPP). In May the *Jamaat-i-Islami* party announced that it would be pulling out of Sharif's Islamic Democratic Alliance (IDA), ostensibly because of disagreements over the government's Afghanistan policy, which shifted support from Gulbuddin Hekmatyar's fundamentalists to more moderate forces. More generally, the *Jamaat* was angered by the government's failure to push forward with the Islamicization of Pakistan's legal and economic system that Sharif had promised in 1990.

Sharif's reluctance to accelerate Islamicization lay in the growing contradiction between an Islamic political and economic system and the requirements of a modern capitalist economy. By February, the future viability of financial reforms, including the important liberalization of the economy, as well as two key development projects, were jeopardized by rulings of the Federal *Sharia* Court stating that the payment of interest was against Islam and therefore illegal. Since he could not amend the constitution to reassure both private and foreign investors, Sharif encouraged several private banks to contest the verdict in order to buy time for his economic strategies, which include the privatization of state-owned companies.

The real test for the Sharif government, however, lay in his conduct of centre–state relations. Throughout 1992, Islamabad was concerned about the climate of violence in Sind and the open warfare between indigenous Sindhi speakers, aligned on the whole with the PPP, and Urdu-speaking *Muhajirs*, who had formed their own party, the *Muhajir Qaumi Movement* (MQM) in 1988. Since becoming prime minister in 1990 Sharif had turned a blind eye to the violence. His party was aligned with the MQM in the national parliament, and the Chief Minister of Sind, Jam Sadiq Ali, was a PPP renegade and a trusted associate of the prime minister. In March Sadiq Akli died, throwing the province into turmoil, but Sharif was reluctant to interfere for fear of upsetting a vital component of the national coalition.

By May politically related crimes, such as kidnapping, killings, abductions and hold-ups, had become so endemic in Sind that the army's Inter-Service Intelligence Unit (ISI), under the newly appointed Lt General Javed Nasir, favoured direct intervention. Later that month, although Sharif disagreed, Pakistan's president and head of the armed forces, Ghulam Ishaq Khan, decided to send the army in to clean up the state's politics.

Sharif tried to target army action against opposition leader Benazir Bhutto, and other personal political opponents such as Mustafa Jatao, the former interim prime minister and a potential rival. The president and army leaned towards a more indiscriminate use of army power. On 19 July the president issued an ordinance that enhanced the army's powers of search and arrest, and granted them immunity from criminal procedures. The army then exposed alleged torture chambers that the MQM used against Sindhis. In protest against what it claimed was government intimidation, and the arrest of MQM MPs, the MQM pulled out of the coalition, further weakening the national government.

The crisis in Sind provided the PPP with its best opportunity to challenge Sharif's national government since it lost the 1990 elections, which it alleges were rigged. It came as no surprise therefore that in July, Benazir Bhutto announced that the PPP was 'abandoning' parliamentary politics and taking to the streets to press for free and fair elections. On 18 November, she led a protest march from Rawalpindi to Islamabad, only to be met by a large police presence and a government determined to use force. While Sharif is clearly anxious to avoid the sort of political stalemate that will bring the army in to play, or force the president to dismiss the government from power, he appreciated that the PPP remains a serious rival to power. In November 1992, with evidence that her campaign was slackening, Sharif held talks with a 'representative' of the PPP and allowed Bhutto to take part in 'national politics' as long as they were peaceful and as long as she stayed in Peshawar. The PPP remains weak and factionalized. Like all South Asian political forces, its strength lies in opposition.

The crisis in Sind has highlighted serious divisions between the prime minister, the army chiefs and the president over which political party should be used to run the province and, more indirectly, which coalition of parties is best able to run the country. Should Sharif lose the confidence of the army and Ishaq Khan, his days in office are limited. Even before the PPP had increased the stakes in November, a new, left-of-centre political alliance, the National Democratic Alliance (NDA), was created in August as a potential alternative to the IDA. The PPP has not yet ruled out the possibility of joining with the NDA in a pre-electoral coalition.

Sharif's credibility and general popularity was further undermined in September. Following heavy monsoons between two and three thousand died in widespread flooding in Punjab and Sind, and 3,000,000 were made homeless. Damage was estimated at between $400m and $2,000m. The national government was criticized by the opposition and by sections of the army for delays in warning areas threatened by flooding, and for holding up relief work.

The Sharif government may have been brought close to the point of collapse during 1992, but the promised restoration of the PPP held out little hope of any significant change for the better, except perhaps in the province of Sind which desperately needs an end to sectarian violence. The crisis of government in Pakistan is essentially a crisis of representation.

Regional Politics

The desecration at Ayodhya had an immediate and debilitating effect on Indo-Pakistani relations, and on India's standing throughout the Islamic world. In August 1992, and more vehemently in December, Pakistan protested both to the United Nations and to the Islamic Conference Organisation (ICO). In Sind and Pakistan's Punjabi districts several Hindu temples were attacked as acts of revenge.

Relations between the two countries had already reached a low ebb. The year had begun with an exchange of pleasantries between Sharif and Rao in Davos, Switzerland, during a January meeting of the World Economic Forum. The two countries even undertook an exchange of intelligence on each other's nuclear installations in accordance with a 1991 agreement. These signs of improvement in relations, however, were soon swamped by new recriminations.

Various statements by Abdur Sattar, Pakistan's High Commissioner to India, over India's 'illegal and illegitimate regime' in Kashmir were published in the Indian paper *The Pioneer* in early February. Expressions of Indian indignation, both publicly and to Sattar by the External Affairs Ministry, did not prevent Pakistan observing a sympathy strike on 5 February in solidarity with their 'Islamic brothers' in Kashmir. This was a useful card for Sharif to play, given the problems over his own Islamic credentials and the ebbing of the Islamic parties from his government coalition.

In a further, more curious twist, the Pakistani government then allowed Amanullah Khan, a leader of the JKLF, to organize a march across the Line of Control (LOC) separating Azad (Pakistani-held) Kashmir, from Indian-controlled Kashmir on 11 February. The JKLF's position on a fully independent Kashmiri state contradicts both India and Pakistan's stated aims towards the province. India seeks to reclaim 'Azad' Kashmir and to integrate it into the Indian Union, while Pakistan seeks to 'reclaim' Kashmir on the basis of the two-nation theory and the fact that Muslims are a majority of its inhabitants.

India briefed the five permanent members of the UN Security Council on its determination to use force to maintain the integrity of the border and cautioned Pakistan to show restraint. On 6 February Sharif 'persuaded' the JKLF not to march into Indian gunfire. Despite his efforts, and the large presence of Pakistani security forces, many JKLF supporters did try to march across the LOC. The affair ended with the Pakistan riposte that by going to the UN India had needlessly internationalized the issue. Given India's sensitivities over the Simla Accord of 1972 and the commitment to bilateralism, if it gained nothing else, Pakistan at least won a clever debating point.

In May relations deteriorated when a senior Indian diplomat was expelled from Pakistan following a statement to an Indian newspaper that he had been kidnapped and tortured for 'spying'. On 25 May the government, still rattled over Kashmir, expelled two senior Pakistani diplomats without adequate explanation. In retaliation, Islamabad cancelled the next round of Indo-Pakistani talks which were to take place in New Delhi on 1 June.

As is so typical of the nature of their relations, however, this outbreak of bad temper was quickly followed by sustained attempts to mediate the crisis. In June both sides agreed to issue a statement over 'diplomatic practice', and by August the air was sufficiently clear to allow the next round of Indo-Pakistani talks to get under way. These were concluded on 19 August with a 'code' of diplomatic conduct and a ban on the use of chemical weapons.

Although Kashmir was discussed at the talks, it was not mentioned in the final communique. It remains a truism that Indo-Pakistani relations will not improve until the Kashmir problem is solved, and in 1992 that solution was as distant as ever. In November the sixth round of Indo-Pakistani talks began in New Delhi, with the foreign ministers attempting to solve the demarcation of the LOC across the disputed Siachen Glacier. The glacier had been scene of serious border violations in 1990–91. Despite encouraging signs, 'technical complications' prevented a breakthrough.

China's Role

During 1991 there had been a few tentative signs that, as a result of the collapse of the Soviet Union and changes in the world security picture, China might be adjusting its relations with India and Pakistan to bring about a better balance than had existed for many years. No real adjustment was carried through, however. Instead, the pace of a Sino-Indian *rapprochement* slackened, while Sino-Pakistani relations, in terms of trade agreements and arms sales, were as close as ever.

In January Pakistan and China announced that they had agreed a new deal on further nuclear cooperation, and the building of a 300-Megawatt nuclear power station at Chashma, a nuclear research institute not far from Islamabad. During a visit to Beijing in October by Nawaz Sharif, it was announced that Pakistan would purchase 40 F-7P Chinese fighter planes. In contrast, although the outgoing Indian Union president visited Beijing in May, the Indian defence minister in July, and a high-level team of diplomats in October for the fifth round of border talks, little of substance seemed to have changed. Nevertheless, the very fact that these meetings, particularly that of the defence minister, took place signalled a significant change of tone in the Sino-Indian relationship.

The ambiguity of these relations, and its consequences for Indo-Pakistani relations generally, were further reinforced on 21 May when China held its largest underground nuclear test. India responded by the second test-firing of its *Agni* intermediate-range missile on 29 May. If armed with nuclear weapons, the missile gives India the delivery system needed to make significant strikes at China. Pakistan used the *Agni* test to argue that, although it was willing to sign the NPT and make South Asia a nuclear-free zone, it could hardly be expected to do so unless India did the same. India continues to insist, however, that it is China, not merely Pakistan, that determines its need for a nuclear option.

Wider Realignments After the Cold War?

As with China, suggestions that India and Pakistan were seeking to adjust their policies towards powers beyond South Asia came to little. The year started with continued efforts to set up a joint US–Indian Army steering committee, and to hold joint naval exercises in the Indian Ocean. In March India resumed high-level talks in Washington over the NPT treaty, and the Missile Technology Control Regime (MTCR) which aims to limit the export of ballistic know-how. In April, Indian Defence Secretary Pawar visited Washington and agreed with his American counterpart, Richard Cheney, on the importance of improving Indo-US relations further.

The US was consequently wrong-footed over an agreement between India and Russia, signed in New Delhi on 4 May, setting up a five-year collaborative project in which Russia would assist India in developing its ballistic and rocket technologies. This, and the *Agni* test in May, clearly violated the spirit, if not the letter, of the MTCR, and jolted American confidence that things had really changed in New Delhi. The test represented not so much India's hostility to the concept of a missile control regime, or the US, but its belief that it had to join a 'ballistics' club before an MTCR freezes out potential membership.

The US responded by threatening to suspend both Russian and Indian aid programmes entirely, and in the interim imposed a two-year ban on 'sensitive' US exports to both countries. In June, however, the Russian Ambassador to India, Anatoly Drukov, confirmed the deal. Indeed, in a statement reminiscent of the 'good old days', a visiting Russian parliamentary delegation to New Delhi, headed by Ruslan Khasbulatov, noted the 'historic ties between India and Russia' and with direct reference to the MTCR noted bluntly that 'no other country will be allowed to interfere' in Indo-Russian cooperation.

It was something of a surprise to some to see how tenaciously India clung to the now separate republics of Russia and Ukraine, with regard to economic and trade agreements, and arms deals. Still anxious about the future of its largely Soviet-made war machine, the defence minister visited Russia in September to conclude a barter arrangement guaranteeing India access to MiG-27 spare parts. Earlier in the year, the

Indian Foreign Secretary J. N. Dixit signed a cooperation and trade agreement which India announced as an extension of the 1971 Treaty of Friendship and Cooperation. Further defence talks took place in Moscow in November between senior members of the Indian air force and navy, amid rumours that India would soon announce the purchase of 20 MiG-29s.

Old allies, even if scarcely recognizable in their new pro-market garb, seemed more reliable than new ones. Talks on the NPT resumed in New Delhi in June, but are unlikely to yield results. Nor is the considerable pressure being exerted by other industrialized countries. Japan told Foreign Secretary Dixit in January that aid would be conditional on India agreeing to the NPT. The UK too, despite signing an extradition treaty between the two countries on 24 September, made appropriate noises about the NPT when Foreign Secretary Douglas Hurd visited New Delhi in mid-January. In September, the French warned the Indian Prime Minister in Paris that extensive technological cooperation with India would only be forthcoming if India signed the NPT and the MTCR. It seems clear, however, that India will not comply until it is satisfied about China's commitment to disarm, and about the true state of Pakistan's nuclear potential.

India's policy towards the new nations in Central Asia also seemed directed as much by the old currents of mistrust over Pakistan, as by any genuinely new and dynamic vision. India reacted mainly to Pakistani initiatives towards the states of Turkmenistan, Uzbekistan, Tajikistan, Kyrgyzstan and Kazakhstan. In February, Pakistan announced that it would maintain embassies throughout the region, and that it would be reviving the joint economic development council set up 27 years ago with Iran and Turkey.

Having identified itself as a main player in Central Asia, Pakistan was quickly engulfed in wider Turkish–Iranian competition. At a post-communist summit held in the capital of Kyrgyzstan on 22 April, the Central Asian republics agreed that their future lay in following a secular, pro-market, essentially pro-Turkish route. If followed through, such a policy would limit Iranian and Pakistani influences which are perceived as being Islamic and confessional.

Nevertheless, in early July, Pakistan signed a trade agreement with Tajikistan, and followed it up on 20 July with an agreement with Afghanistan and Uzbekistan on a road-building and communications programme. In contrast, India's response seemed slow. It was not until September that the Minister of State for External Affairs went on a whistle-stop tour of the Central Asian republics, signing trade agreements with Kyrgyzstan and Uzbekistan, and holding 'joint security' talks with Kazakhstan the next month.

As with India, the continuity in Pakistan's policies within the wider international system is striking. Throughout 1992, Islamabad tried hard to work itself back into the American embrace. Since 1990 Pakistan has faced a problem that mirrors India's. Just as the collapse of Soviet military and economic aid caused difficulties for India's military, the suspension of US military and economic aid threatens Pakistan's military machine with a scarcity of spare parts, especially for its F-16 squadron.

On an official visit to Islamabad in January 1992, US Naval Chief of Staff Admiral Frank Kelso expressed the need for the two countries to come to some 'objective understanding' over the problems posed by the NPT and the Pressler Amendment. Such views were later expressed during a 'private' visit to Washington by Pakistan's Army Chief of Staff, General Asif Nawaz Janjua. That such problems exist were underscored by Senator Larry Pressler's visit to India and Pakistan between 12–15 January, in which he asserted that, in his opinion, Pakistan had the ability to construct one or two fissile devices 'immediately a decision was made'.

The pot was stirred further by a *Washington Post* article on 7 February citing a statement to the Pakistani National Assembly by Shahryar Khan, the Secretary of Foreign Affairs, to the effect that Pakistan was only a screwdriver turn away from the bomb. Khan was, at the time, visiting Washington to convince the US that they did not have it. He later said that the *Washington Post* had quoted him 'out of context'.

Despite these obstacles, Pakistan's single-minded search for arms achieved results. Moreover, in the face of India's intransigence, America's hard stance against Pakistan seemed like bias. By the end of the year, not only had Nawaz Sharif negotiated in Paris for the sale of 40 *Mirage* 2000 fighter bombers, the country had moved close to the French on a whole series of conventional defence contracts. Because of its reservations over Pakistan's position on the bomb, the French government, unlike the Chinese, had drawn the line at assisting Pakistan's civilian nuclear power programme.

Notwithstanding the 'nuclear problem', 25 years of involvement between the US and Pakistan must, and clearly does, remain important. Although a Democratic presidency could reinforce the pro-Indian lobby, Indian attitudes towards Washington may well prove decisive. Moreover, as the US seeks to define its wider regional priorities in the post-Cold War environment, Pakistan may be considered a more useful ally than India.

The Clouds Gather

Given the peculiarities of the region, it should not be surprising that South Asia is slow to respond to broad changes within the international system. Nonetheless, the degree of continuity is unexpected, especially with regard to India. India's fundamental changes in economic strategy seek to bring it through the crucible of the IMF and the World Bank into the international trading system. The recent switch to pro-market strategies, evidenced by the 1992 budget removal of large subsidies, the reformation of the tax system and the lifting in September of ceilings on foreign investment, have wider consequences for India's attitude towards the NPT, and towards Pakistan and China, which have yet to be realized. Admittedly, Japan's attempts to link much-needed aid with Indian compliance with the NPT failed. At a heads-of-state meeting in Tokyo between 22 and 26 June, in the face of Japanese pressure, India garnered pledges of $850m.

Other pressures remain. The IMF's conditions explicitly limit India's defence spending to under 4% of GNP. The Aid to India Consortium, when it announced in April an enhanced aid package, made it subject to India continuing its liberalization strategies. General Motors had signed a $30m collaborative project in February, as have other electrical and telecommunication companies. To antagonize the US administration would be to risk losing access to the types and range of technological equipment India needs not just to be a military power, but to be a modern economy.

The same can be said of Pakistan, where the economy faces problems of the incompatibility of Islamic laws and a free-market economy, as well as persistent levels of social and religious violence. Both states are tarnished by the image of corruption, and suffer the prospects that de-regulation and inexperience will, in the short term at least, increase the opportunities for making black money. Even if both can continue to receive aid and technological help from the West, it is difficult to have much confidence in their ability to overcome their economic failings.

The most serious crisis for South Asia as a region lies, however, in the ramifications of the Ayodhya debacle. It is not just a crisis for India, but for Indo-Pakistani relations in particular, and for South Asia's position in the world generally. Pakistan has provided a model for the tragic misuse of Islamic ideology to create a bogus state structure, authoritarian, unresponsive to provincial needs, and with little claim to legitimacy. That another such undertaking, tied to the even more elusive concept of the Hindu *Rashtra*, may soon begin in India fills many Indian commentators with near despair. There is a great danger that the long Nehruvian adventure, which combined economic development with secularism and democracy, is coming to a close.

REALIGNMENT IN CENTRAL ASIA

Ethnicity and factionalism, rather than the ideologies that set the tone of the last decade, appear to be reshaping Central Asia. Fundamentalism and communism, the avowed opponents during the Afghan War, no longer play a significant role. Yet, although national identities will develop from ethnic lines, this process is just barely under way. At the moment, local loyalties, patron–client relationships, tribalism and factionalism based on geographic origins are slowing and hampering

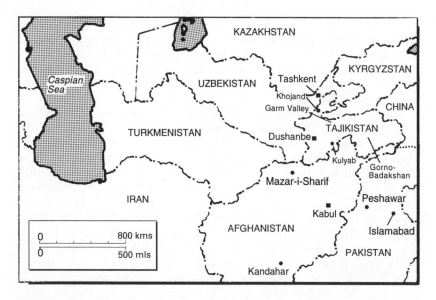

the general reshuffling along ethnic, linguistic and sectarian (Shi'a/ Sunni) lines.

This can be seen most clearly in Afghanistan, but it is a common evolution throughout Central Asia. To succeed in the traditional societies which exist in Central Asia, communist regimes had to root themselves in ethnic nationalism and tribal or clan loyalties. Islamic fundamentalism, after its peak in the 1980s, has turned from a political factor to a more socio-cultural instrument, which can be played by any regime. The promotion of Islamic symbols, such as mosques and the veil for women, has little to do with political programmes and alliances.

Fundamentalist parties have lost their specific ideological clout. In Afghanistan, the Tajik commander Ahmed Shah Masud and the Pashtun leader Gulbuddin Hekmatyar, both Islamic fundamentalists, have allied with former communists from similar ethnic backgrounds to fight each other. In Tajikistan, the vicious fighting is not so much a question of 'Islamicists' against 'communists' as a settling of accounts between geographical entities (Khojent and Kulyab against Garm and Pamir). The disintegration of the grasp of ideologies on developments has been vividly illustrated by the recrudescence of traditional ethnic, tribal and geographic passions in the recent history of Afghanistan and Tajikistan.

From the Collapse of Communism . . .

On 25 April 1992, the Afghan *Mujaheddin* seized Kabul, putting an end to a communist regime that the USSR had installed and supported for 14 years. The regime had been doomed from the collapse of the

Soviet Union; it was only a matter of how long it would take. Until the end of 1991, Benon Sevan, the UN special envoy who was trying to negotiate a political settlement, had advocated a role for President Najibullah. But even he acknowledged in February 1992 that the president's fate was sealed, thus contributing to undermining his remaining power.

Even so the suddenness of Najibullah's fall came as a surprise. A vital contributing factor was the realignment of the political coalitions opposing one another from ideological bases (communism versus Islam) to ethnic identities (mainly Pashtun versus non-Pashtun). This trend, which had lain dormant during the effort to oust the Soviet troops from Afghanistan, re-emerged when they withdrew in February 1989.

The final crisis was triggered by a move by President Najibullah in February 1992 to enhance Pashtun control over his northern troops and militia-men. He appointed a Pashtun general in Mazar-i Sharif in place of the Tajik general Abdul Momin, and tried to reduce the influence of Rashid Dustom, the leader of the northern pro-government Uzbek militia. Both men, joined by another previously pro-regime local leader Sayd Jaffar Naderi, head of the Persian-speaking Ismaïli militia posted on the northern end of the Salang Pass, revolted in April. The three made an alliance with the Tajik Masud, leader of the *Mujaheddin* 'Supervisory Council' which controls the main part of north-east Afghanistan.

This non-Pashtun northern coalition quickly took the regional capital Mazar-i Sharif and headed south towards Kabul. The remaining communist leaders there also split along ethnic lines: Tajikis, like General Mohammed Nabi Azimi, commander of the Kabul garrison, and Abdul Wakil, Minister of Foreign Affairs, helped the northern coalition to take the city, while Pashtuns, like Interior Minister Mohammed Pakteen, gave support to Gulbuddin Hekmatyar. Such a realignment along ethnic lines had been anticipated by Hekmatyar as early as 1990 when he had made an alliance with the former Minister of Defence Shahnawaz Tana'y, a hardline communist but also a die-hard Pashtun.

Dustom and Masud established a joint military command in Kabul on 25 April, but declared that they were ready to accept any government set up by the *Mujaheddin* coalition. Although the Peshawar-based *Mujaheddin* parties were not prepared for the sudden fall of Kabul, most of them, encouraged by Pakistan, were surprisingly prompt to answer the call. They settled on Professor Seghbatullah Mojaddedi as president of a provisional Leadership Council. He arrived in Kabul on 29 April, appointed Masud Minister of Defence and made Dustom a full general. Hekmatyar, who opposed this arrangement, was driven out of Kabul after a few days of battle. He established his bases in Logar Province and began a regular shelling of the capital.

Hekmatyar has since fought against all the governments established in Kabul. He has used both ideological arguments, condemning the coalition between Masud and former communist leaders like Dustom, and ethnic loyalties, criticizing the share of control of non-Pashtuns over the new government.

Despite this, Hekmatyar has been unable to unite Pashtuns against the northern coalition. Six of the seven parties based in Peshawar are mainly Pashtun; the exception is the *Jamiat-i Islami* under the leadership of the Tajik Burhanuddin Rabbani. The constituencies of these parties combine ideological and tribal loyalties which prevent the construction of an all-Pashtun coalition. Among Pashtuns the tribal factor remains a key element. The core of Hekmatyar's support comes from the Ghilzay and eastern Pashtun tribes. The southern Durrani tribal confederation, which formed the Afghan dynasties from 1747 to 1978, is strongly opposed to Hekmatyar, who lacks connections with this traditional tribal aristocracy. And he could not even count on full support from all the Ghilzay and eastern Pashtuns. Jadran, Safi, Wardak and some other tribes supported their own local commanders. Some Pashtun leaders, like Abdul Rab Sayyaf and Jellaluddin Haqqani, get direct foreign support from Pakistan and Saudi Arabia, and have been eager to keep a certain distance from Hekmatyar.

While the struggle for the capital raged for almost a year, the provinces remained relatively stable and peaceful. The endurance of the local powers is remarkable, particularly when compared with Kabul. The *Mujaheddin* commanders who took control of the regional provinces in 1992 are the same men or their sons (i.e., Ismaïl Khan in the west or the son of Hajji Latif in Kandahar) as those who had held the surrounding areas since 1980. These regional powers are not separatist. They all acknowledge that there should be a central, if weak, government in Kabul, while they themselves have no interest in contending for the central power.

... To Anarchy in Kabul

This complex situation provided much room for political manoeuvres, based on a constant reshuffling of tactical alliances among the different actors. The Afghan Islamic Government, established by the *Mujaheddin*, was headed from May to June 1992 by Mojaddedi, and then by Burhanuddin Rabbani. The government was merely a nominal umbrella organization. Ministries, as well as Kabul districts, were distributed, or sometimes simply taken by arms, along political and sectarian lines. The capital was consistently shelled by Hekmatyar's troops, while internecine feuds regularly broke out, opposing former allies and bringing together former foes. The main military forces in Kabul were Masud's troops (Tajiks from the north-east *Mujaheddin* forces and from the former communist army), Dustom's Uzbek militia, armed Shi'a groups from *Hisb-i Wahdat*, Pashtun tribal fighters from

Sayyaf's *Ittihad* (backed by Wahhabis from Saudi Arabia) and, out in the suburbs, Pashtun radical fundamentalists headed by Hekmatyar. At one time or another, any of these groups within Kabul could have been found fighting against the other three.

There were repeated calls for the convening of a great *shura* or *jirgah* (a council of religious and traditional leaders) to meet under UN auspices to appoint a coalition government. But these calls could not surmount the political and ethnic fragmentation. In December, Rabbani was confirmed as president by a *shura* whose legitimacy was denied by almost all the other leaders, except Sayyaf. Rabbani took up his post in Kabul, which for the next three months came under increased shelling from Hekmatyar. Although initially Rabbani was only supposed to have the post for three months, he insisted on his right to stay on. This led to such intensified shelling that Kabul was threatened with complete destruction.

The acute danger galvanized President Rabbani and Hekmatyar to re-examine their positions. In February 1993 they agreed a cease-fire and met in Islamabad, under the auspices of Pakistan, Iran and Saudi Arabia, to discuss a peace formula. In March, the eight *Mujaheddin* leaders in Islamabad signed an accord which reserved the post of prime minister for Hekmatyar and allowed Rabbani to remain as president for 18 months from his initial elevation to the post on 29 December 1992 when new elections will be held.

The settlement should not obscure the fact that the whole arrangement is very unstable. Neither the powerful Defence Minister Masud, nor General Dustom, were involved in the deal. Without their agreement, however, no permanent peace can be reached in Afghanistan. Other groups have also refused to approve the settlement. Since the agreement does not address the ethnic, linguistic and sectarian antagonisms in the country, the bloodshed can be expected to go on. Factionalism and peace remain a contradiction in terms in Afghanistan.

The Role of Foreign Powers

The two major opposing foreign powers distanced themselves from involvement in Afghan affairs once Soviet troops had pulled out of the country. After the collapse of the USSR, Russia retained only two residual concerns: the fate of the remaining Soviet prisoners of war; and the danger of an Afghan spill-over in Central Asia. The US also lost its interest in Afghan political and military affairs. It left the almost impossible task of finding an agreement among the Afghan factions to a UN team of negotiators.

Four regional actors, Pakistan, Iran, Saudi Arabia and Uzbekistan, remained directly involved in the Afghan situation, however. Although the official policy of each is to have a stable, neutral Afghanistan, headed by a coalition government, and although none has any territorial claim, each strove to maintain a foothold in the country and to uphold their clients, while not hesitating to support tactically some other groups, thus undermining the possibility of constructing a stable Afghanistan.

Saudi Arabia's priority was to fight Iranian influence. For this reason, the Saudis were strongly opposed to the Shi'a Hazara. They also opposed the Tajiks because, while they are Sunni, they speak Persian as do the Iranians, and the Saudis feared that the pull of linguistic heritage would be stronger than sectarian alliance. Saudi Arabia supported the Pashtuns, and among them the more fundamentalist, including Hekmatyar and the pro-*Wahhabi* Sayyaf. Uzbekistan discretely supported General Dustom's militia, both because of his former communist orientation and because he is an Uzbek.

Pakistan openly supports the Pashtuns in general, and the fundamentalists in particular. Until 1991, Hekmatyar was the main recipient of most foreign aid channelled through Pakistan. In 1992, the Pakistan foreign ministry, anxious to have a stable government in Kabul, dropped its support for Hekmatyar. Nevertheless, some military and political Pakistan circles, such as the Inter-Service Intelligence Unit (ISI), the military services and the *Jamiat-i Islami* kept up their support for him.

There are a number of reasons why Pakistan does not feel threatened by Pashtun nationalism spilling over the border and causing trouble at home. The long war neither encouraged the development of an all-Pashtun identity nor solidarity. The Pakistani Pashtuns resent the cost and inconvenience of the presence of millions of their Afghan brothers as refugees. There is no 'Pashtun nationalism' that might contest the border between Afghanistan and Pakistan; Pakistani Pashtun nationalist groups have not done well in the elections which followed the death of General Zia in 1988. The only role Pashtun solidarity has played is in the construction of smuggling networks on both sides of the border. Pashtuns are effective in dealing in weapons and drugs, and the war gave a tremendous boost to this traditional traffic. But this has not led to political solidarity. After all, smugglers need borders.

Iran is a multi-ethnic state in which loyalty to the central government is based on Shi'ism, not on a 'Persian' identity. Thus it is logical that Iran has not promoted ethnic solidarity among Persian-speakers in Afghanistan, but instead has concentrated its support on the Afghan Shi'as, united in the *Hisb-i Wahdat* party. Tactically Iran gave some help to General Dustom in 1992. This was due to the outbreak of civil war in Tajikistan, where the so-called Islamic-democrats opposed the former communists, who denounced Iranian influence. To have given their exclusive support to the Islamists in Afghanistan would have antagonized Uzbekistan, which remains the key to any Central Asian policy. Thus the need to placate Tashkent might explain why Iran supported Dustom instead of Masud in Afghanistan.

The Struggle for Tajikistan

Iran was not alone in its deep concern over the deteriorating situation in Tajikistan, which in the latter half of 1992 descended into full-scale civil war. The sense of alarm was even more pronounced in the other Central Asian states of the former Soviet Union, which feared that the collapse of the Tajik state might be the start of a general unravelling of the Central Asian political structures bequeathed from the Soviet period. For the former communist leaders of these states, in particular, the Tajik civil war represented an immediate threat, since it provided the first direct evidence of the potential mobilizing power of political Islam. The Uzbek president, Islam Karimov, was especially sensitive to this perceived threat, given the strength of Islam amongst his own people, and he repeatedly urged Russia and the other Central Asian states to intervene directly in Tajikistan to prevent an ostensibly inexorable spread of Islamic fundamentalism.

As in Afghanistan, the Tajik civil war was not so much driven by ideological motives, whether communist or Islamicist, as it was by a complex regional power struggle. Ever since the birth of the Tajik republic in 1924, political and economic power had been concentrated in the north around Khojand (Leninabad). In the south, the Khojand leadership formed an alliance with the Kulyab oblast, in order to resist demands from the other regions of the south for greater political representation and economic investment.

Such demands were most strongly made by the powerful clan from the Garm valley, where dissatisfaction with the ruling regime was translated into support for the Islamic Renaissance Party. In these demands, the Garm Tajiks were supported by the Gorno-Badakshan autonomous region, where the indigenous population of Ismaïli Pamiris have felt themselves culturally and socially distinct and whose demands for greater autonomy have been repeatedly rebuffed by the central authorities.

With the disintegration of the Soviet Union at the end of 1991, these regional tensions were further exacerbated by the precipitous decline in the national economy. Tajikistan had been the poorest of the Soviet republics and had been dependent on substantial subsidies from the Union budget. Without these subsidies and with the general drop in trade and production, living standards rapidly deteriorated and added economic discontent to the political alienation.

Throughout 1992, the Tajik president, Rakhmon Nabiyev, tried to preserve the traditional Khojand–Kulyab hegemony whilst being forced to make a number of concessions to the opposition. Emboldened by the fall of Najibullah in spring 1992, the opposition staged a series of demonstrations which grew in size to nearly 50,000 people. Reluctantly bowing to this pressure, Nabiyev agreed in May to include a number of opposition figures in his government.

This attempt at a national reconciliation government failed to stem the escalating crisis. Khojand and Kulyab refused to accept the government and the Islamic-democrat opposition increased its demands to include Nabiyev's resignation. In early September, the opposition effectively carried out a *coup d'Etat* and forced Nabiyev to resign – at gunpoint. The country split and a bloody civil war erupted. The savagery of the following four months of war was intense: 40,000 to 60,000 people were killed; 600,000 refugees were driven out; 150,000 houses were destroyed; and there was economic damage estimated at around 200 billion roubles.

The result of this blood-letting was the gradual but effective resumption of power by the traditional Khojand–Kulyab communist coalition and the retreat of the Islamic-democratic opposition into the inaccessible Pamiri mountains. On 19 November, the communist-dominated Supreme Soviet reconvened and elected a Kulyabi, Imolali Rakhmonov, as the new head of state and approved a new cabinet which excluded any opposition figures.

This military and political victory was greeted with relief by the neighbouring Central Asian states, most notably by Uzbekistan which had given logistical and material support to the pro-communist armed factions. The Russian forces in Tajikistan – principally the 201st Motor-Rifle division – had also undoubtedly contributed to the success of the *ancien régime*, although it was consistently maintained that these forces were obeying strict neutrality between the armed factions. In early 1993, this division became the basis of a CIS peacekeeping force, which had the *de facto* mission of ensuring the security of the Rakhmonov government from any further armed attacks by the Islamic-democratic opposition.

For the leaders of the other Central Asian states, the containment and suppression of the Tajik opposition has been a source of considerable relief. They feared that any other outcome would set off the many contradictions and sources of instability in the region – all mobilized through Islamic protest groups. The awful example of the tribal and clan warfare which has racked Afghanistan for the last decade was ever present in their minds.

The events in Tajikistan have shown how potentially unstable is the rest of Central Asia. It has also illustrated the difficulties of containing such threats without severe repression. In Uzbekistan and Turkmenistan, the political clamp-down on all forms of protest makes it clear that the present leaderships are intent on preserving stability at any cost. Whether they have the strength and perseverance to do so has yet to be answered.

The Shape of Things to Come

Another difficult question to answer is whether there is any longer a real *raison d'être* for Afghanistan. The fall of the USSR and the end of the Cold War cancelled the need for it as a buffer state, one of the major reasons for its previous existence. The appearance of new states in the region based on ethnic nationalism is in itself a challenge to the very existence of a multi-ethnic Afghanistan.

There is a congruence between the ethnic crystallization in Afghanistan and the regional countries, all of which support their own favourite ethnic group: Hazara for Iran, Pashtuns for Pakistan and Saudi Arabia, Uzbeks for Uzbekistan. Regional powers are thus enhancing ethnic identities in Afghanistan. This polarization along ethnic lines is also embodied in the newly independent republics in Central Asia.

The emergence of those countries can be expected to play a role in the assertiveness of ethnic identities in Afghanistan. Although in many cases they were artificially designed by Stalin, ethnic-national identities have struck deeper roots than has yet occurred in Afghanistan. As in Afghanistan, the breakdown is along linguistic lines, but it has taken a more precise form. The key factor is the strength of Uzbek nationalism. Uzbekistan is the most populated republic in Central Asia (it has 20 million inhabitants, versus 16 million in Kazakhstan and Afghanistan, and 5 million in Tajikistan and Turkmenistan). The weight of Uzbeks is not counterbalanced by the Russians, who are leaving, nor by the Kazakhs, who are avoiding involvement in the south. The continuing devolution of power from Moscow to Tashkent is enhancing its position.

Tashkent has been openly supporting General Dustom in Afghanistan and the former communists in Tajikistan, using local armed militias in the two countries as tools. At the moment it does not seem to have territorial ambitions, and this position may be maintained for the forseeable future. But a growing ethnic assertiveness on the part of Uzbeks living in Afghanistan, as well as in Tajikistan, may bring a change of assessment in Tashkent which provides a lodestar for identification and a base for support.

Dushanbe does not provide the same kind of model for Afghan Tajiks. On the contrary, the repression of the opposition movement in Tajikistan has brought tens of thousands of Tajik refugees to northern Afghanistan. The open ethnic opposition between Tajiks and Uzbeks in former Soviet Central Asia has, until now, contrasted with their common opposition to the Pashtuns in Afghanistan. This may, however, soon change.

Despite much talk about an Afghan spill-over to Central Asia, there has in fact been a reverse flow, both of people and of concepts. In a real sense history has described a large circle and the late twentieth century is repeating the sixteenth century when three Muslim empires (the Iranian, Uzbek and Moghol, now Pakistan) were using what is today known as Afghanistan as a battleground. There is a race on between the Afghans who wish to re-establish an independent buffer state between these regional empires and the heavy pull of growing ethnic awareness which would link Afghan ethnic groups closer to their foreign ethnic patrons. The shape of Afghanistan and of Central Asia will depend on the outcome.

Africa

Over 30 years of 'state-building' in Africa has still not led to much 'politics-creation'. In 1992–93, the process of democratization continued in most of those African countries sufficiently at peace with themselves to allow a measure of competition through the ballot box. While losers sometimes honourably accepted their fate, as was the case of Kenneth Kaunda in Zambia, highly dubious electoral practices, or simple lust for power, just as often meant that elections were followed by displays of violence. Rioting followed elections in Cameroon, leading in turn to the imposition of a state of emergency. The UNITA leader Jonas Savimbi rejected the results of the elections in Angola and reignited the civil war.

Some leaders showed disdain for the whole idea of democracy. President Mobutu continued to hang on to power in Zaire despite increasing Western pressure on him to compromise. Daniel Arap Moi in Kenya bowed to the idea of multiparty politics, but most observers felt that there was serious rigging of the elections that eventually took place. By the beginning of 1993, the Western states and donor community had lost patience with some of Africa's leaders who were keeping power against the popular will and continuing to sup from the public trough. But the capacity and the will to force genuinely democratic practices was not there, and while most Western leaders concerned about Africa were frustrated by the slow progress towards democracy, they were more shocked by the faster progress of state collapse in those countries where no distinction was made between war and politics.

The continued civil war in Liberia was one example. Despite the efforts of the regional peacekeeping force deployed there (ECOMOG), the power of interim President Amos Sawyer barely extended beyond the capital, and the power of rebel leader Charles Taylor throughout much of the rest of the country was such that most foreign companies who still wanted to invest in the country dealt directly with him. While the Nigerian-led forces were able in early 1993 to grab more territory from Taylor, this hardly brought peace closer. But in 1992/93 the archetypal example of state collapse was Somalia, whose frontiers no longer form the borders of a state, but of a zone of anarchy, which the international community has somehow to police.

The drama of state collapse was therefore greatest in the Horn of Africa, which was also the place where new African states had the greatest prospect of being created. The Eritreans were preparing for a referendum on independence to be held in April 1993, while 'Somaliland' had already declared itself free of Mogadishu's 'rule'. In South/Central Africa, the continued instability in Rwanda, the resurgence of the Angolan civil war and the horrible prospect of Zaire's fracture, invited nightmare scenarios of tribal conflict proliferating across huge tracts of land. It was also a year of woes in the Republic of South Africa where the negotiations between de Klerk and Mandela had more downs than ups, and where those who wanted a share in power were not always keen on power-sharing.

WAR, FAMINE AND DEATH IN THE HORN

The tragedy which Somalia endured in 1992 eclipsed every other problem in the Horn. The overthrow of former dictator Mohammed Siad Barre in January 1991 led the country from civil war, which had started in the late 1980s, directly into total anarchy. With no government, warlords and heavily armed gangsters ranged throughout the country. Large-scale famine due to drought and the fighting made the Somali crisis the worst any state has suffered in recent memory. The dire extent of the disaster, however, belatedly elicited unprecedented international humanitarian response which culminated late in 1992 in an American-led multinational military intervention to ensure delivery of food and medicine.

The world's concentration on Somalia shifted attention away from the catastrophe in southern Sudan. Guerrillas of the Sudan People's Liberation Army (SPLA) continued their fight against the Islamic fundamentalist military regime of General Omar Hassan Ahmed al-Bashir. The southerners' morale was undermined by major splits within the SPLA. As in Somalia, the people of the southern region faced starvation, exacerbated by the policies of Bashir's regime and ethnic clashes among the southerners.

Only by comparison did Ethiopia's problems appear more tolerable. President Meles Zenawi's domestic support diminished considerably, ethnic rivalry increased and the ruling Ethiopian People's Revolutionary Democratic Front (EPRDF) was split. The regional elections of June 1992 created more animosity and the proliferation of political factions ensured that Ethiopian politics remained volatile.

One of Ethiopia's domestic problems was the projected independence of Eritrea. Following a referendum scheduled for April 1993, Eritrea was expected to formalize its sovereign statehood, but there were many Ethiopians who still felt the territory was an integral part of Ethiopia. On the surface, Eritrea appeared quiet, but underneath there were political and ethnic tensions because the unity which most Eritreans enjoyed when they were fighting against the Ethiopian government had dissipated.

Like other states in the region, Djibouti faced ethnic and political problems. Nationalists of the Afar clan remained restless, an insurgency continued and the presidential succession struggle shifted into higher gear. By late 1992 Djibouti had established a multiparty system, but political instability continued.

The Non-State of Somalia

Anarchy reigned in Somalia during 1992. There was no police force, army or government, and there were no schools, hospitals or courts. Instead, there were roving gunmen and clan-based militias who terrorized everyone, with no interest in the many thousands of Somalis who were starving in a famine that was as much caused by the fighting factions as by drought. There were four sets of actors on Somalia's bloodied stage: the warlords and clan elders; relief agencies; the United Nations; and the US-led multinational force.

At least 14 factions and numerous 'freelance' gunmen competed for control. The dominant warlords in the Mogadishu area were 'interim president' Ali Mahdi and his arch-rival General Mohammed Farah Aideed, both from the United Somalia Congress (USC) and the Hawiye clan. They both claimed a mandate to rule and terrorized their opponents whenever they could.

In August 1992, Aideed allied with several other factions and formed the Somalia National Alliance (SNA), an important symbolic step towards his goal of establishing a multi-clan political authority. Mahdi also crafted a trans-clan coalition which included the Somalia National Front (SNF), led by Siad Barre's son-in-law and former defence minister, General Mohammed Said Hersi 'Morgan', and the Majerteen-based Somalia Salvation Democratic Front (SSDF). While Mahdi was doing this, his Abgal clan of the Hawiye group split into three factions, leaving him with a very narrow power base.

Despite widespread insecurity, non-governmental organizations (NGOs) continued to provide help. The International Committee of the Red Cross (ICRC), the Save the Children Fund, CARE, World Vision, Oxfam, *Médecins sans Frontières*, Concern and several others supplied medicine, food and clothing. Because of their neutrality, NGOs provided assistance to all sides in the conflict. This did not prevent numerous difficulties, however, including a lack of security for their personnel and severe logistic problems in the unloading, storage and transport of supplies. Some of the supplies were left unloaded for months because of disputes among competing clans. Having been unloaded, much of the aid was stolen from warehouses or *en route* to the starving.

Relief workers were subjected to extortion, blackmail and robbery. Warlords and merchants demanded 'protection' money. To get the food where it was needed the NGOs had to pay militias to escort it. Convoys of trucks taking food to distribution centres in the interior were often accompanied by men in jeeps (nicknamed 'technicals') armed with assault rifles and roof-mounted anti-aircraft guns. These convoys were routinely looted, often by the escorts themselves. By the time Western governments began to send relief supplies in mid-1992, nearly all children in rural areas were said to suffer from malnutrition. In December 1992 it was estimated that the death toll from starvation for the year had reached 400,000.

The UN also played a role in Somalia. It had been criticized for waiting until very late before committing its resources, and indeed it had not begun to consider Somalia seriously until Boutros Boutros-Ghali had become Secretary-General in January 1992. Then it organized and provided humanitarian assistance, but was soon forced to realize that it was treating the symptoms rather than the causes of the problem. Starvation in Somalia is a consequence of the civil war; which, in turn, is a result of corruption, misguided macroeconomic policies, clan feuds and power struggles.

According to Security Council Resolution 733 of 23 January 1992, the UN's objectives were to: arrange a cease-fire between warring factions; organize and deliver humanitarian assistance; and promote national reconciliation and a political settlement. By the end of 1992, the UN mandate had been expanded to include the rebuilding of Somali institutions.

Mainly because there was no mandate for the UN troops to enforce their efforts, the peacekeeping attempts in 1992 achieved nothing. Because alliances shifted frequently and the political factions did not trust each other, no cease-fire could hold for long, and this destroyed any possibility of creating conditions conducive to national reconciliation. For instance, in January 1992, the UN Under-Secretary-General for Political Affairs, James Jonah, went to Mogadishu to try to persuade USC factions to negotiate peace. In the same month, the Security Council imposed an arms embargo on Somalia and called on the combatants to 'cooperate' with the UN and relief agencies in their humanitarian efforts. Representatives of the rival USC factions went to New York in mid-February 1992, and although they refused to negotiate with each other face to face, they agreed to end the fighting. But, as always, they had agreed to this cease-fire only to flout it. Another cease-fire agreement was signed on 5 March, and this held for a few months.

In April 1992 the UN Secretary-General appointed an Algerian diplomat, Mohammed Sahnoun, as his special representative to Somalia to provide overall direction of UN activities and facilitate a political settlement. The Security Council authorized the creation of the UN Operation in Somalia (UNOSOM) to provide security for humanitarian activities in Mogadishu in April 1992. It also approved the deployment of 50 unarmed military observers to monitor the cease-fire. Sahnoun was successful in arranging a reconciliation between various groups, but he was frustrated by the slow response of the UN and the international community. It was only after Boutros-Ghali had complained to the Security Council in July 1992 that the Council took the Somali tragedy seriously.

The UN needed a peacekeeping operation to deliver relief assistance, but the problem was how to send such a force to a country without a government and where cease-fires were not respected. Mahdi agreed to the UN deployment, but he had virtually no authority in much of the country. The fact that he requested a UN peacekeeping force made his adversaries view such an operation as partisan. Sahnoun made contact with warlords in some parts of Somalia, but in others, he found it hard to obtain permission for the deployment of UNOSOM. In some areas where agreements were reached with local warlords, they were more often violated than not.

In late July 1992 the Security Council warned that if the factions did not cooperate, it could 'not exclude other measures to deliver humanitarian assistance'. It also approved a peacekeeping force of 500 troops to escort food convoys in Mogadishu and the surrounding area, but this force was far too small for the task. The UN agreed to increase UNOSOM troops to 3,500 in late August 1992, but opposition from some warlords who wished to continue their profitable looting and protection rackets kept these forces from being deployed. UNOSOM troops were deployed on the principle of non-use of force except in self-defence, but this was its greatest weakness, because the situation required peace-enforcement rather than peacekeeping. Even after the 500 Pakistani troops arrived in October 1992, they were kept in barracks for weeks without clear instructions.

The sharpest critic of UN operations in Somalia was the Secretary-General's own representative, Sahnoun, who was frustrated by the bureaucratic obfuscation and delays of the UN and its agencies. When Boutros-Ghali hit back and criticized Sahnoun publicly, Sahnoun resigned on 26 October 1992 and was replaced a week later by the Iraqi (Kurdish) diplomat, Ismat Kittani. Shortly after taking office, Kittani prepared a report for the Secretary-General detailing the difficulties UNOSOM was facing. This report formed the basis of Boutros-Ghali's decision in late November 1992 to seek US involvement and an expanded military presence.

The American-led Unified Task Force (UNITAF) of about 40,000 troops from more than 20 nations is the first humanitarian intervention force in UN history. The Security Council authorized it after determining that the human tragedy in Somalia constituted a threat to international peace and security under Chapter VII of the UN Charter. The task force was the result of a temporary convergence of interests between Boutros-Ghali and former US President George Bush. Both argued that they were concerned that the aid which the UN and industrialized countries were providing did not reach those it was meant to help. No doubt both felt something had to be done to alleviate the suffering, but they had other agendas as well. Boutros-Ghali sought an opportunity for the UN to demonstrate its interventionist capability, and Bush hoped to help protect the US defence budget after he left office by demonstrating the financial costs of US leadership of the 'new world order'.

The Security Council gave the Unified Task Force the right 'to use all necessary means to establish as soon as possible a secure environment for humanitarian relief operations'. It was to secure the main ports, open supply routes and prepare the way for UNOSOM II to take over. The Task Force was initially criticized by some relief agencies because they felt it might undermine the reconciliation that had been achieved. However, by February 1993, the effect of UNITAF appeared positive. There was increased relief delivery to ports and major distribution centres in the country. Virtually all supply routes had been secured, the port and airport of Mogadishu were functioning and the bandits had disappeared from the city. The looting of relief supplies and the protection rackets operated by merchants had ceased. As a result, humanitarian assistance has reached many people who would have perished, and the death toll from starvation has dropped. Rival leaders started talking and a meeting of 14 factions in Addis Ababa in January 1993 agreed to a nationwide cease-fire, general disarmament and the holding of a national reconciliation conference on 15 March 1993.

By March 1993, a new UNOSOM, with the power of enforcement, was preparing to take over from the task force. With factional squabbles continuing, it appeared the UN would have no alternative but to compel warlords to come to the negotiating table. Even after bringing them to the table it will not be easy to find an acceptable compromise. One possible solution mooted is to zone or cantonize the country along clan boundaries. The UN, however, will have tremendous difficulty establishing peace amongst Somali clans; few Somali leaders have been able to create acceptable political compromises amongst the clans without using force or terror. Since the Congo operation of the early 1960s, the UN has had little experience in the creation of a normal political process in countries that live by tribal rules.

More Horrors in Sudan

The political, economic and humanitarian situation in Sudan has gone from bad to worse. The nine-year-old civil war between the Sudan People's Liberation Army (SPLA) in the Christian south and government forces from the Muslim north, the internecine fighting between the main wing of the SPLA, led by John Garang, and breakaway factions, and the continuing deterioration of the economy have led inevitably to increasing humanitarian problems.

As in the recent past, the imposition of the *Sharia* (Islamic law) remained the main determinant of public policy. National Islamic Front (NIF) members continued to dominate national politics, the economy, the civil service, the armed forces and commerce and trade. There were sharp divisions within the NIF in mid-1992, but the party's leader, Hassan Turabi, who also acted as the *de facto* head of state, visited several African, Middle Eastern and Western countries to drum up support for the fundamentalist regime, while also making no secret of his party's ambition to spread Islamic fundamentalism to other parts of Africa and the Middle East.

Earlier in 1992, government forces took advantage of the split within the SPLA, which had occurred in August 1991, to launch an intensive dry-season offensive against the southerners. By mid-1992 they had recaptured many towns in the south, including some which had been held by the SPLA for about nine years. It was after scoring these military victories that Sudan's leader, General Bashir, hoping to negotiate from a position of strength while the SPLA was suffering from major internal splits and military defeats, agreed to have talks with the SPLA in the Nigerian city of Abuja.

Prior to the talks, Sudanese officials met clandestinely with leaders of the SPLA breakaway faction – the Nasir group (named after a town on the banks of the Salongo river) – in January 1992 and reached a tentative agreement on a settlement of the southern problem. They agreed that after they signed a peace accord, there should be special constitutional status for the south within a united Sudan for an unspecified transitional period. The agreement also vaguely mentioned the possibility of a referendum after this period for the south to choose its own political and constitutional status.

Once the talks got under way, however, the government delegation's arrogance and intransigence compelled the Nasir group to join forces with Garang's faction. The government, which had underestimated the rebels' political acumen, took a firm line. The only conciliatory proposal it made was a federal system in which the southern region would be exempt from *Sharia*. The Nasir faction adamantly demanded self-determination for the south, but the government delegation could not agree to include this issue on the agenda. The government then tried to woo the Garang faction by conceding that the Sudanese constitution need not mention Islam as the official state religion. The Garang faction, however, insisted that there should be either unity under a secular democratic system or self-determination for the south. All parties agreed to a final communiqué that recognized Sudan as a 'multi-ethnic, multi-lingual, multi-cultural and multi-religious' state. Although they also agreed to consult their supporters with a view to resuming talks aimed at an interim constitutional arrangement acceptable to all sides, fighting in the south resumed as soon as the meeting was over.

After the Abuja meeting, the Garang and Nasir factions of the SPLA went different ways. There was another split in the Garang faction, led by William Nyoun, a Dinka like Garang, who formed a group called Forces of Unity. Three other senior Dinka commanders are reported to have deserted the Garang faction in mid-January 1993.

The Sudanese government, which has been virtually isolated by the international community, maintains close links with Iraq, Libya and Iran. Iran has supplied it with oil, weapons and army vehicles. In addition to offering training to Sudanese government fighters, Iran also provided revolutionary guards to fight alongside the Popular Defence

Forces, the government's alternative army. It also financed Sudan's purchase of more weapons from China.

Sudan's human rights record has not improved; government opponents continued to be detained and tortured in 'ghost houses'. The rebel forces' record is hardly better. As a result of the constant fighting, there were also nearly one million displaced persons in the country, most of them having fled the civil war in the south. The government continued to harass displaced persons, holding them in overcrowded camps with inadequate amenities. It also tried to frustrate the UN's *Operation Lifeline* and continued to conceal the extent of the suffering in the south, with a view to discouraging relief agencies from providing aid. By early 1993 the threat of famine in southern Sudan had grown greater than the threat of war, and the region faced a humanitarian disaster as serious as that in Somalia.

Disappointment in Ethiopia

Observers who might have thought that Ethiopia would enjoy peace after the departure of Mengistu Haile Mariam in 1991 were wrong. Ethiopia remained a politically unstable and economically poor country. President Meles was challenged from within, and the international goodwill towards his regime was wearing thin.

Most of Ethiopia's political problems stem from ethnic competition and the flawed regional elections of June 1992. The elections, which were designed to give rival ethnic groups control over their own affairs, were a fiasco. They could not be held in the Harar area, or in Somali and Afar regions, because these regions were considered too unsafe. Where they were held, some parties boycotted the polls while international observers denounced abuses that took place during the voting. In general terms, the elections entrenched ethnicity as the central element in the political process.

Ethiopia contains more than 64 different ethnic groups. The Ethiopian People's Revolutionary Democratic Front (EPRDF) which had formed a government when Mengistu left, had decided that it could best avoid conflict by embracing ethnicity instead of subsuming it. The main political factions had agreed in 1991 that each major ethnic group would get autonomy within its own region, including police powers and the right to use local languages. The government emphasized self-determination with democracy at the local and national levels. The lack of democratic experience, however, meant that ethnic feuds would continue.

Serious differences between the EPRDF and the Oromo Liberation Front (OLF) drove the OLF from participation in the interim administration. The Oromo make up about 40% of Ethiopia's population, and although not all of them support the organization, it claims to speak for all Oromos. Citing EPRDF intimidation, the OLF had boycotted the regional polls. It also claimed that the EPRDF manipulated registration and other preparations for the election, a claim which was supported by international observers. The EPRDF, which was seen by other political groups as heavy-handed, had also backed minor Oromo groups, including the Oromo People's Democratic Organization (OPDO), as part of its efforts to undermine the OLF. The flaw in voting aroused new passions, threatening a civil war. The US government expressed concern over the conduct of the polls and warned that without free and fair elections, some aid might be withheld.

The EPRDF continued to accuse the OLF of hiding food and selling it at high prices and claimed that it was anti-democratic. The OLF, on the other hand, claimed the EPRDF had been taking land from Oromo peasants near Addis Ababa at gunpoint and had tortured OLF members and officials. In October 1992, the two parties met in Asmara, Eritrea, under the chairmanship of the Eritrean People's Liberation Front (EPLF), but they were unable to resolve their differences. By this time, they were both beginning to come apart. Within the EPRDF, the Tigrayan People's Liberation Front (TPLF) was pitted against the OPDO, while moderate/conservative and radical element in the OLF could not see eye to eye.

When the EPRDF took power in 1991, the country was bankrupt, industry was neglected and thousands of people were starving. Meles promised to pursue a free-enterprise system which appears to have impressed some Westerners who have provided various forms of economic support. In 1992, the World Bank and other donors pledged $657m in emergency aid, to be provided over a 30-month period. Despite these pledges of aid, there has been little improvement in the economy.

Although, on balance, the Ethiopian political system began to open up in 1992, and there was more freedom of expression than before, the future looks far from rosy. The regional elections that were supposed to be part of a pluralist political system turned out to be a major embarrassment for Meles. By early 1993, the signs of continuing political instability could not be hidden, and the government was clearly unable to maintain order in some parts of the country.

Uncertainty in Djibouti

Continued fighting in Djibouti between government forces and the rebel *Front révolutionnaire pour l'unité et la démocratie* (FRUD), which was formed in 1991, drew France, Djibouti's main aid donor, into the conflict. Unhappily for the government, which had expected unquestioned backing, differences between Paris and Djibouti were exposed. The government was then forced to accept the necessity of establishing a multiparty system. Adroit manipulation of the process, however, left the question of Afar participation in an Issa-dominated structure unresolved and threatens renewed violence.

As guerrilla activities increased in early 1992, the Djibouti government sought military assistance from France under the 1977 agreement between the two countries, claiming that FRUD was a foreign invasion force. The French took the view that it was a domestic problem that needed an internal solution. In January 1992, the French Minister Delegate for Foreign Affairs, Alain Vivien, met with FRUD leaders in Sana'a, the capital of Yemen. Vivien, who had also visited Egypt, Eritrea and Ethiopia to obtain views on the continued French military presence in Djibouti and to gain a regional perspective of Djibouti's crisis, insisted that the Djibouti government should open a dialogue with the rebels. However, Djibouti's Foreign Minister, Moumin Bahdon Farah, argued that Djibouti could continue the 'war logic' and that Vivien's visit had achieved nothing. Nevertheless, in February 1992, FRUD and the Djibouti government declared a cease-fire and France agreed to deploy a peacekeeping force.

After a visit to France in November 1992, President Gouled agreed with Mitterrand that he should talk to FRUD and scheduled a meeting with its leaders. This was an abortive gesture, for he soon cancelled the meeting because the guerrillas refused to release all their prisoners, mostly government soldiers. FRUD insisted that the government also held political prisoners, including Ali Aref, the former Chief Minister, who had been sentenced to ten years in jail in July 1992 after being convicted of plotting to overthrow the government. The government refused to acknowledge that Aref was a political prisoner. The standoff in Djibouti generated conflicting responses from Paris. There were differences between the French military in Djibouti, the presidency and the foreign ministry over what to do. Some elements within the French military wanted Gouled to step down.

Behind the scenes the French government pressed Gouled to move towards multiparty democracy. Early in 1992, Gouled had appointed a 14-member committee to draft a multiparty constitution. The committee presented the preliminary draft of the new constitution to the government in April 1992, but opposition parties criticized it as inadequate. In particular, they opposed the establishment of a strong executive presidency.

Under pressure from France, internal opposition from among the Issa and the guerrilla war, Gouled agreed to submit the multiparty constitution to a referendum in September 1992. It was overwhelmingly approved. The new constitution restricted the number of political parties to four. By November 1992 only two parties, both led by Issas, had been registered – the ruling *Rassemblement populaire pour le progrès* and a new party, the *Parti du Renouveau Démocratique*, headed by former Finance and Health Minister, Mohamed Djama Elabe. FRUD and seven other parties which had been grouped under *Front Uni* were not registered. *Front Uni* had called for a boycott of the referendum insisting on substantial decentralization, updated electoral registers and a curb on presidential powers. Under the new constitution, Gouled was permitted to stand for presidency in 1993.

The country's first multiparty election was planned for 20 November 1992, but it was later postponed to 18 December. Despite this supposed introduction of pluralism, Afar participation in the political process was still very limited. Since lack of Afar participation is one of the basic causes of the conflicts in Djibouti there is little reason to expect that the hint of multiparty politics will do much to reduce the high level of instability in the country.

Grim Prospects

It is hard to feel any confidence in the possibility of peace and prosperity in any of the countries of the Horn. Eritrea's referendum is likely to result in a strong vote for independence, but ethnic and political problems remain and it will be many years before they can be resolved. There is likely to be a gradual return to a fragile peace in Djibouti, but that will largely be determined by the result of the presidential election due in spring 1993 and the level of political participation for the Afars. If the expected happens with Gouled re-elected and the Afars still politically marginalized, uncertainty will continue. Under the best of circumstances Ethiopia's multiparty system would take years to develop, and in the interim the EPRDF government is certain to be challenged by its former allies. It would not be surprising if Meles felt it necessary to adopt draconian measures to remain in power.

In Somalia, while the immediate crisis has been blunted by the presence of the international force under American leadership, a national reconciliation process has hardly begun. Even after a new government has been chosen it will certainly require significant foreign military support to survive. In Sudan, divisions within the NIF and the SPLA have ensured that the strength needed for reconciliation is completely lacking. The north and south appear condemned to continue unproductive warfare which military force will not easily win, but civilians are certain to lose. In the Horn of Africa it is all too easy to believe in the four horsemen of the Apocalypse.

SOUTH AFRICA: TO THE ABYSS AND BACK

The slogan on a popular T-shirt, '1993 – the nightmare continues', encapsulated the national mood in South Africa at the end of 1992. It was an amalgam of despair, resignation and corrosive cynicism and it marked a precipitous descent from the confident heights of the March referendum, when South Africa's white population voted two out of three in favour of sharing political power with the country's black majority. From that moment of optimism on 17 March 1992, when President F. W. de Klerk claimed a convincing victory over his enemies on the far right of the white establishment, everything seemed to go wrong.

De Klerk's momentous decision in February 1990 to dismantle the barricades of the apartheid state and to negotiate with its enemies kindled great (possibly too great) expectations. Far from realizing these, the most complex state and most sophisticated economy in Africa seemed instead about to descend into political anarchy, civil war and economic collapse.

Constitutional negotiations – the focus of hope of the vast majority of South Africans – broke down and the vacuum was filled by internecine massacre, by the seamy and often murderous antics of the security establishment's 'dirty tricks' brigade and by seemingly endless disclosures of private fraud and public sector corruption as an army of skeletons began to tumble out of the decaying apartheid closet.

De Klerk himself ended the year in a weakened state, as a steady procession of cabinet ministers pleaded exhaustion and quit the political scene, and an increasingly fractious National Party (NP) began to realize, possibly for the first time, that the end of white rule was truly at hand. Some Nationalist MPs were openly critical of de Klerk for not keeping them fully informed and others decided to throw their weight behind Chief Mangosuthu Buthelezi's Inkatha Freedom Party. Certainly the mood within the NP – so very different from the triumphalism which had marked its victory over the far right during the March referendum – illustrated South Africa's dilemma: the need to outpace the forces of disintegration by maintaining the momentum of change had to be balanced against the time needed to devise a new constitution that would win the widest possible support in this fractured country.

Sniffing the Brimstone

The fate of the Convention for a Democratic South Africa (CODESA), the multiparty negotiating forum convened in the wake of the March referendum, was itself an apt illustration of the dangers of trying to rush constitutional fences before the major parties were ready to take the jump. CODESA was expected to usher in the brave new democratic South Africa. Instead, it broke up in May amid mutual recriminations of cynicism and bad faith between the African National Congress and the National Party. The two key opponents were condemned to go at least one more bruising round before both realized that neither could survive without the other. By the year's end, however, they had accepted that the future was foreclosing on both of them and that South Africa itself would not survive as a functioning economy without major concessions from both sides.

In March 1993 a multiparty convention re-launched the search for a lasting settlement. 'A torch of hope had been lit', said ANC Secretary-General Cyril Ramaphosa; but 1992 had been a dark and a sobering year.

The National Party's negotiators carried much of the blame for the break up of CODESA. Flushed with their referendum success, they had tried to front load the constitutional negotiations by insisting that the powers and borders of the regions of a future South Africa would be decided by a 75% majority in an elected constituent assembly which, it was envisaged, would be charged with the task of drawing up South Africa's democratic constitution. It was a move designed to emasculate the constituent assembly (in which the ANC would probably enjoy an overwhelming majority), and to commit the country to a highly devolved form of federation.

In the event, the ANC, which had agreed to most of the government's demands, jibbed at this final hurdle and CODESA was suspended. There was evidence that the breakdown was not unwelcome to the ANC leadership, worried by accusations from its more radical members that it had lost touch with its rank and file. Certainly, the degree of trust between the two main negotiating partners had been damaged by the fact that both were already campaigning vigorously and somewhat prematurely for victory in the first post-apartheid elections.

Initially the hiatus seemed to provide both with a much-needed pause for reflection. Within a month, however, South Africa's *annus horribilis* began in earnest when, on the night of 17 June, more than 40 men, women and children were slaughtered in Boipatong township, 40 miles south of Johannesburg, by marauding hostel-dwellers in a reprisal for a similar massacre in April, when a large number of Inkatha sympathizers had been hacked or burned to death by ANC supporters. Not only was Boipatong the latest in a dismal roll-call in the five-year civil war between Inkatha and the ANC, but it further poisoned the political climate. The police and army, widely suspected of being in sympathy with Inkatha, were accused of conspiracy in the massacre, and when de Klerk tried to visit the township to show sympathy for the bereaved, he was hounded out by angry youths.

The ANC, echoing the charges of government conspiracy and bowing to the demands of its radicals, announced a programme of 'mass action' to mobilize its supporters in a rolling series of stay-aways, sit-ins, protest marches and mass demonstrations. As the civil war between Inkatha and the ANC plumbed new depths of frenzied barbarity, the government complained that mass action was ratcheting up the political temperature. Although a mass demonstration outside the Union Buildings, the heart of government in Pretoria, passed off peacefully, 40 deaths marred a national stay-away on 3 August, when four million striking black workers brought most of the country's industries to a standstill.

A growing awareness of the damage inflicted on South Africa's weakening economy by political instability had begun to persuade the political leaders to scale down the rhetoric and to renew contacts, when Boipatong was joined in the annals of mayhem by Bisho, the capital of Ciskei, one of South Africa's four quasi-independent home-lands. The radical faction in the ANC, led by a militant communist Ronnie Kasrils, had sworn to 'liberate' Ciskei from its military leader, Brigadier Oupa Gqozo. Kasrils, who had made little secret of his contempt for the ANC leadership's willingness to negotiate with the government, believed that Pretoria was vulnerable to the 'Leipzig option' (a reference to the events in East Germany in 1989) and that a popular uprising would deliver power to the popular forces in South Africa. On 7 September, as a group of ANC demonstrators led by Kasrils attempted to break out of a football stadium to march on Bisho, they were fired on by Ciskei troops, leaving 28 dead and more than 200 injured.

The incident brought down upon South Africa and Ciskei the re-newed opprobrium of the world. The liberal South African judge, Richard Goldstone, whose inquiry into the causes of political violence made him the world's busiest judge, condemned both the Ciskei sol-diers and government and, to a lesser extent, Kasrils and the leaders of the march.

Clawing Back

Awash with guns and alight with feuds, the whole cauldron vigorously stirred by semi-detached military and police hit-squads prosecuting their own dirty war against the peace process, South Africa seemed about to implode. The shock of the Bisho massacre, however, appeared to bring home to both President de Klerk and Nelson Mandela how close South Africa had drifted to the edge of the abyss. They pulled back. Contacts between the government and the ANC were renewed and, by 26 September, a chastened Mandela and de Klerk met to issue a joint Record of Understanding.

The agreement was, in essence, a three-fold undertaking which committed the government to fence off migrant workers' hostels, which the ANC saw as nothing more than barracks for Inkatha *impis*; to ban the carrying of so-called traditional weapons in public areas; and, an undertaking by both the government and the ANC to facilitate the installation of an interim government of national unity and elec-tions for a constituent assembly.

In the outrage following Boipatong, Mandela had set 14 conditions for the resumption of negotiations. These had now shrunk to three. One of the original conditions had been for international monitors. In a major reversal of policy which had long insisted that South Africa's internal affairs were out of bounds to the rest of the world, the South African government invited the assistance of the international commu-nity. By the end of 1992 the country had played host to teams of observers from the United Nations, the EC and the Commonwealth. At the request of the UN Secretary-General Boutros Boutros-Ghali, Cyrus Vance had taken sufficient time off from peace brokering in Bosnia for a hurried visit to South Africa and, at the South African government's invitation, UK expert on policing, Peter Waddington, joined the hard-pressed Judge Goldstone in his ever-widening inquiries.

These inquiries eventually led to a raid on the secret offices of the Department of Military Intelligence by police investigators working for Goldstone. They seized files showing that secret agents, who had formerly worked for the discredited 'Civil Cooperation Bureau', had been re-employed by Military Intelligence's Department of Covert Collection to infiltrate the ANC with the aid of drug dealers and prostitutes.

Cleansing the Security Forces

When Goldstone went public with these disclosures, President de Klerk appointed the Chief of Staff for the Defence Force, Lt General Pierre Steyn, to investigate further and, on 19 December, summarily purged 23 senior military officers (including two generals), and a large number of civilians. At least 70% of the officers were from Army Intelligence. A seemingly shaken de Klerk said that Steyn's preliminary findings indicated that maverick military men had been involved in a serious attempt, which possibly included murder, to undermine South Africa's peace process. He continued to deny, however, that this was evidence of a widely alleged, officially sanctioned 'Third Force' in South Africa's security establishment, whose major aim had been to foment violence between Inkatha and the ANC.

Some military sources, however, believed that the purge had been planned long in advance as part of a carefully orchestrated campaign by de Klerk to assert control over the South African security forces and to weed out those elements hostile to the integration of the security forces and the ANC's military wing, *Umkhonto we Sizwe*. This belief was based on a number of indications that the government had been planning to clamp down on securocrats in the SADF and the police by forcing officers who could threaten the negotiation process into premature retirement. Nineteen police generals had been purged in August following a highly critical report by Peter Waddington, who advised that the high command of the South African Police should be restructured as part of the country's negotiated settlement.

Equally, the Further Indemnity Act which de Klerk pushed through parliament in October in the teeth of opposition from all political parties and widespread condemnation, was believed to be part of his strategy. Although the amnesty for political crimes applied to everyone, offering it to members of the armed forces could be seen as a necessary pre-condition to ease right-wing conservatives out of the security forces. On the other hand, the president's determination to ram the bill through did nothing to allay persistent doubts about the extent of cabinet knowledge of Military Intelligence's campaign against the very organization with which the government was now attempting to negotiate South Africa's future.

In 1992 an inquest into the 1985 murder of an ANC activist, Matthew Goniwe, and three of his colleagues, had heard that the State Security Council, on which several cabinet ministers sat, had authorized the 'permanent removal' of Goniwe. In a related development Transkei leader, General Bantu Holomisa, released documents alleging that the Chief of Military Intelligence, General C. J. van der Westhuisen and the Chief of the SADF, General A. G. Liebenberg, had been implicated in a plot to consolidate the two Xhosa homelands, Ciskei and Transkei, which could have involved the murder of former Ciskei leader, Lennox Sebe.

At the very least the allegations reinforced doubts over whether a generation of officers, who had devoted their careers to 'destabilising' the ANC both at home and abroad, would accept the fact that the government was now treating with the enemy, let alone preside over the necessary integration of *Umkhonto we Sizwe* into the SADF. Evidence of past misdemeanours and continuing dirty tricks, together with aggressive, anti-ANC statements by the Chief of the Army, General George Meiring, fuelled fears of a possible security force coup against the de Klerk government. A far more likely scenario, however, was that senior officers who had been sacked or had quit a shrinking SADF would feel free to make common cause with the more violent elements of the far right.

Although South Africa's destabilizing of its neighbours had long since ceased, a series of reports at the beginning of 1993 provided an apt illustration of how far the disintegration of an authoritarian regime in South Africa mirrored similar events in Russia and Eastern Europe. South African soldiers – particularly from Special Forces and the disbanded 32nd Battalion, which had spent 10 years operating behind the lines in Angola on behalf of UNITA – were being recruited by the MPLA to fight as mercenaries against their former ally, UNITA, in the resumed civil war in Angola. At the same time, there were unconfirmed reports of Aeroflot transport aircraft flying arms from South Africa to resupply UNITA via Zaire.

The government was not alone in being confronted by embarrassing ghosts from its recent past. Two reports on ANC detention camps in Africa, one by Amnesty International and the other an internal inquiry by the ANC itself, revealed that a regime of brutality and murder had been inflicted on ANC dissidents during the organization's years in exile. In a response not dissimilar to President de Klerk's reaction to Judge Goldstone's disclosures, Nelson Mandela roundly condemned those responsible, but refused to name the miscreants. Thus far no senior ANC official has been dismissed or disciplined. The ANC also admitted concern over the activities of its so-called Self Defence Units in the townships and particularly in Natal, which some senior officials alleged were out of control.

Uncovering Corruption

The morale of the ordinary South African was also eroded by a seemingly never-ending stream of reports of bureaucratic corruption as the kleptocracy which had been sustained by 40 years of apartheid was uncovered in inquiry after inquiry. White South Africans who had long used comparisons with corrupt governments in the rest of Africa to provide justification for continuing white rule, were shaken to discover that their civil servants were equally well-versed in bribery and corruption.

The old South African society was falling apart politically, socially and economically. Some reports put the cost of white collar crime committed in the country over the previous eight years at more than R380 billion, a figure well in excess of the total annual GDP. Some of the corruption was undoubtedly a product of political uncertainty as white South Africans, faced with a loss of political power, sought to maintain economic privilege and security through other means. Much of it was the product of apartheid itself. For more than four decades the government had stuffed millions of rands into the mouths of the black homeland satraps to maintain the myth of grand apartheid.

During 1992 a number of trials and commissions of enquiry uncovered a worm bed of economic crimes and misdeeds. Government scandals, which involved R5bn of taxpayers' money, ranged from a diversion of homeland 'development' funds (including R200m in Lebowa alone), to a billion rand Ministry of Transport fraud, to more than 200 doctors who had allegedly defrauded the state of considerable sums through the abuse of medical aid schemes. Crimes of this magnitude might have brought down many a Western government. In South Africa, however, although 35 government officials were under investigation and six had been convicted, no Cabinet minister had been sacked, forced to resign, or otherwise held accountable.

The climate of corruption that had flourished in the last days of the apartheid regime had also undoubtedly been stimulated during the years of isolation by the belief that any action was justified to defend the pariah state. This ranged from sanctions-busting to the diversion of billions of rands in slush funds to secret military intelligence operations and hundreds of front companies, unaccountable to the public *fiscus*. It is a matter of some irony that when President de Klerk tried to dismantle these operations they were simply 'privatised' and continued to function and undermine his reform strategy.

The scandals which continued to rock the regime also eroded de Klerk's authority, which was further hampered by the departure of some of his most trusted aides and cabinet ministers – including the Chairman of the National Party, Stoffel Botha, and the Minister of Constitutional Affairs, Dr Gerrit Viljoen – all of whom seemed to be suffering from political exhaustion. One of those who departed pleading nervous collapse was the Minister of Finance, Barend du Plessis. He was succeeded, however, by a non-politician and one of the country's most successful industrialists, Derek Keys, who brought much-needed discipline to the management of an economy which had been in recession since 1989.

Pressured by Dismal Economics

Real GDP had declined 3% since 1990. Although a strict monetary policy had been applied by the Governor of the Reserve Bank, Chris Stals, which had effectively succeeded in squeezing inflation down to below double figures for the first time in 14 years, both the government and the ANC began to realize that only a political settlement and the promise of political and social stability would stop the economy moving into a permanent downward spiral, from which there would be no recovery. Indeed, as violence continued unabated, the South African economy shrank at an annualized rate of over 5% during the third quarter of 1992.

In the 1992–93 budget Barend du Plessis had predicted economic growth of one per cent in 1992, but within weeks of his statement the full horror of the worst drought to afflict Southern Africa in living memory began to manifest. The persistent decline in economic growth had a dismal effect on state revenues and a decline in income, together with spending overruns by government, amounted to an 8% deficit in the 1993 budget.

Despite major cuts in the defence budget, it was becoming evident that the post-apartheid dividend would be much smaller than anticipated and that the new South Africa would be critically dependent upon foreign investment. Informed estimates suggested that the country would need in the region of R20bn of foreign capital a year to achieve a four per cent economic growth rate to cater for the existing workforce and keep new jobs coming on to the market. Such was the rate of decline that most estimates suggested that more than 50% of the economically active population in South Africa was no longer in formal employment.

With the constitutional negotiations on hold for much of the year and with the country racked by political violence (by the end of the year the death toll from politically related murders since 1990 had risen to 9,000), it was noteworthy that the stream of international visitors brought note books rather than cheque books. South Africa had restored open trading relations with most of the world; indeed, in 1993 Beijing planned a 'Chinese Trade Fair' in Johannesburg. If negative internal growth and healthy exports meant that the current account remained in surplus, however, it was obvious that foreign investment would wait until the country got its political house in order.

It was symptomatic of the country's plight that, while substantial foreign investment was conspicuous by its absence, South Africa received almost R1bn from various governments, including the UK, in overseas development aid in 1992, making it one of the world's largest recipients of project aid. These projects, such as those for the education and training of black leaders, were directed more at the ANC than the government.

Despite the fact that the post-apartheid reconstruction of South Africa would have to be underpinned by prodigious economic growth, the International Monetary Fund forecast that 1993 would bring, at best, growth of around one per cent. Eventually, recognition that political delay and its attempt to cripple the economy through mass action and continued sanctions would ensure only that it would inherit an economic wasteland drove the ANC leadership back to the negotiating table. It also persuaded the organization to announce that it would appeal for the lifting of sanctions the moment a transitional executive was in place and a date set for elections to the constituent assembly. Although sanctions were largely in abeyance, the ANC remained the gate-keeper to access to IMF funds.

New Negotiations – New Compromises

The resumption of bilateral talks with the government which resulted in September in the 'Record of Understanding' led, however, to an immediate outbreak of verbal hostilities from an outraged Chief Buthelezi, who believed that the government and the ANC were preparing to cut him out of any constitutional deal. He responded by threatening the secession of Natal-KwaZulu. Relations between the NP and Buthelezi continued to deteriorate as he sought common cause with other traditional homeland leaders and with the far right Conservative Party, insisting that any future constitution would have to be built around a semi-independent Natal-KwaZulu which retained only the slenderest confederal links with the centre.

Nevertheless, as fence-mending discussions with Buthelezi broke down amid mutual accusations of bad faith, the government and the ANC persisted with behind-the-scenes negotiations and, by November, de Klerk was able to unveil a timetable for transition which would have appeared hopelessly optimistic only a few months previously. In December and January two government/ANC 'bosberade' (bush councils) culminated in an agreement, brokered on the back of a document drawn up by South African Communist Party Chairman, Joe Slovo, and following suggestions by ANC moderate Thabo Mbeki.

The plan accepted the fact that the stability of any constitutional dispensation was critically dependent on the attitude of the SADF, the police and the public services, and that the white bureaucracy would require tangible assurances of job security if their support was to be secured. Even more important, the document also accepted the premise that, even after the adoption of the new constitution, 'the balance of forces and the interests of the country as a whole may still require a government of national unity'. It was a phrase which became the basis of a classic compromise between the government and the ANC and, when President de Klerk rose to address the Opening of Parliament in January 1993, it was almost universally accepted that he was opening the last full session of parliament in which black South Africa would not be represented.

He revealed that multiparty negotiations, the successor to last year's doomed CODESA, would probably resume at the beginning of March; that the transitional executive council (effectively a transitional non-racial government) could be in place by June; and that the interim constitution, under which South Africa's first fully democratic elections will be held probably before April 1994, would be completed by September 1993.

The last full session of the present parliament would be devoted to dismantling the tricameral parliament, clearing away the last remnants of South Africa's discriminatory laws, contracting the civil service in preparation for it to serve one nation instead of apartheid's divided state, and promoting acceptance of a Bill of Rights.

To frightened South Africans of all races he promised a crackdown on the violence and criminality which was claiming 20,000 deaths a year. To white South Africans, however, he promised no more than to negotiate for 'power-sharing, a strong regional government, checks and balances, the sensible accommodation of our country's cultural and linguistic diversity'.

Within days the outline of the compromise forged between government and the ANC became apparent when the ANC's national executive announced its acceptance of a five-year coalition government of national unity which could carry South Africa through to the end of the century. In exchange, the government appeared to drop its demand that compulsory power-sharing would be written into the constitution. The government had also abandoned the principle of a bicameral parliament and agreed that any decision on the powers of the regions in a federal system be delayed until the constituent assembly.

The wild card in this new accommodation remained Inkatha and its leader, Chief Buthelezi. The priority of both the ANC and the government was to bring him into government as a junior partner; but both sides made it clear that he would not retain the right of veto over a constitutional settlement. If necessary, the two main partners in South Africa's new deal would rule without him.

Many Boulders in the Path

That prospect raised the possibility that South Africa's new government might have to resort to authoritarian measures to contain the resulting unrest. A white oligarchy would transform itself, not into full-blown democracy, but into a multiracial oligarchy. Once again, full democracy in South Africa might be postponed and civil liberties, just beginning to emerge after decades of repression, could once again disappear.

Whether or not that prophecy is fulfilled depends on whether the government and the ANC can strike a deal on real federalism. There is every reason – save one – why federalism, with the maximum devolution of powers to regional and local authorities, should be accepted as the answer to South Africa's potent ethnic mix and its mutually suspicious and fearful minorities. But the ANC, having striven to win the keys of Pretoria and all the patronage that entails, is unwilling to deny itself the prize, especially as it sees in the government's desire for federalism simply a device once more to divide and rule the black majority.

Neither is it likely that Chief Buthelezi will give up without a struggle his plans for a semi-autonomous Natal-KwaZulu. Nevertheless, when a two-day conference was held at the beginning of March 1993 to plan for a new multiparty convention to be held at the beginning of April, Inkatha's representatives were present and conciliatory.

The conference was remarkable for including, for the first time, among the 28 parties, the two extremes of the South African political spectrum, the far right Conservative Party and the black radical Pan Africanist Congress. Their attendance was all the more remarkable for the fact that, at the end of 1992, the PAC's military wing APLA (the Azanian People's Liberation Army) had launched a series of raids on white farms in the Orange Free State and the North-eastern Cape, and the khaki commandos of the far right had not been slow to promise reprisals.

The March meeting postponed the contentious issues for the later, more substantive talks. Nevertheless, both the ANC and government negotiators hailed it 'a great success'. South Africa's non-racial government was, however, still far from its destination along the rocky road. In the months that lie ahead the ANC and the government will certainly squabble over the appropriate division of the spoils while attempting to cope with threats as diverse as an estranged Winnie Mandela and her army of youthful radicals, the APLA terrorists, the diehard racists of the right, the former spies of the 'dirty tricks' brigade, the Zulu *impis* of Inkatha and the murderers who gunned down six Inkatha school children on the eve of the March talks. But those threats are the reason why, between the government and the ANC at least, a deal has been done, and why it will probably stick. For they also represent the price of delay. After the 'nightmare year' of 1992, both the government and the ANC appear to have decided that it is a price neither they nor South Africa can afford.

As President de Klerk put it during his 1993 address to parliament, every South African faced a choice: 'either to support constitutional change and everything reasonably required for its success, or to retire into the *laager* and prepare for an armed and bloody struggle'. By April 1993 it appeared that, for the two main parties at least, the choice had been made.

ANGOLA: FROM BALLOT BOX TO BATTLEFIELD

On 29 and 30 September 1992, Angolans confounded the sceptics when they turned out peaceably and in large numbers to vote in the country's first ever competitive national elections. This was the culmination of a tense transitional period following the conclusion of a peace accord between the governing MPLA party and the UNITA movement at Bicesse in Portugal, in May 1991.

The transition from civil war to civilian elections had been dogged by problems with military demobilization, accusations and counter-accusations of accord violations by the competing political parties and outbreaks of political violence. Yet, the cease-fire had held, relatively free campaigning had been undertaken by the parties and international observers had monitored the voting and the count.

The overall organization of the elections had been far from perfect, but they proceeded more smoothly and fairly than could have been reasonably expected in a country which had not been at peace for over 30 years and which had never held democratic elections. Despite initial suspicions about the sincerity of the signatories to the peace accord (the MPLA, led by President José Eduardo dos Santos, and UNITA, led by Jonas Savimbi), the Angolan people had taken the election very seriously. Over 91% of the electorate had voted. There had been little debate of issues during the elections – the policies of the MPLA and UNITA were surprisingly similar and the smaller parties were acknowledged to have little chance of challenging their bids for power – but the electorate had a very clear choice between the formerly Marxist but increasingly pro-free market MPLA and the conservative and authoritarian UNITA movement.

As the count started, most Angolans, along with the peace accord guarantors (the United States, Portugal and Russia), the UN monitoring team (UNAVEM II) and the other international monitors, were congratulating themselves and looking forward to the inauguration of a popularly elected president, government and parliament. Just as the conduct of the election had confounded sceptics, however, so the electoral aftermath confounded such hopes. As the first results emerged, showing a clear lead for the governing MPLA, the whole vote was rejected as fraudulent by Jonas Savimbi. He demanded that the UN and the peace guarantors uphold his denunciation, even though the chief US liaison officer in Angola, Jeffrey Millington, and the UN special envoy, Margaret Anstee, had already praised the conduct and the fairness of the process.

Savimbi's pronouncement was accompanied by a thinly veiled threat to go back to the bush if the results were not declared null and void. The UN refused to condemn the elections as fraudulent and so UNITA mobilized its forces for war and seized control of several provincial capitals. There was a slow military response from what remained of the MPLA forces, but on 30 and 31 October fierce fighting erupted in the capital, Luanda, and civil war was effectively resumed.

Breaking with the Past: Bicesse to Ballot Box

The backward step to war destroyed all that had been achieved by the peace accord and during the transition period after the war. It also shattered the fragile peace that was being established across southern Africa after years of regional conflict, civil war, destabilization and liberation struggles.

The Bicesse accord itself grew out of the process of regional reconciliation started in 1988, after the South Africans and UNITA failed to defeat the MPLA and their Cuban allies at the siege of Cuito Cuanavale in southern Angola. This process had led to independence in Namibia, the withdrawal of South African forces from there and from southern Angola and a phased withdrawal of the 50,000 Cuban troops from Angola. Many thought that the removal of this large-scale international intervention from the Angolan civil war would automatically bring an end to the conflict. It did not. It took two and a half years from the signing of the Namibia deal to find a peace accord acceptable to the MPLA and UNITA. The decline in international and regional intervention had not mitigated the hatred and suspicion between them.

The accord failed to account for this lasting hatred and to provide for an armed UN presence sufficiently large and with sufficient powers to ensure the disarmament and demobilization of the warring armies and to provide a stable and nationally effective government during the transition. Instead, implementation of the accord took place with the MPLA government in power but working alongside a joint political and military commission – including MPLA, UNITA, American, Russian and Portuguese representatives – and with a UN force of 350 military observers and 90 police monitors (augmented by 400 election supervisors in the run-up to the elections). No measures were taken to enable the government to extend its administration to UNITA-held areas.

The small UN force had to oversee the confinement of 124,000 government troops and 23,000–70,000 UNITA guerrillas in assembly points, their disarming and the eventual demobilization of the entire armies. A new army was to be formed totalling 40,000 men (20,000 from each of the opposing sides). This was an impossible task. First, UNITA did not give accurate details of the size of its force, concealing tens of thousands of guerrillas and their arms in remote areas. Second, demobilization was slow and was not completed prior to the elections. And third, UNITA refused to allow the extension of government control to areas it occupied. The result was that by the elections, only 45% of government troops had been demobilized and 24% of the forces assembled by UNITA had given up their weapons. Most of the

UNITA army was therefore intact and the government had thousands of soldiers and the paramilitary police at its disposal.

The existence of these forces was disastrous. When UNITA contested the results of the election (which gave dos Santos 49.57% of the vote to Savimbi's 40.07% in the presidential election – necessitating a run-off between them – and the MPLA 53.74% to UNITA's 34.10%, with ten other parties getting 12.16%, in the parliamentary poll) it had the military muscle to go beyond verbal protests. At election campaign rallies, Savimbi had said that any result other than a clear victory for UNITA would indicate that the voting had been rigged; most Angolans and the international observers had taken this as bombastic rhetoric, but to Savimbi it had been a statement of intent.

Return to Battle

UNITA said it would respond vigorously to a 'rigged' election victory for the MPLA and it did. In October it withdrew from the integrated army and prepared to take by force what it had failed to obtain through the ballot box. Attempts by the UN and the United States to avert violence failed. South Africa's Foreign Minister, Pik Botha, was similarly unsuccessful in mediating, especially as the MPLA government accused South Africa of continuing covertly to supply UNITA with arms and other assistance.

UNITA's military response consisted of a widespread mobilization of forces to capture as many towns as possible. During the civil war, it had been successful as a rural guerrilla army but had failed to capture and hold urban areas. Now, it went all out to change that. It seized Caxito (the capital of Bengo province) and N'dalatando (the capital of Cuanza-Norte province) and on 30 October attempted to gain control of Luanda's international airport. The latter move brought a swift and bloody reaction from the MPLA government. Its forces were less prepared for war than UNITA's on a national basis. More of them had been disarmed, many had deserted and conscripts were not keen to fight on. They were strong, however, in and around Luanda. The paramilitary police beat back UNITA attacks in Luanda and the government distributed arms to its supporters there. A bitter fight followed and UNITA was effectively expelled from the city.

Savimbi had already moved his headquarters down to Huambo, Angola's second largest city. Although many of Savimbi's military and political high command were captured or killed in the Luanda fighting, disrupting his command structure, UNITA gained the upper hand in the first few months of the fighting. It seized nearly 70% of the country and challenged MPLA control of the northern provinces, the coastal regions and the crucial central and southern towns of Huambo, Cuito, Menongue and Luena.

The MPLA government was slow to respond, but when it did a full-scale war developed. The paramilitary police were the main strike

force, but were soon joined by re-formed military units and, in the towns, by armed MPLA cadres. There was fierce fighting in December and January around the coastal towns of Lobito and Benguela and the southern town of Lubango. In the north, using Zairean territory as a base, and with the reported support of Zairean troops and white mercenaries, UNITA captured the vital coastal oil installations at Soyo. The rebels threatened to move into the chief oil-producing province of Cabinda. This offensive was only stalled by a stern warning from the new Clinton administration in Washington that it would not tolerate any attacks on the US oil companies in Cabinda. Clinton was expected to recognize the MPLA government, but by March 1993 had failed to do so and had done little to influence the conflict, apart from confirming that the US had stopped supplying aid to UNITA after the elections.

The heaviest fighting centred on the town of Huambo. It is in the heart of the Ovimbundu-populated central plateau from which UNITA derives most of its support. Although Savimbi had set up his HQ there in October, the MPLA controlled much of the town. From December 1992 onwards, a battle raged around and within the town. The MPLA force there numbered several thousand and was supported by aircraft and artillery. By March 1993, 12,000 UNITA troops were fighting the increasingly beleaguered MPLA garrison. At least 6,000 people had been killed in the battles for the town and even higher casualties were expected as 10,000 MPLA troops advanced towards it from the west. They never reached it; on 7 March the MPLA announced that it had 'withdrawn' from the town.

The War Can Spread

In March 1993, UNITA still retained control over 60–70% of national territory but the MPLA government held Luanda, Cabinda and many of the major towns. Neither side looked as if it could achieve a military solution. A long drawn-out war of attrition seemed the most likely outcome. Prospects for a negotiated settlement were poor. The MPLA-led government (which included members of opposition parties elected in September) was committed to achieving a cease-fire and the resumption of the transitional process. It was also prepared to fight, and there was a strong faction within the MPLA and the army which favoured a military solution. UNITA, on the other hand, was committed to war. The only dissenting voices were those of UNITA commanders captured in Luanda who had taken up seats in parliament and, whether under duress or of their own free will, had called for a truce. Savimbi and his supporters based around Huambo showed no interest in peace.

Two attempts by the UN and the peace guarantors to get talks under way in Addis Ababa failed – the first round in January 1993 because of a UNITA refusal to agree to a cease-fire as a starting point, and the second round in February because most of the UNITA delegation failed to turn up, despite UN efforts to assist them and ensure their security.

The continuation of the war is a disaster for Angola and is a danger for the whole southern African region. UNITA has already accused Namibia of helping the MPLA government and there is considerable evidence that the SADF and South African Military Intelligence, with or without government approval, have been flying arms to UNITA bases in central Angola.

Zaire is also closely involved. Until the Bicesse accord, it provided the main conduit for US military aid to UNITA. Now, it is the main conduit for UNITA's diamond smuggling operation. Some $500m-worth of diamonds are mined illegally in northern Angola annually, and UNITA has access to an unknown proportion of these diamonds and can finance its war effort through the funds gained by selling them on the international market or through Zairean middle-men. President Mobutu of Zaire and his increasingly lawless army may be involved in the trade and may also be providing troops to enable UNITA to hold the coffee-, diamond- and oil-producing areas of northern Angola.

Zaire: Descent into Anarchy

Zaire's interest in the conflict in Angola is increasingly financial, although its ties with UNITA date back to the civil war. These were never severed totally, and Zairean forces undoubtedly assisted Savimbi's post-election bid for power by allowing UNITA to continue to use bases in Shaba province and other parts of Zaire bordering Angola.

The financial incentive is provided by the role Kinshasa has played as a market-place for the diamonds smuggled out of northern Angola by UNITA and by independent smugglers. In the longer term, Mobutu and his military commanders undoubtedly hope that with a UNITA government beholden to them, Zaire would be linked economically to an oil-rich and reconstructed Angola.

The financial aspect is vitally important to Mobutu and the Zairean army as the political struggle continues between the president and the interim government headed by Etienne Tshisekedi who led the Union for Democracy and Social Progress (UDPS), the strongest party within the opposition coalition. The economy of the country is in chaos as a result of the conflict, and smuggled diamonds are a valuable commodity.

Zaire has now suffered three years of political conflict and widespread violence following Mobutu's reluctant move in April 1990 to start a process of democratization. This was forced on him by domestic pressure from opposition groups, and international pressure from trading partners and aid donors (notably Belgium, France and the United States). In 1991 a national conference was convened to draw up a more democratic constitution; it was soon dominated by the opposition coalition, known as the Sacred Union.

Conflict between the conference and Mobutu, who did all he could to block progress on reform, led to violent clashes between the opposition and the army in September 1991. Kinshasa descended into anarchy, and violence and looting became the norm. French and Belgian troops were flown in to help suppress the rioting. Foreign pressure impelled Mobutu to appoint Tshisekedi as prime minister. His government lasted less than two weeks before it was dissolved by Mobutu, who appointed a new government which lasted a month, and then another, headed by breakaway opposition leader and effective head of Shaba province Nguza Karl-I Bond. Nguza worked with Mobutu to undermine the national conference, which Nguza tried to suspend in January 1992.

Foreign pressure in April led to the reinstatement of the national conference which proceeded to declare itself sovereign with legislative and executive powers, although it accepted Mobutu as head of state. It was unable, however, to exercise its powers and the conflict continued, and increasingly much of provincial Zaire was left without any semblance of government.

In August, the conference appointed a new government headed by Tshisekedi. Nguza was forced out of power and reacted by declaring that resource-rich Shaba province would not accept the sovereignty of the government (there followed vicious attacks on Tshisekedi supporters in Shaba). Shaba, formerly Katanga, has a history of political violence and attempts at secession. In late 1992, the national conference renamed itself the High Council of the Republic (HCR) and drew up an interim constitution which reduced President Mobutu's powers considerably and made the presidency a largely non-executive post. Mobutu has resisted and continued to try to govern over the heads of Tshisekedi and the HCR.

In November 1992, Mobutu attempted to control economic policy by introducing a new five million zaire banknote (with inflation running at 1,000% annually the zaire is practically worthless). The Tshisekedi government declared the note illegal and ordered banks not to accept it for payment. On 28 January 1993 the army garrison in Kinshasa rioted when the now useless notes appeared in their meagre and infrequent pay-packets. Mobutu's presidential guard suppressed the violence, killing up to 1,000 of the mutinous troops and numerous civilians.

Some semblance of order was restored in February, but the political conflict continued. The governments of Belgium, France and the US met during the month to put pressure on Mobutu to hand over power to the HCR and the government. They could do little to influence him because economic anarchy in the country made talk of economic sanctions pointless and because of Mobutu's control over the few organized troops.

During late February, troops thought to be loyal to Mobutu besieged the HCR. building and the home of its chairman, Archbishop Monsengwo Pasinya. The siege was ended after the HCR promised to solve the problem of army pay. Army Chief of Staff General Eluki Monga Awundu warned that if in future army demands were not met and peace insured, 'the Zairean armed forces will assume their responsibilities'. These have thus far chiefly centred on looting, violence and anarchy. Those three evils look to be Zaire's lot for the foreseeable future as Mobutu and the opposition fight for political power, while the army fights for whatever loot it can get.

While two of Central Africa's most powerful leaders, Savimbi and Mobutu, are unable to acquire power through consent they will continue to seek it by force. The result is likely to be further descent into chaos for two of Africa's largest countries.

Arms Control

FROM NEGOTIATION TO IMPLEMENTATION

In the wake of the Cold War, arms control negotiations have flourished. Agreements on nuclear, chemical and conventional weapons have been reached in rapid succession, and new issues have crowded the arms control agenda. At the same time that reaching agreements on limiting or eliminating certain types of weapons has become much easier, however, their implementation has become far more difficult. The emergence of democratic debate and parliamentary independence in the states of the former Soviet Union has made ratification of arms control agreements uncertain. Even when ratified, the new states are finding it difficult for economic and technical reasons actually to implement the sweeping arms reductions that have been agreed.

This phenomenon is likely to slow future arms control negotiations, with states concentrating instead on implementing the gains achieved to date. And these achievements are enormous: the elimination within seven years of all strategic nuclear arms from the non-Russian republics; a 70% cut in US and Russian strategic forces; the possible complete elimination of chemical weapons worldwide; an end to biological weapons research in Russia in violation of the 1972 Biological Weapons Convention (BWC); and deep reductions in conventional forces in Europe. Western countries, and especially the United States, will be called upon to extend financial and technical assistance to the newly independent states of the former Soviet Union and other countries to ensure that these arms control gains will in fact be realized.

While the traditional arms control agenda is likely to concentrate on securing the implementation of already reached agreements, the overall agenda may expand into more complex areas. Moving to the forefront will be such issues as ensuring the actual destruction of weapons to be reduced under various agreements, developing new and more cooperative patterns of verification to increase mutual confidence, and negotiating non-discriminatory restrictions on military capabilities to strengthen international non-proliferation norms. None of these issues will be easy to resolve. The number of players involved will increase and the issues are apt to be more complex than those tackled during the Cold War years. None of this will make reaching agreement any easier.

Strategic Nuclear Arms

The bilateral strategic nuclear arms control agenda was finally completed in 1992. A quarter-century of negotiations has brought Washington and Moscow back to where they began: the agreement to reduce their strategic forces to 3,000–3,500 weapons each is a return to the levels the US and the USSR deployed in the mid-1960s and mid-1970s respectively. Most importantly, both countries agreed to eliminate multi-warhead (or MIRVed) land-based missiles, which had been the central focus of strategic arms control ever since negotiations first began in November 1969. The Strategic Arms Reduction Talks (START) II Treaty incorporating these historic achievements was signed by US President George Bush and Russian President Boris Yeltsin in Moscow on 3 January 1993.

But implementation of START II is conditional upon the entry into force of its predecessor, the START I Treaty, which was originally signed by the Soviet Union and the United States in July 1991. Following the break-up of the USSR in December 1991, Belarus, Kazakhstan, Russia and Ukraine, on whose territory Soviet strategic weapons were based, pledged to adhere to and implement the US–Soviet treaty. How this was to be done without according the three non-Russian states *de jure* status as nuclear powers was the subject of intense negotiations in the first half of 1992.

On 23 May 1992, in Lisbon, the four countries and the United States signed a protocol to the START I Treaty that legally resolved the matter. Under the Lisbon protocol, the four former Soviet republics were identified as the bilateral US treaty partner under START I, and the three non-Russian states agreed to sign the Nuclear Non-Proliferation Treaty (NPT) as non-nuclear weapons states 'in the shortest time possible'. In separate, legally binding letters to the US president, the same three countries further pledged to eliminate all strategic weapons on their territory within the seven-year implementation period of the Treaty.

The Lisbon formula appeared to have settled the matter. Kazakhstan ratified START I in July 1992, and the United States, Russia and Belarus followed in October, November and February 1993 respectively. Ukraine balked in the latter half of 1992. While continuing to pledge that it would ratify START I and sign and ratify the NPT, Kiev made parliamentary action conditional on obtaining adequate security guarantees from Russia and the US, receiving financial compensation for the dismantling of weapons on its soil, and settling the issue of control over the weapons that were still on its territory.

Whether the concerns behind these conditions were real or merely designed to respond to growing pressures within Ukraine to retain the nuclear weapons on its territory forever, Moscow and Washington have attempted to address them directly. Both have indicated that they would guarantee Ukraine's security, the United States by reiterating the positive security guarantee it has extended to all non-nuclear signatories of the NPT, and Russia by stating openly that it would give 'a guarantee to preserve and safeguard the territorial integrity of Ukraine and its borders and defend it from nuclear attack'. Washington has also offered to provide $175m in direct assistance for the dismantling of nuclear weapons and missiles on Ukrainian soil, while Russia has indicated that it will share the proceeds of the sale of highly enriched uranium recovered from dismantled weapons. The issue of control remains unsettled. Physical control over the weapons remains in the hands of the Russian president and the commander of the strategic forces of the Commonwealth of Independent States (CIS), but Kiev continues to assert 'administrative' control over the forces.

Whether the differences between Ukraine and the other parties to the START I Treaty can be worked out remains to be seen. Kiev may have been holding out in return for substantial private and public investment. But rising nationalist sentiment in Ukraine, mixed signals from Moscow and Washington, and a general lack of urgency have thrown the issue into considerable doubt.

Without a resolution of the Ukrainian issue, START II cannot be implemented. Because START II is a truly historic achievement, finding a solution to this issue becomes all the more urgent. The basic framework for the treaty was established during the Bush–Yeltsin Washington summit in June 1992 when it was agreed that US and Russian strategic forces would be reduced in phases to 3,000–3,500 within a decade. All MIRVed ICBM warheads would be eliminated, and warheads on submarine-launched ballistic missiles (SLBMs) would be limited to 1,750 on each side. Unlike START I, air-delivered weapons would be counted according to the number for which heavy bombers were actually equipped. Each country could also exclude up to 100 bombers from the count by reorienting them to conventional roles.

The START II framework was hailed in the West as a major arms control achievement. In Russia, however, it came under sustained attack, mainly because the agreement cuts land-based missiles which are the backbone of Russia's strategic forces. Without a substantial investment, which it clearly could not afford, Russian ICBM warheads would by the end of the decade account for only about 15% of its strategic weapons, compared to 65% before START. At the same time, the lax rules governing heavy bombers would provide the United States with appreciable advantages.

How to resolve these concerns was the subject of intense negotiations in the months leading up to the signing of START II in January 1993. In the end, Washington made a number of significant concessions. It allowed Russia to retain 90 SS-18 missile silos to be used by smaller, single-warhead missiles, provided Russia agreed to destroy all SS-18 missiles. The United States also agreed that Russia could remove five of the six warheads on 105 SS-19 missiles in order to implement the ban on MIRVed intercontinental ballistic missile (ICBM) warheads. In this way, Russia could retain up to 195 silo-based ICBMs at little cost, in addition to the mobile, single-warhead SS-25 it already deployed. In the end, Washington agreed to limit the reorientation of heavy bombers from conventional to nuclear roles to one time only and acceded to Moscow's request to inspect the B-2 bomber to see how many weapons it actually carried, a provision Washington had rejected during the START I negotiations.

Although these US concessions met many of the Russian concerns, ratification of the START II Treaty is threatened by political turmoil in Russia and the growing strength of the hardline opposition. It will take much skill and hard work to ensure that the agreement is ratified and implemented.

Chemical and Biological Weapons

On 13 January 1993, 130 nations gathered in Paris to sign the Chemical Weapons Convention (CWC), which had been under negotiation in the UN Conference on Disarmament since the early 1970s. The CWC, which bans the possession, acquisition, production, stockpiling, transfer and use of chemical weapons and mandates the destruction of any CW stocks that exist within ten years of the Convention's entry into force, is the most ambitious disarmament agreement ever negotiated. The CWC's verification regime is also the most comprehensive to date. It not only mandates routine and *ad hoc* inspections of civilian industries and military sites, but allows challenge inspections with guaranteed access to any suspect site, although the degree of access is subject to negotiation between the inspected state and the inspectors. The CWC will enter into force 180 days after the 65th signatory has ratified the convention, but in no case earlier than 13 January 1995. By mid-February 1993, 136 countries had signed the Treaty.

Full implementation of the CWC will face two challenges: destroying the 40,000 agent tonnes of Russian chemicals; and ensuring that all countries believed to possess chemical weapons sign it. Unlike the United States, Russia lacks an operational facility to destroy the former Soviet chemical weapons stockpile. It faces both financial obstacles and public opposition to the construction of an environmentally sound destruction facility. The cost of destroying the stockpile will run into billions of US dollars and so far has not been a high priority. Public opposition has also delayed construction, and accounted for the closure of the only existing Soviet facility.

The United States has appropriated $25m for the design of a facility to be built in Russia that meets environmental standards, but construction will require Western financial assistance. Without any destruction facility it is unlikely that Russia can meet the Convention's ten-year timetable for destroying CW stocks. The Convention, however, allows for a five-year extension of the timetable.

A second problem is to convince all states believed to possess chemical weapons to sign. Nine of the 15 countries, in addition to the US and Russia, which are known or believed to possess chemical weapons have now signed the Convention. These signatories include China, India, Iran, Israel and Pakistan. Israel's accession is especially significant, not only because in so doing it will subject itself to intrusive inspections for the first time, but also because with the notable exception of Iran, Saudi Arabia and Kuwait, no other Middle Eastern country signed the CWC. The absence in Paris of the major Arab states, including Egypt, Iraq, Jordan, Libya and Syria, was especially disappointing, since all but Jordan are believed (or, in the case of Iraq, known) to possess chemical weapons. Convincing these states (as well as North Korea, the only other presumed CW state not to sign) to join the Convention will be a difficult, but essential task to ensure the total abolition of chemical weapons.

There were also developments in the biological weapons area, with Russia acknowledging that the Soviet Union had violated the BWC ever since its entry into force in 1975. In a US–Russian–British statement on 14 September 1992, Moscow agreed to allow 'visits to any non-military biological site at any time to remove ambiguities'. US and British visitors would have unrestricted access to the facilities, and subsequent Russian visits to US and British facilities would also be held. This agreement should go a long way towards resolving long-standing US charges of Soviet non-compliance with the BWC.

The tripartite agreement also underscored that greater openness, including through regular and reciprocal inspections, could strengthen the BWC, which lacks any verification provisions. In September 1991, the parties to the BWC agreed to set up an experts group to study whether adding a verification protocol to the BWC would be desirable. Although the Bush administration opposed the negotiation of a protocol because it believed that effective verification is impossible, the tripartite agreement leaves open the possibility that the Clinton administration may support adding a verification protocol to the BWC.

Conventional Forces

The Treaty on Conventional Armed Forces in Europe (CFE) officially entered into force in November 1992, two years after it was signed. On 15 May 1992, the eight former Soviet republics with territory in the treaty's zone of application reached agreement in Tashkent on how to divide among themselves the Soviet allocation of treaty-limited equipment (TLE). The bulk of the allocation went to Russia, which received somewhat over 50% of the tanks, armoured combat vehicles and helicopters, slightly less than 50% of the artillery, and well over 50% of the aircraft. Ukraine received between 20 and 30% of the TLE, with five other states receiving the remainder.

The Tashkent agreement opened the way for an extraordinary conference of those states now taking part to amend the CFE Treaty so as to reflect the dissolution of the Soviet Union, an original party to the treaty. During the Conference on Security and Cooperation in Europe (CSCE) summit in Helsinki, the now 29 parties to the treaty agreed to its provisional entry into force on 7 July 1992, even though Armenia and Belarus had yet to ratify it. Baseline inspections of declared TLE holdings were completed on 14 November, five days after the Treaty formally entered into force. Mandated reductions in TLE will have to be completed by 13 November 1995.

The Helsinki CSCE summit also welcomed the conclusion of two additional treaties. On 10 July 1992, the 29 parties to the CFE Treaty signed the politically binding CFE-1A agreement, which sets a ceiling on the number of military personnel each country may deploy within the Atlantic-to-the-Urals area at levels declared by the parties themselves. Earlier, on 24 March 1992, all NATO and former non-Soviet Warsaw Pact states, plus Belarus, Georgia, Russia and Ukraine, signed the Open Skies Treaty, under which each party is allowed to overfly the entire territory of other parties. Annual quotas, calculated on the basis of territorial size, are set for the number of flights each country can make and must receive.

At the Helsinki summit the 52 CSCE member-states (Yugoslavia having been suspended) agreed to convene a Forum for Security Cooperation (FSC) to discuss and negotiate new arms control, disarmament, confidence- and security-building, security cooperation and conflict-prevention measures. The programme for immediate action sets out 14 areas for negotiation, including harmonization of obligations concerning arms control, disarmament, and confidence- and security-building measures, new stabilizing measures, global exchanges of military information, cooperation in respect of non-proliferation, regional security issues, and cooperation in defence conversion, force planning and verification. The FSC opened in September 1992 in Vienna and initial discussions focused on harmonization and military information exchanges.

The New Agenda

The traditional engine of arms control is running out of steam. The arms control successes of the last few years have left many states overwhelmed, and securing the gains achieved to date will be the priority for the foreseeable future. That is why cooperative arms control and disarmament, designed to implement agreements achieved to date, is now deemed more important than negotiating additional force-reduction agreements. The need to help poverty-stricken former Soviet republics dismantle their nuclear, chemical, biological and conventional weaponry amassed during 40 years of Cold War confrontation has been clearly recognized. In November 1991, the US Congress allocated $400m to assist in the dismantling of Soviet weapons of mass destruction. In October 1992, Congress appropriated an additional $400m for this purpose.

As of January 1993, one-quarter of these funds had been allocated to specific projects. These included helping Russia in the transportation and storage of nuclear weapons and materials, the design of chemical weapons destruction facilities, the accounting and control of fissile materials, the creation of a centre to employ weapons scientists on civilian projects and the provision of accident response equipment. Ukraine and Belarus also received funding for some of these purposes, as well as to help both new states to establish export controls. The aim of these projects is both to ensure that agreements to eliminate weapons of mass destruction are implemented in a secure, safe and environmentally sound manner, and to reduce the likelihood of weapons, materials or knowledge spreading to other countries through sale, theft or bribery.

Another priority of the new arms control agenda is to halt the proliferation of weapons of mass destruction and advanced technologies. In recent years, traditional non-proliferation regimes, based primarily on export controls, have been strengthened to address this concern (see *Strategic Survey 1991-1992*, pp. 200-211). At the same time, there is a growing recognition that relying on export controls alone may not be enough: they may slow the acquisition of military technology, but they are unlikely to stop it. Regional arms control and non-discriminatory arms limitations are increasingly seen as useful complements to export controls.

While proliferation is generally discussed as a concern that affects the entire Third World, the real problem is located in a few specific regions: the Middle East, South Asia and North-east Asia. In most of the remainder of the world, proliferation never has been, or no longer is, of real concern. In Latin America, for example, amendments to the 1967 Treaty of Tlatelolco were adopted in August 1992, satisfying Argentinian, Brazilian and Chilean concerns. As a result, the Latin American nuclear-free zone will soon become a reality.

Active diplomacy is therefore focused on the regions of most concern. An arms control dialogue has been started in the Middle East as part of the peace process. Various confidence-building proposals affecting conventional forces have been discussed and some limited progress has been made. Israel's signing of the CWC, and intense private discussions between the US and Israel about the latter's nuclear programme, have led to hopes for greater transparency in this area as well. In South Asia, the United States has begun bilateral discussions with India and Pakistan in order to address the nuclear problem. Although the gulf between many of the countries involved remains wide, the discussions may open the way to five-power talks on nuclear proliferation that would also involve Russia and China. The burst of activity in the two Koreas in late 1991 and early 1992 has not been followed by any further progress on how to curb Pyongyang's nuclear ambitions or the massive conventional forces deployed by both sides along the demilitarized zone. North Korea allowed International Atomic Energy Agency inspections of its declared nuclear facilities, but in March 1993 it refused requests for inspections of a suspect facility at Yongbyon. In a sudden explosion of anger North Korea became the first country to withdraw from the NPT which it had joined in 1985, leaving the question of its nuclear intentions even more shrouded in doubt.

As the CSCE experience in Europe has demonstrated, regional arms control cannot achieve results overnight. However, the fact that countries in these three regions are engaged in a dialogue is important in and of itself. Dialogue may create a greater mutual awareness of security concerns and lead all sides to identify more clearly the areas of agreement and disagreement.

In addition to regional dialogues, non-discriminatory arms limitation approaches may also be needed. Clearly, the time is not yet ripe for the declared nuclear powers to approach nuclear weapons in the same manner as they have chemical and biological weapons – that is, to seek their complete elimination on a worldwide basis. But some non-discriminatory restrictions on their nuclear capabilities may be possible, particularly in the area of nuclear testing, where prospects for a complete ban are today brighter than they have been at any time since the late 1950s.

The impetus for a comprehensive test ban (CTB) has come from unilateral actions by Russia, France and the United States. In October 1991, the then Soviet President Mikhail Gorbachev declared a one-year testing moratorium, which was reaffirmed by Russian President Yeltsin in January 1992. The following April, France announced that it would suspend testing for the remainder of the year. In October the US Congress voted to suspend US testing until July 1993, limiting testing thereafter to 15 tests over a three-year period for safety and reliability purposes only, and declared that the United States would halt testing by September 1996, unless another nuclear power were to test first.

With President Clinton firmly on record in favour of a CTB, prospects for negotiating a ban in time for the 1995 NPT review conference have brightened. France and Russia have declared that they, too, will suspend testing until July 1993, and both support a CTB. China and Britain are the only declared nuclear powers to maintain that they must continue testing. But since Britain does so at the Nevada testing site, US policy on the issue will likely determine British policy as well. Following on the heels of the deep nuclear reductions of START II, a CTB would be powerful evidence that the nuclear powers are finally beginning to fulfil their commitment under Article VI of the NPT to end the nuclear arms race and begin the process of disarmament. This will strengthen efforts to extend the NPT indefinitely, an issue that must be decided at the 1995 review conference.

It has been said that with the end of the Cold War, the need for arms control has disappeared. There is some truth in this statement: the spectacle of tense summits and years of intense negotiations in Geneva and Vienna is clearly a thing of the past. Nor are the successes or failures of arms control any longer the barometer of the state of relations among major powers. But none of this had anything to do with arms control, which involves the mutual regulation of armaments in an effort to reduce the probability of their ever having to be used. That goal is clearly not a thing of the past, as the agreements of the last two years have shown and the large remaining agenda attests. Arms control as a circus has disappeared, and that is for the better; what remains is arms control as serious business, and it would be best if everyone knuckled down to the task.

Chronologies

UNITED STATES AND CANADA

January
22–23   40 donor governments meet in Washington to coordinate aid to former USSR republics; President Bush announces proposed $600m increase.
23   US Secretary of State James Baker announces two-week emergency food airlift to USSR beginning 10 February.
29   Bush announces FY 1993 defence budget of $291bn, ending production of B-2 bomber, *Seawolf* submarine and sea-based missiles.
30   Bush announces plans to close 83 military installations in Europe.

February
1   Bush holds talks with Russian president, Boris Yeltsin.
11   Bush announces cessation of production of ozone-destroying chemicals by end of 1995.
25   Canada announces it will withdraw its troops from Europe by 1994.
26–27   In San Antonio, Bush and leaders of Colombia, Bolivia, Peru, Ecuador, Mexico and Venezuela meet to discuss drug trafficking.

March
10   General Manuel Antonio Noriega, ousted Panamanian president, refuses to testify at US trial.
17–   Bush rejects congressional compromise on aid to Israel that might go for building settlements in Occupied Territories; US offers $300m in housing loan guarantees (18).
26   US Secretary of Defense, Dick Cheney, announces plans to reduce National Guard and reserves by 250,000 before end of 1997.

April
1–   Bush offers $600m in humanitarian/technical aid and $1.1bn in loan guarantees to the former Soviet Union for grain purchases; Deputy Secretary of State Lawrence Eagleburger certifies to Congress that Russia, Ukraine and Belarus are eligible to receive $400m in aid for dismantling nuclear weapons and retaining scientists (28).
19   Bush tightens 30-year economic Cuban blockade by barring cruisers or cargo ships from visiting Cuba.
26   At Washington meeting, G-7 nations agree to $6bn rouble stabilization fund for Russia.

May
22   US Defense Department announces the closure or reduction of 61 European and two South Korean bases.
28   US announces future publication of provisional list of more than $1bn-worth of EC goods subject to protective tariffs.

June
3   US House of Representatives votes to cut troops abroad to 228,000 by end of 1995 and the defence budget by $3.5bn.
4   Senate approves legislation to tighten Cuban sanctions.

6–8   Bush hosts three-day meeting with UK Prime Minister John Major at Camp David.

15   US Supreme Court condones abducting foreigners for trial.

16   Caspar Weinberger, ex-Secretary of Defense, indicted on criminal charges in Iran–Contra affair.

16–   Bush and Yeltsin begin two-day Washington summit; sign agreement calling for creation of Euro-Atlantic peacekeeping force (17).

July

1   Japanese Prime Minister Kiichi Miyazawa begins three-day visit to US.

2   Bush announces completion of withdrawal of all ground and naval tactical nuclear weapons from outside the US.

5   US and Russia conduct first joint naval exercise in Barents Sea.

8   Canadian federal government and nine provinces conclude agreement on constitutional change to reshape Senate and status of Quebec.

13   Bush announces cessation of plutonium production.

August

5   US army announces that in 1993 it will withdraw 115 units, totalling 11,900 troops, from Germany.

12   Canada, Mexico and US conclude agreement on formation of North American Free Trade Area.

13   Bush moves US Secretary of State Baker to White House to run election campaign; Eagleburger named Acting Secretary of State.

20–   Canadian national and provincial governments agree restructuring of federal parliament; Quebec agrees (22).

September

1–   US agrees to buy from Russia at least 10 tons of weapons-grade uranium per year for five years, and 30 tons thereafter, for conversion for use in nuclear power stations; US offers Russia $1.15bn in loan guarantees and other assistance for food (14); Senate approves a link of aid to troop withdrawals from the Baltic, and the $12bn Bush requested as IMF contribution (24).

14   Senate and House of Representatives votes to link renewal of China's MFN status with human rights progress.

20   Senate favours US armed forces cuts in Europe to 100,000 by September 1996, but not to go below 150,000 until 1995, and authorizes $274bn defence bill (FY 1993).

24   Senate Appropriations Committee approves $14.3bn foreign aid starting October 1992, including $10bn housing loan guarantees for Israel.

30   US closes base in Søndre Strømfjord in Greenland and returns Subic Bay naval base to Philippines.

October

1   US Senate fails to overturn Bush's veto on imposing conditions on renewal of China's MFN status.

26   Canadian referendum results in overwhelming negative vote on constitutional reforms.

November

4   Arkansas Governor Bill Clinton elected 42nd President of the US.

December

5   Bush sends letter to Ukrainian President Leonid Kravchuk offering political and economic aid and $175m for dismantling nuclear warheads if Ukraine agrees to become nuclear weapons-free state.

10–   President-elect Clinton names Lloyd Bentsen as Secretary of Treasury; Les
       Aspin as Secretary of Defense and Warren Christopher as Secretary of State
       (22).
14   Bush authorizes US companies to open offices in Vietnam.
17   Bush, Canadian Prime Minister Brian Mulroney and Mexican President
       Carlos Salinas sign NAFTA.
25   Bush pardons ex-Secretary of Defense Caspar Weinberger and five other
       Reagan aides involved in Iran–Contra scandal.

CENTRAL AND SOUTH AMERICA

January
1–   El Salvadoran government and FMLN agree cease-fire terms to be enforced
       on 1 February; troops and FMLN clash in north (2); peace talks resume in
       New York (6); peace agreement signed in Mexico (16).
8   Deposed Haitian president, Jean-Bertrand Aristide, accepts René Theodore
       as new prime minister after talks in Venezuela.
24   Bolivian President Jaime Paz Zamora and Peruvian President Alberto
       Fujimori sign agreement allowing bilateral transit for goods without custom
       formalities through corridor giving landlocked Bolivia free port facilities.

February
1   El Salvadoran cease-fire begins.
4–   US announces intention to lift trade embargo on Haiti; deposed President
       Aristide signs agreement with leaders of Haitian National Assembly, paving
       way for his return, following OAS-sponsored talks (20–23).
10   Argentinian air force formally transfers *Condor* II missiles project to civilian
       control.

March
28–   Jamaican Prime Minister, Michael Manley, retires; Percival James Patterson
       replaces him (30).

April
5–   Peruvian President Alberto Fujimori dissolves Congress and suspends the
       constitution; Prime Minister Alfonso de los Heros and his cabinet resign,
       opposition leaders are placed under house arrest (6); US suspends $320m aid
       and OAS calls for return to democracy (7); OAS decides not to impose
       economic sanctions (13); Vice-President Maximo San Roman is sworn in
       symbolically as rival constitutional president (21).
13   Haitian Defence MFMLNinister, Colonel Gracia Jean, resigns.
23   Colombian government establishes three-day state of emergency to counter
       electricity crisis.

May
17   No candidate receives absolute majority in first round of Ecuador's presiden-
       tial elections; next round scheduled for 5 July.
23–25 Colombian rebels clash with government forces near Dabeiba.
27   EC environment commissioner Carlo Ripa di Mena announces he will not
       participate in planned Rio Earth Summit because of industrial nations' re-
       fusal to commit to environmental protection.
28   US closes its ports to ships breaking Haitian embargo.

June

3– UN 12-day Earth Summit opens in Rio de Janeiro; Convention on Climate change agreed (4); declaration passed committing UN members to environmental protection measures (11); biodiversity treaty signed (12); declaration of principles on developmental and environmental needs signed (14).

11– Haitian parliament approves Marc Bazin as prime minister; sworn in (21).

11 Bush's visit to Panama marred by anti-US demonstrations.

30 In El Salvador FMLN demobilizes two-fifths of its forces.

July

5 Sixto Durán Ballen wins second round in the Ecuadorean presidential election.

10 Former Panamanian president, General Manuel Noriega, sentenced to 40-years imprisonment in US.

22 In Colombia Pablo Escobar, Medellín drug leader, escapes from prison.

August

3 Surinamese government and Surinamese Liberation Army conclude peace accord.

7 At five-day talks in Mexico, Guatemalan government and Guatemalan Revolutionary National Unity agree restrictions on army-sponsored 'civil defence' patrols.

16– In El Salvador army finishes demobilizing one of five insurgency battalions; FMLN and government agree new peace agreement timetable following four-day visit by UN peace negotiator, Marrack Goulding (17).

26 Peru suspends membership of Andean Pact, assumes observer status until end of 1993.

27 Cuba announces willingness to share nuclear information with any neighbouring country.

September

1– In Brazil, impeachment proceedings against President Fernando Collor de Mello are formally initiated; Collor is suspended from power, and government resigns *en masse* (29).

5 In Nicaragua, President Violeta Chamorro dismisses top police chief, René Vivas, in bid to secure US aid.

9– Russia and Cuba begin discussions on withdrawal of 16,000 CIS troops; they agree completion date in first six months of 1993 (16).

11– ICJ settles 'Soccer War' border disagreement between El Salvador and Honduras giving Honduras two-thirds of land and ruling they must share Gulf of Fonseca with Nicaragua.

12 In Peru, *Sendero Luminoso*'s leader Abimael Guzman Reynoso captured.

21 Mexico and the Vatican re-establish diplomatic relations.

21 FMLN demobilizes another two-fifths of its forces.

October

7– In Peru, Guzman Reynoso sentenced to life imprisonment for treason; *Sendero Luminoso* kills 44 in La Mar province (10); 10 alleged members arrested including Marta Huatay, member of the Association of Democratic Lawyers (17).

8– In Colombia three escaped members of Medellín cartel surrender to authorities; Brance Munoz, Medellín military leader, shot dead (28).

16 Rigoberta Menchú, Guatemalan human rights activist, wins Nobel peace prize.

28– In El Salvador, President Alfredo Cristiani announces that he has suspended all steps to reform, purge and demobilize the army.

November

6– In Colombia, guerrilla groups launch renewed offensive against government; President Cesar Gaviria declares 90-day state of emergency following weekend violence (8).

10– Guatemalan Constitutional Court upholds decision to recognize Belize; Guatemalan Congress endorses resolution clearing 130-year-old dispute with UK and Belize (26).

13 Attempted coup against Peruvian President Alberto Fujimori fails.

15 In Panamanian referendum voters reject constitutional reform outlawing maintenance of an army.

27 Attempted military coup in Venezuela foiled.

December

2– In El Salvador, FMLN begin destroying weapons; Atlacatl battalion dismantled (8); demobilization completed (14); end to civil war formally declared (15).

2– In Brazil, senate votes to indict President Fernando Collor de Mello for corruption and influence peddling; Collor de Mello resigns and Itamar Franco sworn in as president (29).

26–28 In Peru, 20 dogs used as dynamite bombs in capital by *Sendero Luminoso* and several car bombs explode in three-day violence.

EUROPE

January

1– In Georgia, fighting resumes in Tbilisi; rebels overthrow President Zviad Gamsakhurdia and set up military council (2); he flees (6); clashes ensue in Idzhevan (8); supporters of Gamsakhurdia agree truce (21); government troops take Tskhinvali (22) and seize Poti (28).

1– Ukraine frees prices; cuts military communication links with Russia (8).

3– Russia abolishes state-set prices; compromise solution on Black Sea Fleet agreed at talks between Ukraine and Russia (13); 12 former officials charged with conspiring to seize power in August coup (14); Russia announces end of nuclear targeting of US (26); and of UK (30).

3– In the former Yugoslavia, federal army and Croatian leaders begin cease-fire; Serbs in Bosnia-Herzegovina declare independence (9); Vatican recognizes Croatia and Slovenia (13); EC follows suit (15); cease-fire violated in Osijek and Slavonia (18–19); Macedonia votes to withdraw representatives from federal parliament (22).

16 In Estonia, state of emergency imposed; Estonian Prime Minister Edgar Savisaar resigns.

17– Former Greek prime minister, Andreas Papandreou, acquitted of bribery and corruption; Greece establishes diplomatic relations with Armenia (20).

19 President Zhelyu Zhelev wins final round of Bulgarian presidential election.

19 South Ossetia votes for independence from Georgia.

20 Finland and Russia sign trade and friendship pact.

30 10 former Soviet republics (Armenia, Ukraine, Belarus, Moldova, Tajikistan, Uzbekistan, Kyrgyzstan, Kazakhstan, Turkmenistan and Azerbaijan) join CSCE.

February

2— In Nagorno-Karabakh, Armenians open new attack; Azeri armed forces launch effort to recapture lost ground as Azeri and Armenian leaders agree to talks (3); following Moscow peace talks Armenian and Azeri foreign ministers call for cease-fire (20); Azeris seize munitions from Russian camp near Agdam (24); Azeri rockets pound capital, Stepanakert, and Armenian forces seize Azeri town, Khojaly (26).

3— EC lifts sanctions against Croatia; Croatian president, Franjo Tudjman, allows deployment of UN peacekeepers (6); Serbia and Montenegro agree plan to create new Yugoslavia following secession of Croatia and Slovenia (13); Krajina's president, Milan Babic, accepts use of UN peacekeepers (17); UN Security Council votes to dispatch 14,000 peacekeepers for 12 months (21).

3 Foreign ministers of Black Sea Economic Cooperation Zone (Turkey, Russia, Azerbaijan, Ukraine, Bulgaria, Romania, Armenia, Georgia and Moldova) meet in Turkey.

5— Mary Robinson becomes first Irish President to visit Northern Ireland; Albert Reynolds replaces Charles Haughey as Irish prime minister (6).   5— Russian President, Boris Yeltsin, visits France; signs friendship pact (7).

9 US Secretary of State Baker leaves for 10-day tour of Russia and Central Asia; announces $14m to found science centre to employ scientists who worked on Soviet nuclear programmes (17).

14 11 leaders of CIS meet in Minsk.

27 Germany and Czechoslovakia sign friendship treaty.

March

1— Bosnia-Herzegovina votes for independence in referendum; Serbs march on Sarajevo as President Alija Izetbegovic declares independence (3); EC and US agree to coordinate Yugoslav policy (10); Muslims, Serbs and Croats from Bosnia-Herzegovina resume EC talks (16); advance UN teams start move into Croatia to prepare for peacekeeping troops (16); at EC talks Bosnian warring factions agree to separation of territory into ethnic regions (17); Bosnian Muslims call for UN protection as Serbs proclaim own constitution (28); three Bosnian factions resume EC talks in Brussels (29–30).

2 Eight former Soviet republics (Armenia, Azerbaijan, Moldova, Kazakhstan, Kyrgyzstan, Uzbekistan, Tajikistan and Turkmenistan) join UN.

2— Violence flares in Moldova between ethnic Russians and Romanian majority; Moldovans seize weapons from Ukrainian barracks in Dniestr region (3); Russian minority granted until 17 March to surrender weapons (15); Slav minority declare state of emergency in Dniestr region (16); Ukranian President Leonid Kravchuk orders deployment of forces on Moldovan border (17); Moldovan President Mircea Snegur declares state of emergency and curfew (28); fighting continues in Koshnitsa as Dniestr and Russian cossacks attack (30); Ukrainian, Russian, Romanian and Moldovan foreign ministers meet to resolve conflict (30–31).

2— Last CIS soldiers withdraw from Nagorno-Karabakh; Azeris demand resignation of their president, Mutalibov (5); he resigns (6); Azeris attack Stepanakert, capital of Nagorno-Karabakh, as Armenians counter-attack Shusha, whilst at meeting of the 35-nation North Atlantic Cooperation Council (NACC) in Brussels they agree jointly to solve conflict (10); Armenian and Azeri foreign ministers sign draft peace accord in Tehran (15); fighting continues in Lachin and Shusha in Azerbaijan (16); UN special envoy, Cyrus

Vance, arrives in Azerbaijan on peace mission (17); Armenia declares state of emergency (18); both sides agree to representation at CSCE-sponsored peace talks (24); Azeris bomb Stepanakert (29–30); Iran announces cease-fire extension of two weeks (27).

5–6 Baltic Council (Norway, Denmark, Estonia, Finland, Germany, Latvia, Poland, Russia and Sweden) established in Copenhagen.

10 Ten CIS republics join NACC.

10– In Georgia, Eduard Shevardnadze appointed as transitional prime minister; Georgian armed forces loyal to Zviad Gamsakhurdia, deposed Georgian president, agree withdrawal from Mingrelia region (17); EC establishes diplomatic relations with Georgia (23); US follows suit (24).

12– Ukrainian President Kravchuk suspends nuclear weapons transfer to Russia; parliament approves withdrawal from rouble zone and establishment of own customs (24).

18– Russia announces willingness to renegotiate status of Chechnia; Tatarstan votes in favour of self-rule (21); 18 republics, excluding Tatarstan and Chechnia, sign federal treaty in Moscow (31).

18 Parliament in Belarus votes to establish own armed forces.

26– Germany halts arms exports to Turkey alleging Turkish use of weapons against Kurds; Defence Minister Gerhard Stoltenberg resigns over issue, is replaced by Volker Rühe (31).

27 Russia and 13 former USSR republics join IMF.

April

1 At NATO defence ministers' meeting in Brussels, former Warsaw Pact members and NATO agree to undertake joint training and manoeuvres.

1– Moldovan troops launch attack in Dniestr region during two-day peace talks with Russia, Ukraine and Romania; at foreign ministers' meeting between Moldova, Russia, Ukraine and Romania cease-fire agreed (6); cease-fire begins as President Mircea Snegur announces request for Ukrainian troops to enforce it (7); fighting erupts again (18).

1– Clashes ensue between Georgian forces and former President Gamsakhurdia's forces; diplomatic relations established with Germany (13).

2 Lithuania and Belarus conclude bilateral cooperation treaty.

2 French President François Mitterrand names former economics minister Pierre Bérégovoy to replace Edith Cresson as prime minister.

3– Cease-fire broken in Croatia; EC recognizes Bosnia-Herzegovina (7); Serb leaders declare independent Bosnian republic and Yugoslav jets launch rocket attacks (7); US recognizes Croatia, Slovenia and Bosnia and UN Security Council approves peacekeepers' deployment (7); Bosnian government orders consolidation of local militias into fledgling army as Serbs bombard Sarajevo (8); Bosnian warring factions agree cease-fire following two days of EC-sponsored talks (12); fighting re-erupts in Bosnia-Herzegovina (13); Serbs bombard Sarajevo (21–22); new Yugoslavia declared by Serbia and Montenegro (27); Serb–Bosnian talks to negotiate army withdrawal begin (26).

3– Albanian President Ramiz Alia resigns; parliament elects Sali Berisha as President (9).

7– Russia and Ukraine both claim jurisdiction over Black Sea Fleet; suspend claims (9); agree to continue Black Sea Fleet talks in Odessa (30).

7– Yeltsin announces Russia will take control of all former USSR forces in East Europe, Baltic and Transcaucasia; parliament approves federation treaty

(10); parliament places three-month limit on Yeltsin's emergency powers (11); government tenders resignation (13); Yeltsin averts crisis by gaining extension of direct governmental control (14); G-7 nations approve $24bn aid to Russia (26).

9–   In Ukraine, parliament refuses to hand over nuclear weapons to Russia; Foreign Minister, Anatoli Zlenko, announces resumption of weapons transfers to Russia for destruction (14); Crimea recognized as autonomous republic (22).

9   Conservative Party wins UK parliamentary elections with John Major as prime minister.

17   Hungary, Czechoslovakia and Poland establish free-trade zone with EC.

23   Germany and Russia sign agreement recreating autonomous Volga German republic; Foreign Minister Hans-Dietrich Genscher announces resignation (27); Free Democratic Party (FDP) elect Klaus Kinkel to replace him (28).

May

1–   In Yugoslavia fighting erupts in Sarajevo; Yugoslavia rejects responsibility for Serbian forces in Bosnia-Herzegovina as cease-fire is announced (5); Sarejevo fighting resumes (7); EC announces withdrawal of Belgrade-based ambassadors in protest (11); Serb leaders declare five-day unilateral cease-fire as US withdraws ambassadors from Belgrade (12); Security Council adopts resolution to continue peace efforts (15); UN peacekeepers leave Sarajevo (17); three-week cease-fire announced (18); Serbia refuses to withdraw from eastern Croatia (21); Slovenia, Croatia and Bosnia-Herzegovina join UN (22); EC agrees trade embargo against Serbia (26); UN approves sanctions against Serbia (30).

3   EC and EFTA nations sign European Economic Area (EEA) agreement.

3–   Azeri forces capture heights near Stepanakert in Nagorno-Karabakh; peace talks resume in Iran (6); cease-fire agreed (7); Armenians take Shusha as fighting continues (9); Mutalibov, reinstated as Azeri president, declares state of emergency (14); Azeri nationalist opposition (APF) seizes control of strategic points in Baku (15); after two days of fighting Armenia opens land corridor to Nagorno-Karabakh (18); Abulfaz Elchibey announces Azerbaijan first republic to leave the CIS (20).

5–   Crimea declares independence from Ukraine; Ukraine completes transfer of tactical nuclear weapons to Russia as Crimea rescinds decision (6); Ukrainian parliament annuls independence declaration (13).

7   Yeltsin signs decree creating Russian army.

11–   Moldova refuses to attend CIS summit in Tashkent; fighting in Dniestr region resumes (18); Moldovan president Snegur accuses Russia of aggression (20); Yeltsin announces Russian army withdrawal (27).

15   At CIS Tashkent summit, Russia, Armenia, Kazakhstan, Tajikistan, Uzbekistan and Kyrgyzstan sign collective security agreement.

22   Poland and Russia sign friendship pact during Polish President Lech Walesa's visit to Moscow and agree withdrawal of remaining former Soviet Union troops by 15 November 1992.

22   France and Germany announce agreement to form 35,000 joint European Army Corps.

26   UK Prime Minister John Major begins four-day tour of Central Europe in Poland; visits Czechoslovakia (27–28); and Hungary (29).

27   Two-day NATO defence ministers' meeting in Brussels approves NATO peacekeeping role under CSCE.

June

1   Albania signs friendship treaty with Turkey, ending 500-year impasse.

1–   In Yugoslavia fighting continues in Sarajevo; Serbs attack UN-escorted aid convoy near Sarajevo (2); UN Security Council agrees to send 1,100 troops to Sarajevo (8); Croatia and Bosnia-Herzegovina sign military alliance against Serbia (17); EC-brokered peace talks resume in Strasbourg (25); French President Mitterrand visits Sarajevo (28); UN takes over Sarajevo airport as Serbs withdraw (29); Radovan Karadzic, leader of Bosnian Serbs, announces unilateral cease-fire (30).

1–   Russian Defence Minister General Pavel Grachev announces foreign intervention in neighbouring states seen as military threat; troops complete withdrawal from Chechnia (8); Yeltsin appoints Egor Gaidar as acting prime minister (15).

2–   Denmark rejects Maastricht Treaty in referendum; at Bonn meeting UK Prime Minister Major and Chancellor Kohl of Germany agree to delay ratification (5); Ireland endorses Treaty (18).

6–   In Czechoslovak election, Movement for a Democratic Slovakia wins in Slovakia and Civic Democratic Party in Czech Republic; President Vaclav Havel appoints Vaclav Klaus to form new federal government (7); Slovak Civic Democratic Party leader Vladimir Meciar and Klaus agree to prepare for nation to split (20); Meciar becomes Slovakian prime minister (24); federal government resigns (26).

10–   In Georgia fighting for South Ossetia breaks out again; Shevardnadze signs South Ossetian peace accord with Yeltsin (24); armed forces bombard South Ossetia (28).

11   Austria accepts autonomy for South Tyrol ending 30-year dispute.

20–   Estonia adopts own currency; and new constitution (28).

21–   After two-day battle, Moldovans capture Bendery; cease-fire declared (22); Moldovan forces use air power in Dniestr region for first time (23); at Black Sea economic summit, Russia, Romania and Moldova agree indefinite cease-fire in Dniestr region (25); Russian army downs Moldovan plane, breaking cease-fire (26); Moldovan government resigns (30).

30   Ukrainian parliament grants Crimea wide-ranging autonomy.

July

1–   In Yugoslavia first French unit joins UN peacekeepers in Sarajevo; US starts relief flights to Sarajevo (3); Bosnian Croat leaders proclaim independent state of Bosnia-Herzegovina (4); WEU and NATO launch joint naval operation in Adriatic enforcing UN sanctions (10); UN lifts 71-day siege in Dobrinja (12); Milan Panic elected Yugoslav prime minister (14); Macedonian government resigns (16); Bosnian warring factions sign cease-fire and agree to place weapons under UN supervision during 14-day cease-fire, beginning 19 July (17); Sarajevo fighting continues (19); EC negotiator Lord Carrington announces will negotiate no more Bosnian cease-fires as UN convoy delivering aid stopped by Serbs (23); convoy abandons efforts (26); Serb Bosnian parliament announces separate Serb state (26).

1–   Czechoslovak President Vaclav Havel names new federal government with Jan Stasky as prime minister; Havel fails to win first round of presidential elections (3); Slovakia declares sovereignty (17); Havel resigns (20); Czech Prime Minister Klaus and Slovakian counterpart Meciar agree on division of country (23).

5   IMF announces $1bn loan to Russia.

6–   At CIS summit in Moscow presidents of 10 republics agree to create joint peacekeeping force for deployment in Moldova; Moldova and Russia sign peace pact and agree to send joint military force to Dniestr region (21); fighting continues in Dniestr region (22); peacekeeping forces move into area (29).

14   Russia and Georgia deploy peacekeeping troops to South Ossetia.

29   Turkey signs defence cooperation agreement with Albania.

August

1–   In Yugoslavia, Franjo Tudjman wins Croatian presidential election; US confirms existence of Serbian detention camps (3); UN demands Red Cross inspection and suspends aid flights for three days (4); Russia recognizes Macedonia (5); federal Prime Minister, Milan Panic, announces closure of all Serbian prison camps in Bosnia-Herzegovina (7); Red Cross accuses all three ethnic groups of violating Geneva Convention (13); Brussels peace conference collapses (14); UN mine-clearers rescue relief convoy trapped in eastern Bosnia (16); UN suspends aid flights to Sarajevo over threats and Karadzic signs agreement placing weapons under UN control (18); aid flights resume (20); UN investigation team refused entry into Serbian prison camp (22); Lord Carrington resigns as head of EC peace effort (25); Lord Owen replaces him (27).

3   In Yalta, Yeltsin and Kravchuk agree to postpone decision on Black Sea Fleet for three years.

4–   In Georgia, Shevardnadze lifts state of emergency in Tbilisi; fighting ensues in Abkhazian capital Sukhumi (14); cease-fire negotiated and broken (15); government troops recapture Sukhumi (18); government and rebels agree to end military operations (29).

4   On two-day visit to Bulgaria, Yeltsin signs friendship treaty.

9–   Lev Petrossian, Armenian president, appeals for CIS aid; Azeri fighters bomb Stepanakert (18); Armenia and Azerbaijan agree cease-fire beginning 1 September (27).

26   Slovak leader Meciar and Czech counterpart Klaus agree to division of Czechoslovakia from 1 January 1993.

September

1–   Slovak parliament approves draft constitution; Slovak Prime Minister Meciar signs new constitution (3).

1–   Nagorno-Karabakh cease-fire announced; fighting begins again in east (18–20).

2–   NATO agrees to provide 6,000 troops to support UN aid deliveries in Bosnia-Herzegovina; missile hits Italian aid aircraft near Sarajevo and UN suspends aid flights (3); Croatian government and Serbian-held region of Krajina in eastern Croatia agree economic cooperation (9); UN Security Council votes to send 6,000 troops (14); UN refuses assignment of Yugoslavian seat to rump Yugoslav state (19); Greek government announces lifting of oil embargo on Macedonia (22); Croatian and Bosnian presidents announce defensive cooperation (23).

3–   At talks in Moscow, Georgian leader Shevardnadze, Yeltsin and Abkhazian counterpart Vladislav Ardzinba agree cease-fire; fighting breaks out again (5); talks reconvene in Sukhumi (6); new cease-fire agreed (9); 30 soldiers killed in landmine explosion in Abkhazia (10).

4   In Bulgaria, former president, Todor Zhivkov, sentenced to seven years imprisonment for misappropriation of state property and embezzlement.

8–   Russia agrees withdrawal of 20,000 troops from Lithuania by August 1993;
        Lithuania announces establishment of own currency (23).
15–   At London meeting UK and Spain resume Gibraltar negotiations; Gibraltar's
        chief minister, Joe Bossano, announces Gibraltar and Falkland Islands to
        establish economic and political cooperation (14).
20–   In referendum France narrowly approves Maastricht Treaty.
23   President Kravchuk of Ukraine claims to have control of nuclear weapons on
        his territory.
27   Russia imposes 60-day state of emergency in republic of Kabardino-Balkaria
        after demonstrations demanding release of Confederation of Caucasian
        Mountain Peoples' leader Moussa Shanibov.

October
1–   Serb authorities in Bosnia-Herzegovina release 500 Muslim prisoners; UN
        resumes airlift (3); UN Security Council votes for preparation of evidence for
        war criminal trials (6); UN imposes ban on military flights over Bosnia-
        Herzegovina (9); federal Prime Minister, Milan Panic, calls for Serbian
        President Slobodan Milosevic's resignation and elections (13); NATO or-
        ders AWAC fleet to monitor 'no-fly' zone (15); Serb police seize control of
        federal interior ministry (19); leaders of Bosnian and Croat Serb territories
        meet to form 'Union of Serbian States' (31).
2–   In Georgia, Abkhazian separatists take town of Gagra; Georgia demands
        Russian troops leave territory as Georgian plane shot down by Russians (5);
        Abkhazians and north Caucasian forces rout Georgian troops; Shevardnadze
        wins legislative elections (11); Russia dispatches warship to region (13).
2–   NATO formally activates 12-nation Rapid Reaction Corps; defence ministers
        agree to draw up plans for peacekeeping operations in Europe with former
        Warsaw Pact (20).
11–   Czech and Slovak prime ministers agree to establish separate currencies by
        mid-1993; agree customs union from 1 January 1993 (26); at London talks
        Hungary and Czechoslovakia agree four-point plan settling Gabcikovo dam
        dispute (28).
12–   In Russia Yeltsin signs cooperation treaty with Azeri President Elchibey; last
        of ex-Soviet army troops withdraw from Poland (28); Yeltsin signs order for
        temporary halt to withdrawal from Baltic (29).
20   Russia, Ukraine, Uzbekistan and Kazakhstan agree to abide by quotas on
        uranium shipments to US.
27–28   In London, Czechoslovakia, Hungary and Poland hold first summit with EC,
        agree to consult on foreign policy.

November
1–   In Germany repatriation of illegal Romanian immigrants begins; massive
        anti-Right demonstration held in Berlin and other cities (8); former East
        German leader Erich Honecker goes on trial (12); National Front banned
        (27).
1–   EC–US trade talks begin in Chicago; EC chief agriculture negotiator Ray
        McSharry resigns over Commission President's alleged interference (5); he
        withdraws resignation (10); EC and US reach agreement (20).
1–   Russia deploys troops between North Ossetian and Ingush fighters, cease-
        fire agreed; Russia declares state of emergency in both regions (2); Chechnia
        protests at Russian troop deployment and threatens retaliation (10); Russia
        and Chechnia sign agreement to withdraw troops from border area (15).
4–   UK parliament passes preliminary vote in favour of Maastricht Treaty; Spain
        ratifies Treaty (25).

9– Russian President Yeltsin visits UK and signs friendship treaty; Russian Constitutional Court upholds the ban of the Communist Party (30).

15– In Lithuania Democratic Labour Party wins second round of legislative elections; Algirdas Brazauskas re-elected as head of state (25).

16– UN Security Council votes for naval blockade of Adriatic to enforce embargo against Serbia (16); NATO forces begin blockade (22).

17– Czech and Slovak republican parliaments authorize split from 1 January 1993; Czech and Slovak delegations agree to split federal army (23); federal parliament agrees separation (25).

19– Norwegian parliament votes to join EC; application made (25).

25 Irish legislative elections won by Labour Party led by Dick Spring.

December

2– At two-day emergency meeting in Jeddah, Organization of the Islamic Conference (OIC) calls for UN use of force against Serbia and lifting of arms embargo against Bosnia; fighting intensifies in Sarajevo as Serbs seize main road linking capital and airport (8); Sarajevo airport reopens (9); Security Council orders peacekeepers to Macedonia (11); Slobodan Milosevic wins Serbian presidential elections (20); federal parliament passes no-confidence vote in Prime Minister Milan Panic and Radoje Kontic replaces him (29).

3– Albania becomes member of OIC; applies for NATO membership (16).

6– In Germany agreement is reached to tighten asylum laws; government bans German alternative neo-Nazi party (10); Alliance of German Comrades banned (21); National Offensive banned (22).

9– Russian parliament rejects Egor Gaidar as prime minister; Yeltsin calls for referendum on the principles of the new constitution; parliament bans referendum (11); Yeltsin proposes Viktor Chernomyrdin as prime minister and parliament approves (14).

17– Manfred Wörner reappointed head of NATO; NATO and former Warsaw Pact countries agree establishment of joint peacekeeping monitors in Europe (18); NATO approves Franco-German corps (22).

17– Azerbaijan president Abulfaz Elchibey declares state of emergency (17); withdraws from peace negotiations (18).

21 Poland, Hungary and Czechoslovakia establish regional trade zone.

MIDDLE EAST

January

7– Israeli forces shoot dead a Palestinian and wound 20 in Gaza over expulsion of 12 activists: Tehiya party resigns from government (15); troops in Occupied Territories increased by 20% as expulsions go ahead (21); government survives no-confidence vote (27).

16– Second round of bilateral Middle East peace talks end in Washington; two-day multinational talks on status of Palestinians resume in Moscow without their participation (28).

February

4– Iraq breaks off talks with UN on resumption of oil exports; UN sanctions renewed over non-cooperation with nuclear inspections (5).

16– Israeli armed forces assassinate Sheikh Abbas Moussawi, leader of *Hizbollah*, in southern Lebanon; Ron Arad, Israeli navigator, killed by Lebanese captors (16); *Hizbollah* rocket Galilee and Israeli-controlled border zone (19); Israelis launch largest attack since 1989 (20).

16–   At Iranian meeting Azerbaijan, Turkmenistan and Uzbekistan join Economic Cooperation Organization; President Hashemi Rafsanjani announces establishment of Caspian Council including Russia, Turkmenistan and Azerbaijan (17).

23   Middle East peace talks resume in Washington as US Secretary of State Baker announces Israel must stop building settlements in Occupied Territories to receive $10bn US loan guarantees.

March
1–   Turkish forces begin two-day bombing of Kurds in Hakurk, Iraq; Turkish Kurds clash with troops in south-east Turkey as PKK defy curfew (22); Iraq begins shelling Kurds (25); Turkish Prime Minister Suleyman Demirel rules out autonomy for Turkish Kurds (30).

4   Fourth round of Washington Middle East peace talks end with little progress.

18–   UN gives Iraq until 27 March to draw up programme for destruction of ballistic missile factories; UN inspectors begin verification of demolition of weapons of mass destruction (22); IAEA orders Iraq to destroy nuclear facilities at al-Atheer (25).

19–   Israel bars Palestinians in Gaza Strip from entering country.

April
1–   Israeli armed forces clash with Palestinians in Gaza; fighting continues (2–3); 28 Palestinians killed in Occupied Territories demonstrating in favour of Colonel Gaddafi (16).

7–   Baghdad agrees to destruction of Iraqi nuclear facility at al-Atheer; allies warn Iraq not to use missile radars and warplane flights in northern protection zone (9); UK, France and US tell Iraq to remove anti-aircraft missiles from north or face retaliation (14); Iraq launches offensive against Shi'i in southern marshlands (15).

27   Middle East peace talks resume in Washington, with Israel's offer of elections in Occupied Territories; Palestinians turn down proposals (28); fifth round of peace talks end (30).

May
5–   In Lebanon demonstrators protest against currency collapse; three-day general strike begins and government resigns (6); trade unions announce strike suspension (7); Rashid Solk becomes prime minister (13).

8   Iranian President Rafsanjani's party, Association of Combatant Clergy, gains majority in legislative elections

13–   Middle East water talks held in Vienna; Israelis and Palestinians agree to exchange water resources information (14).

14–   Turkey bombards northern Iraq (14); 65 killed in Turkish–Kurdish clashes in south-east Turkey (24); UN Security Council votes to maintain sanctions against Iraq (27).

21–   In Lebanon, Israeli aircraft bomb *Hizbollah* in south (21–26); Israeli soldier killed in bomb attack (27); training camp and villages shelled (29–30).

27–   Israeli forces contain violence in Gaza Strip over killing of rabbi by Palestinian; Islamic fundamentalist gunman kills security guard at Red Sea (30).

June
4–   Israeli helicopters fire into offices of PLO near Tyre, Lebanon (4); attacks launched against *Hizbollah* in south (10); Lebanese National Resistance ambushes Israeli patrol (11); last two Western hostages freed (15); PLO local commander, Colonel Anwar Madi, assassinated in Sidon (30).

8–   Israel allows Palestinians in Gaza Strip back to work in Israel; general
        restrictions in Gaza relaxed (9); Labour Party wins Israeli legislative election
        (23); Prime Minister-elect, Yitzhak Rabin, announces freeze of Jewish settle-
        ment in some areas of the Occupied Territories and cuts in state subsidies to
        existing settlements (26).
22–   Four-day talks on oil trade resumption between Iraq and UN end in impasse.
22–   Turks and Kurds clash in south-eastern Turkey; Turkish parliament renews
        allied Kurdish protection mandate (24).
26   UN experts travel to Baghdad to begin destroying military production equip-
        ment.

July
2–   Iraqi coup attempt thwarted; UN inspectors prevented from examining Min-
        istry of Agriculture (5); government begins air attacks on Shias (22); con-
        frontation over UN weapons inspections resolved (26); new UN inspection
        team arrives in Baghdad (28); James Baker meets Iraqi dissidents in Wash-
        ington (29); UN inspectors search Ministry of Agriculture finding no weap-
        ons-related material (28–29).
7–   PLO and Islamic fundamentalists clash in gun battles in Occupied Territo-
        ries; Prime Minister Yitzhak Rabin forms coalition (13); four-day military
        siege of Najah University in West Bank resolved (17); all planned future
        construction in West Bank and Gaza stopped (23).
21   Israeli Prime Minister Rabin visits Egypt.

August
2–   Iraqi media claim Kuwait as part of Iraq on second anniversary of invasion;
        UK, France and US agree to impose air exclusion zone in south Iraq below
        32nd parallel (18); enters into effect (26).
2–   In Israel two Arabs appointed deputy ministers for first time; soldiers kill
        three infiltrators from Jordan to West Bank (4); 800 Arab prisoners released
        and restrictions eased on Palestinians in Occupied Territories (23); Rabin
        revokes expulsion order on 11 Palestinians accused of inciting terrorism
        (24); 185 Palestinians released (31).
23–   Lebanon holds elections, boycotted by Christians; Foreign Minister, Faris
        Bouez, resigns in protest at cabinet decision not to cancel elections or nullify
        results, run-offs set for October (26).
24–   Middle East peace talks resume in Washington; Israeli Foreign Minister
        Peres hints at territorial concession on Golan Heights, Israel proposes Pales-
        tinian self-rule in Occupied Territories (25).

September
9   In Israel, Prime Minister Rabin announces territorial concessions on the
        Golan Heights in exchange for peace.
10–   Iran repeats its claim to sovereignty over the Abu Musa and Greater and
        Lesser Tunb islands; talks on island dispute held in Abu Dhabi (27–28).
10–   Iraqi aircraft intercepted entering UN air exclusion zone in Kurdistan;
        Kurdistan Democratic Party and Patriotic Union of Kurdistan agree to merge
        (15); 82 killed as Turkish Kurds attack border point in Hakkari (29).

October
1   Qatar government suspends 1965 accord with Saudi Arabia over border
        dispute.

2–   Security Council votes to seize frozen Iraqi oil assets for Kurdish relief and war reparations; Kurdish parliament votes for federative state in northern Iraq (4); The PKK enforces economic blockade on northern Iraq (11); PKK begins peace talks and agrees to abandon bases in northern Iraq (27); Turkish military capture PKK base, killing several hundred people (30–31).

5–   In Kuwait, opposition wins legislative election.

7–   In Israel, 90 Palestinians shot and wounded in clash with soldiers in Gaza Strip; Palestinian prisoners end two-week hunger strike, 24-hour curfew introduced in Gaza Strip following outbreak of violence (11); six Palestinians wounded in West Bank fighting (16); army seals off West Bank (18); two Israeli soldiers ambushed in West Bank (21).

8–   Israel accepts participation of Palestinians from outside Occupied Territories in Middle East peace talks; seventh round of talks begins in Washington (21).

11–   In Lebanon *Amal* and *Hizbollah* win legislative elections; Rafik al-Hariri replaces Prime Minister Rashid al-Solh (22); five Israeli soldiers killed in south by *Hizbollah* (25); Israel retaliates and targets north (26–27).

November

2–   Turkey continues attack on Kurds in Iraq; foreign ministers of Turkey, Iran and Syria condemn creation of *de facto* Kurdish state (14).

4–   In Lebanon, Southern Lebanese Army clashes with *Hizbollah* in Dabshe area; *Hizbollah* fire rockets into northern Israel in retaliation for Israeli warplanes attack on *Hizbollah* base (8); Israeli jets attack Hizbollah village in south (11).

8–   Middle East peace talks reconvene in Washington; Israel walks out of refugee talks in Ottawa objecting to Palestine National Council presence in Ottawa (11); talks resume (12).

29   Turkmenistan, Kyrgyzstan, Tajikistan, Uzbekistan and Azerbaijan join Economic Cooperation Organization (ECO).

December

4–   Israeli troops shoot 10 Palestinians in Gaza Strip; three soldiers killed in ambush in Gaza Strip and three border policemen wounded in West Bank (7); troops enforce curfew in Gaza Strip (8); general strike marking fifth anniversary of *intifada* mounted (9); *Hamas* kidnaps border guard demanding release of leader, Sheikh Ahmed Yassin (13); security forces seal off West Bank and Gaza Strip (14); border guard found dead outside Jerusalem (15); 415 suspected *Hamas* members deported to Lebanon (17); Arabs boycott scheduled peace talks in Washington (17); UN Security Council condemns deportation as Lebanon refuses to admit deportees (18); armed forces kill seven Palestinians in Occupied Territories (20); Supreme Court rejects appeal to return deportees (22); UN envoy James Jonah begins three-day visit to help resolve issue of deportees (27); Lebanon prevents him visiting deportees (28).

7–   In Iraq six bombs found on UN truck carrying aid to Kurds; third UN aid truck convoy bombed in north (16); Iraq rejects UN request to escort aid lorries (23); US shoots down MiG fighter in no-fly zone (27); US aircraft carrier *Kitty Hawk* deployed to region (28); UN-escorted relief trucks start deliveries again (29).

20   Qatar signs border dispute agreement with Saudi Arabia.

EAST ASIA AND AUSTRALASIA

January
2–   Bush ends three-day visit to Australia; visits Singapore (3–5), South Korea
      (5–6) and Japan (7–9).
7   South Korea announces cancellation of annual *Team Spirit* military exercises
      with US.
19–21 Cambodian *Khmer Rouge* repulses governmental attacks in Kompong Thom
      Province.
22–   During four-day visit to Beijing by Israeli Foreign Minister David Levy,
      Israel and China establish diplomatic relations.
28–   At two-day ASEAN summit in Singapore, Indonesia, Malaysia, Philippines,
      Singapore, Thailand and Brunei sign agreement to set up free-trade area in 15
      years.
30   North Korea signs agreement for IAEA inspections.

February
19   North and South Korea sign declaration to end formally their 40-year con-
      frontation.
26–   In Cambodia, *Khmer Rouge* shoots down UN helicopter; UN agrees to
      dispatch 15,900 peacekeeping troops to Cambodia (28).

March
5   At end of two-day talks US agrees to provide extra $3m aid to Vietnam and
      Vietnam agrees to speed up pace of accounting for MIAs.
14–   North and South Korea conclude new agreement allowing inspection of
      suspected nuclear weapons sites; South Korean Democratic Justice Party
      wins legislative elections (24).
16–   Thai jet fighters ordered to attack Burmese aircraft invading airspace in hot
      pursuit of Karen guerrillas; Burmese border positions bombed (17); Thai
      troops drive Burmese soldiers out of Thailand (19).
29–   Cambodian troops launch offensive against *Khmer Rouge* in north; army and
      Khmer Rouge open peace talks north of Phnom Penh (31).

April
1–   UN sends 194 peacekeepers to central Cambodia to monitor cease-fire;
      Khmer Rouge joins other Cambodian factions in signing UN convention on
      human rights, invites UN to inspect limited areas in its zones (20).
6–   Chinese Communist Party chief, Jiang Zemin, begins five-day visit to Tokyo.
7–   Thailand's coup leader, General Suchinda Krapayoon, named prime minis-
      ter; protestors demand Suchinda's resignation (20).
23–   Burmese Prime Minister, General Saw Maung, resigns; General Than Shwe
      replaces him (24); after four days of talks, Burma agrees to take back
      refugees who had fled to Bangladesh (27); government cancels military
      offensive against Karen guerrillas (28).
24   John Major announces Chris Patten to replace Sir David Wilson as governor
      of Hong Kong.
29–   Japanese Prime Minister Kiichi Miyazawa visits France; and Germany (30).

May
4–   Thai opposition leader Chamlong Srimuang announces hunger strike over
      military takeover of cabinet posts; supporters demonstrate in Bangkok de-
      manding Prime Minister General Suchinda's resignation (5–8); demonstra-

tions suspended following compromise requiring prime minister be elected member of parliament (11); more violent demonstrations break out in Bangkok, government declares state of emergency in Bangkok and four provinces (17); troops fire on protestors, dozens killed (17–19); King Bhumipol Adulyadej meets with prime minister and opposition leader, reaches agreement ending violence (20); prime minister resigns (24); state of emergency lifted (26).

11   Fidel V. Ramos wins Filipino presidential elections.
12   UK and Vietnam sign agreement on compulsory return of 55,700 'boat people' in Hong Kong.
31   Indonesian military kill M. L. Prawar, military commander of Free Papua Movement (OPM).

June
1–   Indonesian troops cross Papua New Guinea border at Wutung to destroy rebel camps; New Guinea Prime Minister, Rabbie Namaliu, reinstated in legislative election (28).
9–   Indonesian legislative elections won by ruling Golkar party.
10–   *Khmer Rouge* refuses to join in demobilization of four factions due on 13 June; in Tokyo, 35-nation Conference on Rehabilitation and Reconstruction in Cambodia agrees to provide $880m in aid (22).
15   Japanese parliament approves bill allowing dispatch of peacekeeping troops overseas.
28   Burhanuddin Rabbani replaces Seghbatullah Mojaddedi as interim Afghan president.

July
2–   In Cambodia, at SNC meeting *Khmer Rouge* imposes conditions on compliance with Paris peace accords; at Manila meeting, EC, US, Japan, South Korea, Canada, Australia, New Zealand, Indonesia, Malaysia, the Philippines, Singapore, Thailand and Brunei announce willingness to back UN sanctions against *Khmer Rouge* (26).

August
23–   South Korean foreign minister, Lee Sang Ock, begins three-day visit to China; agreement establishing diplomatic relations signed, and Taiwan severs relations with South Korea (24).

September
7   North and South Korea agree cross-border economic exchanges.
7–   In Cambodia *Khmer Rouge* drops demand for UN verification of Vietnamese troop withdrawals; ends three-month boycott of military meeting with UN (17); first Japanese troops deployed overseas since Second World War join peacekeeping forces in Cambodia (20).
8   Taiwan and Russia agree to exchange permanent missions which will issue visas.
9   Iranian President, Hashemi Rafsanjani, begins four-day visit to Beijing.
13–   In Thai legislative elections four pro-democratic parties emerge with combined majorities; they agree to form coalition including the Social Action Party (14); Chuan Leekpai, leader of the Democrat Party, becomes prime minister (23).
22–   In Philippines, President Fidel Ramos lifts ban on Communist Party; US personnel leave Subic Bay naval base (30).
27   South Korean President Roh Tae Woo begins four-day visit to China.

October

12–   In China, first border-dispute talks with Vietnam open; Japanese Emperor
       Akihito arrives for six-day visit (23).

13–   UN Security Council passes resolution to carry out elections as scheduled
       despite *Khmer Rouge* opposition; Yasushi Akashi, head of UNTAC, an-
       nounces temporary freeze in disarmament effort because of *Khmer Rouge*
       refusal to join (21).

November

3–   In Cambodia, government calls for scrapping of UN disarmament plan; three
       UN election team monitors shot (24); Security Council imposes trade sanc-
       tions on *Khmer Rouge* (30).

4   Japan announces resumption of development assistance to Vietnam.

11–   In Hong Kong, legislature backs Governor Patten's proposals for increased
       democratic participation; China announces that after taking control on 1 July
       1997 it will not adhere to any contracts made without its approval (30).

18   Yeltsin begins three-day visit to South Korea.

20   Xanano Gusmao, leader of East Timor's independence guerrillas, is captured
       by Indonesian troops.

24   US formally hands Subic Bay naval base over to Philippine control.

30   Chinese premier Li Peng begins five-day visit to Vietnam.

December

3–   In Cambodia six UN peacekeepers released by *Khmer Rouge*; *Khmer Rouge*
       boycotts meeting of SNC (8); 21 UN peacekeepers taken hostage in
       Kampong Thom province (15, 17); 46 more detained (17); 11 released (20);
       46 released (18); *Khmer Rouge* declares cannot guarantee security for tres-
       passers in its zone (23); *Khmer Rouge* kills at least 13 ethnic Vietnamese
       (27); refuses to join UN peace plan (28); shells UN troops (31).

17–   Yeltsin begins three-day visit to China; US announces lifting embargo on
       four arms shipments imposed in 1989 (23); China closes French consulate in
       Canton over arms sales to Taiwan (23).

17–   In South Korea, Kim Young Sam wins presidential election; South Korea re-
       establishes diplomatic relations with Vietnam (22).

19   Taiwanese ruling Nationalist Party wins legislative elections.

SOUTH AND CENTRAL ASIA

January

2–   Bangladeshi forces reinforce Burmese border; bilateral talks end in stalemate
       (8).

5   China and Tajikistan establish diplomatic relations.

6–   In India 13 members of People's War Group killed by police in Andhra
       Pradesh; Kashmiri gunmen fire on bus of Hindu nationalists in Kashmir
       Valley (23); curfew imposed (24); Hindus raise Indian flag in Srinagar,
       Kashmir (26); clashes break out when curfew lifted (27).

29   India establishes diplomatic relations with Israel.

February

11–   Sikhs kill hundreds of Hindus in series of attacks in Punjab; JKLF supporters
       attempt to cross 1949 cease-fire line but Pakistan troops open fire, killing

seven (12); Pakistan deploys troops to prevent Muslims again crossing into Indian Kashmir (29); five Kashmiri militants cross border at Muzzafrabad, Pakistan, as police arrest Raja Muzaffar, acting chief of JKLF (30).

18–   Afghan President Mohammed Najibullah offers to hand over power to a UN-backed interim government; UN Secretary-General's envoy, Benon Sevan, arrives in Kabul for peace talks (31).

April

4–   Afghan President Najibullah offers to yield power to transitional neutral council; UN Secretary-General announces new Afghan peace plan which *Mujaheddin* reject (10); Najibullah resigns as *Mujaheddin* take capital (16); Abdul Rahim Hatif replaces Najibullah as president (17); UN special envoy Benon Sevan appeals for cease-fire and amnesty (20); Hatif secures safe passage for Najibullah (21); rival *Mujaheddin* factions infiltrate capital (23); 10 *Mujaheddin* groups agree to form 50-member interim council to take power (24); battle for capital Kabul breaks out (24–27); cease-fire arranged (27); Islamic Council takes power, Seghbatullah Mojaddedi replaces Abdul Rahim Hatif as president (28); Ahmed Shah Massoud named defence minister (30).

22–   In Tajikistan parliamentary speaker, Safarli Kenjayev, resigns after opposition releases 18 politicians taken hostage on 21 April; parliament grants President Rakhmon Nabiyev emergency powers as protestors continue three-day demonstrations in Dushanbe (30).

May

3–   Tajik President Nabiyev reappoints Safarli Kenjayev as speaker; state of emergency declared following violence in Leninski and Yavan (5); opposition takes Dushanbe (6); Nabiyev lifts three-day state of emergency (7); agrees to coalition government (11).

4–   In Afghanistan, intra-*Mujaheddin* fighting breaks out as Gulbuddin Hekmatyar's forces open offensive against transitional government; informal cease-fire agreed (6); Defence Minister Massoud and Hekmatyar agree cease-fire and disengagement of troops from Kabul, decide to hold election within one year (25).

June

1–   In Sri Lanka troops take control of Tamil Tigers base, Alampil, in north-east; take over Senthakulam base in north (11); joint sea, air and ground attack launched (28).

July

17–   In India, all-party talks in Delhi fail to reach consensus over construction of temple at disputed site in Ayodhya; Hindu militants accelerate construction (19); fighting ensues in Kerala and Maharashtra in south (19–20); Supreme Court orders halt to construction (22); *Vishwa Hindu Parishad* party announces suspension of temple construction (24).

27   In Tajikistan, government, opposition and military agree truce.

August

2–   In Afghanistan, *Hizb i Islami Mujaheddin* faction quits leadership council and attacks capital; government jets bombard *Mujaheddin* positions east of Kabul (12); Gulbuddin Hekmatyar offers cease-fire (13); Hekmatyar ousted from coalition (17); *Hizb i Islami* agrees 72-hour cease-fire (27).

11– Indian government announces six-month extension of federal rule in Kashmir; fighting in Kashmir (16); talks begin in Delhi (17); Pakistan proposes talks on issue under Simla Agreement (17); India and Pakistan sign agreement prohibiting use of chemical weapons (19); agree high-level talks on disputed Siachen Glacier (23).

31 In Dushanbe, Tajikistan demonstrators storm presidential palace.

September

1– In Tajikistan, anti-government protestors release 13 of 33 officials held in presidential palace as northern region of Khojand (Leninabad) renews secession pledge; President Nabiyev resigns following airport stand-off with opponents in Dushanbe (7); Tajiks seize CIS weapons from army depots (27); Russia announces an increase of its troop strength to as much as 10,000 (28); Russian troops seize control of Dushanbe airport (30).

October

5 In Kashmir, separatist leader Altaf Ahmed Qurestu killed by Indian security forces.

24– In Tajikistan, state of emergency and curfew declared; forces loyal to ousted President Nabiyev seize parliament in two-day battle (24); they withdraw from Dushanbe (25).

28 Afghanistan interim president Burhanuddin Rabbani resigns.

November

2 India and Pakistan begin talks on Siachen Glacier dispute

11– In Tajikistan government resigns; Imloi Rakhmonov appointed as acting president (19).

18– In Pakistan, former prime minister Benazir Bhutto banished to Karachi over staging of anti-government march; ban lifted (26).

December

4– In Tajikistan fighting escalates in Dushanbe; pro-communist forces take capital (10); fighting continues near Afghan border (17); pro-government forces take Islamic stronghold, Kofernikhon, following three-day fight (20); thousands of refugees flee to Afghanistan (23).

6– In India, Hindus tear down mosque in Ayodhya, government imposes direct rule in Uttar Pradesh; violence erupts all over India, taking security forces five days to regain control (7–11); government bans *Rashtrija Swayam Sevak Sangh* (RSS), *Vishwa Hindu Parishad* (VHP) and *Bajrang Dal* Hindu groups and *Jamaat-i-Islami* and Islamic *Swayamsevak* Muslim groups (10); Prime Minister Narasimha Rao imposes direct rule on Rajasthan, Madhya Pradesh and Himachal Pradesh (15); he survives no-confidence vote (21).

AFRICA

January

1– Chad reinforces troops following attacks at Lake Chad; two towns captured by rebels loyal to Hissène Habré (2); they retreat (6).

2– In Algeria, widespread anti-government demonstrations mounted; army deployed nationwide (8); President Chadli Bendjedid resigns (11); government introduces martial law and cancels second round of legislative elections due on 16 January (12); military council appoints five-man ruling committee, headed by Mohamed Boudiaf (14); Islamic Salvation Front (FIS) leader, Abdelkader Hachani, arrested and assemblies around mosques banned (22); Rabah Kebir, another FIS leader, arrested (28); police open fire on Muslim demonstrators (29).

2   Nigerian President, Ibrahim Babangida, dissolves cabinet.

19–   Zairean Prime Minister, Nguza Karl-i-Bond, suspends National Conference; protestors errect barricades, demonstrate (20); soldiers take over radio station, demanding resignation of President Mobutu Sese Seko, until they are ousted by troops loyal to Mobutu (22–23).

20–   In Congo, troops seize airport and radio station in capital, demanding resignation of Prime Minister André Milongo; he holds talks with rebels (21); replaces foreign and defence ministers (28).

23   Angola and South Africa re-establish diplomatic relations after 17 years.

24–   President Moaouia Ould Sidi Mohamed Taya wins Mauritanian presidential election; curfew imposed (26).

27–   EC lifts sanctions against South Africa; South African police arrest 10 members of Afrikaaner Resistance Movement (AWB) including leader, Eugene Terreblanche (28).

February

2   Libya announces it will allow IAEA inspections.

4–   In Algeria, clashes between army and Islamic fundamentalists break out; state of emergency declared (9).

10   In Liberia, forces of the United Liberian Movement For Democracy, loyal to president Samuel Doe, launch fresh attack in west against Charles Taylor's forces.

12–   Somalian warring factions attend UN peace talks; fighting breaks out in capital (12–13); UN advances cease-fire plan (14); Aideed faction agrees to abide by UN cease-fire (16); all factions agree to cease-fire (27).

20–   South African president, F. W. de Klerk, announces referendum on his reforms, threatening to resign if vote is negative; Russian Foreign Minister, Andrei Kozyrev, visits South Africa (28–29).

25   In Djibouti, French troops leave barracks to quell 15-week rebellion by Afar tribesmen.

March

3–   Somalian president, Ali Mahdi Mohamed, and General Mohamed Farah Aideed sign cease-fire agreement; UN team arrives to conduct peace talks (23).

4–   South African Convention for a Democratic South Africa (CODESA) agrees to form interim multiracial cabinet; whites give strong support to reform in referendum (17).

4–   In Algeria judge orders dissolution of FIS; government dissolves fundamentalist local assemblies (31).

8   Sudanese army launch five-pronged attack on areas controlled by SPLA.

10   Kenyan president, Daniel arap Moi, withdraws constitutional reform proposals; political rallies are banned (19).

12   Mauritius becomes independent nation.

23–   Libya offers to hand Lockerbie bombing suspects to the Arab League; case is taken to the ICJ (26); Arab League appeals to UN Secretary-General not to impose sanctions after talks collapse (29); Security Council votes to impose sanctions from 15 April unless suspects are handed over (31).

April

1– Libyan leader Colonel Gaddafi threatens to sever oil sales and business with nations supporting UN sanctions; EC agrees to support Security Council resolution (6); Libya cuts all communications links with outside world for 24 hours (13); ICJ rules against Libya in Lockerbie crisis (14); UN imposes sanctions (15); UK rejects Gaddafi offer to try suspects in Cairo (23).

4– Sudanese government forces capture town of Bor; after further successes agree to hold peace talks with SPLA on 24 May (26).

6– EC lifts embargoes on South Africa (6); diplomatic relations resumed with Ivory Coast (8); President de Klerk visits Nigeria (9–10); president F. W. de Klerk proposes surrendering office after multiracial elections to three-to-five-member executive (23).

6– Liberian warring factions meet in Geneva for peace talks; Charles Taylor agrees to West African peacekeepers creating a buffer zone between his territory and Sierra Leone's (20).

20 Zambia and Israel re-establish diplomatic relations.

26– United Somalian Congress (USC) captures town of Garbaharrey; Siad Barre flees (29); arrives in Kenya (30).

29– Sierra Leonean armed forces overthrow President Joseph Momoh; he flees to Guinea (30).

May

1– Junta declares state of emergency in Sierra Leone, closes borders; names Captain Valentine Strasser head of 20-member ruling council (2).

4– Nigeria and Israel restore diplomatic relations; riots ensue in Lagos over poverty and fuel shortages (13–14); four-day ethnic fighting breaks out in Kaduna (16); curfew imposed (17).

8– South Africa and Kenya sign an agreement for the establishment of representative offices; creation of 19-member multiparty transitional government agreed at constitutional talks in South Africa (11); President de Klerk begins visit to Russia, Japan and Singapore (31).

14 Somalian port, Kismayu, taken by General Farah Aideed.

14 Libya accepts UN investigation of terrorist activities.

20– Sudanese troops capture town of Liria; government and SPLA open talks in Nigeria (26).

June

4– Sudanese peace talks held with little result; SPLA attacks southern capital, Juba.

9– Kenyan President Moi makes first visit to South Africa ending a 21-year African boycott on official visits to the country; ANC begins peaceful protest (16); over 40 killed in Boipatong massacre (17); ANC breaks off bilateral government talks (21); President de Klerk cuts short visit to Spain (22); ANC withdraws from constitutional talks (23); UN Secretary-General agrees to mediate (27).

16 Chad signs peace pact with southern rebels.

29 Algerian President Mohamed Boudiaf assassinated.

July

2– In Algeria Ali Kafi named president; Prime Minister Belai Adessalem resigns, replaced by Sid Ahmed Ghozali (8); troops and fundamentalists clash in Algiers (17–19).

21–   In South Africa, UN envoy Cyrus Vance arrives in Johannesburg for 10-day
        fact-finding mission; talks between Congress of South African Trade Unions
        (COSATU) and the umbrella employer body, Co-ordinating Committee on
        Labour Affairs (SACCOLA) to prevent a threatened general strike fail (22);
        following an invitation from the ANC, UN observers oversee the announced
        one-week mass action including a two-day general strike (31).
27   15th summit of ECOWAS opens in Dakar.
27   UN Security Council passes resolution approving emergency relief for So-
        malia and deployment of 500 peacekeepers to ensure relief effort.
30   Libya requests UN inspection to ensure no terrorists are in country.

August
2–   In Mozambique, two-day troop mutiny ended following three months' back-
        pay payment; President Alberto Chissano and Afonso Dhlakama, Renamo
        leader, hold peace talks in Rome (4); sign agreement committing them to
        cease-fire by 1 October (7).
3–   In South Africa 48-hour general strike begins one-week protest; government
        approves independent investigation into police and army and stationing of 30
        UN observers (13); Security Council authorizes observers (17); Hernus
        Kriel, law and order minister, announces retirement of 13 generals in police
        purge (27)
4–   In Somalia UN suspends food relief; UN signs agreement with warring
        factions for deployment of 500 troops within 21 days (12); armed looters
        seize part of first UN shipment in Kismayu (16); French aid arrives (20); US
        airlift begins as UN observers wounded in looting (28).
4   In Zaire, National Conference adopts draft constitution changing country's
        name to Federal Republic of Congo.
17   Angola, Botswana, Lesotho, Namibia, Malawi, Mozambique, Swaziland,
        Tanzania, Zambia and Zimbabwe sign treaty creating South African Devel-
        opment Community (SADC).
25–   In Liberia, Charles Taylor's National Patriotic Front of Liberia forces retreat;
        they counter-attack at Kakata (26); UN peacekeeper killed as fighting contin-
        ues (31).

September
1   In Somalia, Somali National Alliance announces prohibition of UN guards
        on relief operations into areas it controls; first UN soldiers arrive to prevent
        looting (14); General Farah Aideed accepts UN troop presence (17); retracts
        acceptance (19).
3–   In South Africa, ANC announces continuation of constitutional talks boy-
        cott; 28 killed in ANC march in Ciskei seeking to occupy Bisho (7); ANC
        agrees to emergency meeting between Nelson Mandela and President de
        Klerk (10); de Klerk announces reforms allowing appointment of black
        ministers, self-government of homelands (17); government announces re-
        lease of 150 political prisoners (25); Mandela and de Klerk hold meeting
        agreeing resumption of CODESA and ANC review of mass action (26);
        Buthelezi, leader of the Zulu Inkatha party, withdraws from constitutional
        talks (27).
4   In referendum Morocco votes in favour of constitutional reform.
8–   In Angola, ruling MPLA and UNITA agree to form coalition government
        following legislative elections; MPLA and UNITA forces form joint armed
        forces (27); legislative elections are held (29–30).

October

1– In Somalia, UN agrees to deploy 750 Canadian troops in north; Somali National Movement approves deployment of UN troops to guard relief operations in north-west (18); UN envoy, Mohammed Sahnoun, resigns and Brigadier-General Imtiaz Shaheen temporarily replaces him (27).

4 In Zaire, troops loyal to President Mobutu deployed around central bank following Prime Minister Etienne Tshisekedi's dismissal of central bank governor, Nyemba Shabani.

4– In Rome, Mozambican President Joaquim Alberto Chissano and Afonso Dhlakama sign peace accord; Mozambique National Resistance (Renamo) violates cease-fire by occupying Angoche port in north (18); Zimbabwean forces begin withdrawal (21).

4– In Angola, Jonas Savimbi, UNITA leader, claiming election fraud, threatens to resume fighting; UNITA withdraws from armed forces (5); fighting erupts in Luanda (11); South African Foreign Minister, Pik Botha, begins two-day visit to mediate war (13); election results show presidential run-off necessary (17); UNITA takes control of provincial capital, Huambo (30).

15– Fighting breaks out in Liberian capital, Monrovia; Nigerian aircraft bombard port of Buchanan; troops loyal to Charles Taylor battle way into Monrovia (21); cease-fire deadline ignored (22).

16 Nigerian government nullifies presidential election results and dissolves executive of Social Democratic Party (SDP) and National Republican Convention (NRC).

November

1– In Angola UN negotiates cease-fire; UNITA takes over provincial capital of Bengo (5); UN Under-Secretary for peacekeeping operations, Marrack Goulding, arrives (6); South African Foreign Minister, Pik Botha, declared *persona non grata* (7); new government installed as UNITA boycotts ceremony (26); government and UNITA agree to honour 1991 peace accords and implement a cease-fire (27); fighting resumes (29–30).

3 In Ghana, Jerry John Rawlings wins presidential elections.

15 Zimbabwe postpones withdrawal of 3,500 troops from Mozambique.

16– In South Africa, Judge Richard Goldstone reveals 'third force' operations to discredit ANC; after three-day national executive meeting ANC proposes national unity government and new peace initiative (25); de Klerk announces multiracial elections by April 1994 but ANC rejects it (26); four whites killed in gunfire and grenade attack (28).

17 In Nigeria, President Ibrahim Babangida announces postponement of handover to civilian rule from January to 27 August 1993.

December

1– UN Security Council authorizes US-led armed forces to Somalia; US marines land and secure Mogadishu airport (9); Ali Mahdi Mohamed and General Farah Aideed agree seven-point peace plan and immediate cease-fire (11); US and French troops deployed in Baidoa (16); US marines take Kismayu in south (20); factions agree to peace at US-brokered talks (26); US seals off potential flashpoints around Mogadishu (30); Bush visits troops (31).

2– In Angola, Prime Minister Marcolino Moco announces formation of new government; UNITA agrees to join government and respect cease-fire (7); following meeting with US Assistant Secretary of State Jeffrey Davidow, UNITA agrees to withdraw troops from captured town in Uige and from Negage air base and resume talks with MPLA (20).

2–   In South Africa, President de Klerk and ANC meet for three-day conference;
        Zulu leader, Chief Buthelezi, agrees resumption of multiparty talks (10); de
        Klerk dismisses 2 generals and 4 brigadiers and 17 other senior military
        officers over conspiracy to undermine reform and murder opposition (19).
2–   Zairean President Mobutu dissolves government; troops surround govern-
        ment building in capital, Kinshasa, accusing him of coup against pro-democ-
        racy administration; troops revolt over pay in Kisangani (20).
8–   In Egypt security forces undertake two-day round-up of Islamic fundamen-
        talists; arrest leader, Aber Ahmad Mohammed Ali (11).
16   UN Security Council establishing fourth major 1992 peacekeeping mission
        authorizes 7,500 troops and civilians to Mozambique.
29   In Kenya Daniel arap Moi wins presidential elections.

ARMS CONTROL

January
21   North and South Korea sign pact promising not to produce or deploy nuclear
        weapons.
29–   President Boris Yeltsin announces Russia will honour any arms-control
        agreements USSR had reached; advocates international agency to oversee
        nuclear weapons cuts and joint global system of defence, replacing SDI (31).

February
1–   At Camp David meeting Yeltsin proposes cutting US and USSR nuclear
        weapons to 2,500; Bush rejects this, but approves joint development of
        global anti-missile defence system (2).
26   In Vienna, IAEA agrees to extend its powers to check for nuclear weapons
        development.

March
4–   At CSCE talks in Vienna 48 nations agree measures limiting land manoeu-
        vres in Europe and information exchanges; at three-day foreign ministers'
        meeting in Helsinki sign *Open Skies* treaty (24); agree CSCE peacekeeping
        role (26).
9   China announces agreement to join NPT.

April
3   In Warsaw, members of 27-nation Nuclear Supplier Group sign agreement to
        limit sales of dual-use machinery and materials.
8   French Prime Minister Pierre Bérégovoy announces suspension of nuclear
        testing in South Pacific until end of 1992.

May
4   North Korea submits list of nuclear assets to IAEA.
15   At CIS summit in Tashkent, Russia and five former Soviet republics agree
        distribution of conventional forces under CFE Treaty.
21   China conducts nuclear test, 37th since 1964.
28–29   At Washington meeting of world's five largest arms suppliers (US, Russia,
        UK, France and China), China agrees again not to transfer missiles banned
        under the MTCR.
29   India test-fires 2,500-km range *Agni* ballistic misssile.

June
4– France announces reduction in nuclear alert status, reduces nuclear subma- rines from three to two; announces closure of missile-tracking station in Azores within four years (17).
5 29 members of North Atlantic Cooperation Council sign CFE agreement.
12 France halts short-range *Hadès* nuclear weapons programme.
15 UK Defence Minister, Malcolm Rifkind, announces elimination of all naval nuclear weapons except *Trident*.
16 At summit in Washington, US and Russia agree to cut long-range nuclear weapons to between 3,000–3,500 by the year 2003 and to eliminate multi- warhead ICBMs.
22 At Geneva UN Disarmament Conference, draft treaty banning CW tabled.
23 US detonates nuclear device at Yucca Flat in Nevada.

July
1– Ukrainian parliament ratifies CFE treaty; becomes effective (17).
10 At two-day CSCE summit in Helsinki, NATO and CIS sign agreement reducing troops in Europe, adopt new peacekeeping role and join other nations in signing new Helsinki accords.
30 US and Russia sign agreement for US to provide $25m to Moscow for destroying Russian CW.

August
3 US Senate agrees to suspend nuclear tests from 1 October for nine months, to limit tests for three years and to ban them permanently by 1996.
7 In Geneva, 39-nation Conference on Disarmament agrees final draft of CBW treaty.
25 France ratifies 1967 Treaty of Tlatelolco prohibiting stockpiling nuclear weapons in Latin America.

September
14– Russia admits it had violated 1972 Convention on Prohibition of the Devel- opment, Production and Stockpiling of Bacteriological (Biological) and Toxic Weapons and pledges to put BW sites under international control.
22 In Paris, UK, France, Germany, Iceland, Norway, Sweden, Finland, Eire, Spain, Denmark, Netherlands, Luxembourg, Belgium and Portugal sign 15- year agreement banning sea-dumping of nuclear waste.
25 China conducts underground nuclear test.

October
6 US and Russia sign agreement granting US aid for storage facilities for dismantling nuclear weapons.
19 Russia extends nuclear test moratorium until July 1993.

November
4 Russian parliament approves START I treaty.
24 UK Armed Forces Minister Archie Hamilton confirms that UK intends to continue nuclear testing.

December
29 US Secretary of State, Lawrence Eagleburger, and Russian Defence Minister, General Pavel Grachev, agree text of START II treaty following talks in Geneva; Ukraine says it needs more time to consider ratifying the START I treaty (29).

Glossary

ALCM	Air-Launched Cruise Missile
ANC	African National Congress
APF	Azerbaijan Popular Front
ASEAN	Association of South-East Asian Nations
ATBM	Anti-Tactical Ballistic Missile
AWAC	Airborne Warning and Control System
BJP	Bharatiya Janata Party (India)
BWC	Biological Weapons Convention
CBM	Confidence-Building Measure
CFE	Conventional Armed Forces in Europe
CIS	Commonwealth of Independent States
CODESA	Convention for a Democratic South Africa
CSCE	Conference on Security and Cooperation in Europe
CTB	Comprehensive Test Ban
CW	Chemical Weapons
CWC	Chemical Weapons Convention
DMZ	Demilitarized Zone
DSP	Democratic Socialist Party (Japan)
EBRD	European Bank for Reconstruction and Development
EC	European Community
ECOWAS	Economic Community of West African States
ECU	European Currency Unit
EEA	European Economic Area
EFTA	European Free Trade Association
EMU	Economic and Monetary Union
EPLF	Eritrean People's Liberation Front
EPRDF	Ethiopian People's Revolutionary Democratic Front
ERM	Exchange-Rate Mechanism
FIS	Front Islamique du Salut
FRUD	Front révolutionnaire pour l'unité et la démocratie (Djibouti)
FRY	Federal Republic of Yugoslavia
FSC	Forum for Security Cooperation
FY	Fiscal Year
G-7	Group of Seven
GATT	General Agreement on Tariffs and Trade
IAEA	International Atomic Energy Agency
ICBM	Intercontinental Ballistic Missile
ICJ	International Court of Justice
ICRC	International Committee of the Red Cross
IDA	Islamic Democratic Alliance
IMF	International Monetary Fund
INF	Intermediate-range Nuclear Forces
IRBM	Intermediate-range Ballistic Missile
ISI	Inter-Service Intelligence Unit (Pakistan)
JKLF	Jammu and Kashmir Liberation Front
JNA	Yugoslav National Army
LDP	Liberal Democratic Party (Japan)
LOC	Line of Control
MFN	Most Favoured Nation
MIA	Missing in Action
MIRV	Multiple Independently-Targetable Re-entry Vehicle
MLRS	Multiple-Launch Rocket System
MPLA	Movimento Popular para a Libertação de Angola
MQM	Muhajir Qaumi Movement (Pakistan)

MTCR	Missile Technology Control Regime
NAFTA	North American Free Trade Agreement
NATO	North Atlantic Treaty Organization
NDA	National Democratic Alliance
NGO	Non-Governmental Organization
NIC	National Integration Council (India)
NIF	National Islamic Front
NPT	Nuclear Non-Proliferation Treaty
OAS	Organisation of American States
OECD	Organisation for Economic Cooperation and Development
OIC	Organisation of the Islamic Conference
OLF	Oromo Liberation Front
ONUMOZ	United Nations Operation in Mozambique
OPDO	Oromo People's Democratic Organization
OPEC	Organisation of Petroleum-Exporting Countries
PAC	Pan Africanist Congress
Perm 5	Permanent Five
PKK	Kurdish Workers' Party
PKO	Peacekeeping Operation
PLA	People's Liberation Army (China)
PLO	Palestine Liberation Organization
PMC	Post-Ministerial Conference
PPP	Pakistan People's Party
Renamo	Resistência Nacional Moçambicana
SADF	South African Defence Forces
SALT	Strategic Arms Limitation Treaty
SDF	Self-Defense Forces (Japan)
SDI	Strategic Defence Initiative
SDPJ	Social Democratic Party of Japan
SFRY	Socialist Federal Republic of Yugoslavia
SII	Structural Impediments Initiative
SLBM	Submarine-Launched Ballistic Missile
SNA	Somalia National Alliance
SNC	Supreme National Council (Cambodia)
SNF	Somalia National Front
SPA	Supreme People's Assembly (North Korea)
SPLA	Sudan People's Liberation Army
SPLM	Sudan People's Liberation Movement
SSDF	Somalia Salvation Democratic Front
SSM	Surface-to-Surface Missile
START	Strategic Arms Reduction Talks
TLE	Treaty-Limited Equipment
TPLF	Tigrayan People's Liberation Front
ULFA	United Liberation Front of Assam
UNAVEM	United Nations Angola Verification Mission
UNDP	United Nations Development Programme
UNITA	União Nacional para a Independência Total de Angola
UNITAF	Unified Task Force
UNOSOM	United Nations Operation in Somalia
UNPA	United Nations Protected Areas
UNPROFOR	United Nations Protection Force
UNTAC	United Nations Transitional Authority in Cambodia
USC	United Somalia Congress
VHP	Vishwa Hindu Parishad (India)
WEU	Western European Union

(for single copy sales see over)

Please tick appropriate box to order

Please enter me a *Military Balance* Subscription for:

❏ 1993 at £35.00/$58.00

Please enter me a *Strategic Survey* Subscription for:

❏ 1993 at £18.00/$29.00

Please enter me a *Survival* Subscription for:

❏ 1993 at £36.00/$50.00

Please enter me an *Adelphi Papers* Subscription for:

❏ 1993 at £83.00/$135.00

Please enter me a *Combined* Subscription for:

❏ 1993 at £166.00/$259.00

*(Combined Subscription includes a copy of **The Military Balance** and **Strategic Survey**, plus four issues of **Survival** and approximately ten **Adelphi Papers**)*

PAYMENT:

❏ Payment enclosed £/$_____   ❏ Bill me

Payment Method: ❏ Cheque ❏ Postal Order ❏ International Money Order
(Please make cheques, etc., payable to **Brassey's (UK) Ltd**)

Credit Cards   ❏ Access ❏ Mastercard ❏ Visa

Card No. ❏❏❏❏❏❏❏❏❏❏❏❏❏❏❏❏

Expiry date _____

Signature (obligatory for credit card orders): _____

Name _____

Address _____

City _____

Country _____

PLEASE PRINT NAME AND ADDRESS CLEARLY

If you are based in an EC country and we do not have your VAT number, we may be required to charge you VAT on publications from 1993 onwards. It is essential therefore, that you provide us with your VAT number.   VAT Number _____

VAT NO: GB 342 1764 71

Signature _____   Date _____

Please return this card, in an envelope, to the appropriate address below:

Residents of ALL other countries: Turpin Distribution Services Ltd, Blackhorse Road, Letchworth, Hants, SG8 1HN, UK, Phone: (+44) 462 672555, Fax: (+44) 462 480947.

Residents of North America: IISS Subscriptions, Turpin Transactions, P.O. Box 9931, McLean, VA 22102, Fax: (703) 790 9063.

SINGLE COPY SALES ORDER FORM

Please tick appropriate box to order. All orders must be prepaid.

☐ *The Military Balance 1992–1993* (Flexicover) 1 85753 027 6 £35.00/$55.00
☐ *Strategic Survey 1992–1993* (Flexicover) 1 85753 003 9 £21.00/$32.00
☐ *Strategic Survey 1991–1992* (Flexicover) 0 08 041784 1 £20.00/$30.00

Please send_____copies of *The Military Balance 1992–1993*
at £35.00/$55.00 (Flexicover) (ISBN 1 85753 027 6)

Please send_____copies of *Strategic Survey 1992–1993*
at £21.00/$32.00 (Flexicover) (ISBN 1 85753 003 9)

PAYMENT:

☐ Payment enclosed £/$_____   ☐ Bill me

Payment Method: ☐ Cheque ☐ Postal Order ☐ International Money Order
(Please make cheques, etc., payable to **Brassey's (UK) Ltd**)

Credit Cards   ☐ Access ☐ Mastercard   ☐ Visa

Card No. ☐☐☐☐☐☐☐☐☐☐☐☐☐☐☐☐

Expiry date _____

Signature (obligatory for credit card orders): _____

Name _____

Address _____   PLEASE
PRINT
City _____   NAME AND
ADDRESS
Country _____   CLEARLY

If you are based in an EC country and we do not have your VAT number, we may be required
to charge you VAT on publications from 1993 onwards. It is essential therefore, that you
provide us with your VAT number.   VAT Number _____

VAT NO: GB 532 5222 78

Signature _____   Date _____

Please return this card, in an envelope, to the appropriate address below:

Residents of ALL other countries: Marston Book Services, P.O. Box 87, Oxford, OX2
0DT, UK, Tel: 0865 791155, Fax: 0865 791927.
Post & Packaging Charges:

	1 Book	Per Extra Book
UK	£1.50	£1.00
Europe	£2.50	£1.50

Residents of North America: Macmillan/Brassey's (US), Book Order Department, 100
Front Street, Riverside, NJ 08075-7500 USA, TOLL FREE TEL: 1 0800 257 5755, TOLL
FREE FAX: 1 800 552 1272. Please add state or local tax and 6% for Shipping/Handling.